the
new world
of
advertising

Compiled by
the editors of
Advertising Age

Edited and with an
Introduction by
Vernon Fryburger

CRAIN
BOOKS

A Division of
Crain Communications Inc.
740 Rush Street
Chicago, Illinois 60611

3/7

Library of Congress Catalogue Card Number: 75-21745
ISBN 0-87251-021-2

Printed in the United States of America

785

CONTENTS

INTRODUCTION

Vernon Fryburger
Chairman, Department of Advertising
Northwestern University

All serious students of advertising and marketing have learned to rely on "Advertising Age" for news about what is going on in the field. They also have learned to expect thoughtful comment on key issues of the times as well as a perceptive surveillance of the relevant political scene. In the November 21, 1973 issue entitled "The New World of Advertising" they got a lot more. What they got is best described by editor James O'Gara in his preface to that issue:

"The New World of Advertising" is an effort to put the changes of the last decade into some perspective; to describe how modern advertising and marketing work; to provide a clear view of what advertising is today—and isn't, of what it can and does do, and what it can't and doesn't do. This volume is designed to give advertising's practitioners a chance to look back and see where they've been so that they might a bit more readily describe where it is they are going. It is designed, hopefully, to broaden and deepen their knowledge of the business, as well as the knowledge of consumerists, critics, regulators, legislators, young people looking to marketing careers, consumers—everybody. We are all of us, finally, consumers."

Apparently, many of us consumers were discerning enough to recognize that "The New World of Advertising" lived up fully to Mr. O'Gara's promise. The demand for extra copies far exceeded the supply.

This book contains twenty selections from "The New World of Advertising." These selections were compiled under the editorial direction of James V. O'Gara and Merle Kingman, "Advertising Age" editors. Some of the selections are timely in nature. These have been updated. This book also contains ten articles from recent issues of "Advertising Age." These have been among the best read, most provocative, and most widely quoted.

All of the authors are authorities in their respective fields. They are thoughtful, articulate and well informed. They are especially qualified to write about the various segments of the advertising business—advertisers, agencies and media. They provide the kind of insights on the planning and management of advertising that only active planners and managers can provide. They are perceptive observers of the state of the advertising business, its continuing concern with consumer welfare, with public service activities, and government regulation. After all, people working in the business are in a unique position to write about what is going on in the business.

For introductory courses in marketing and advertising this book should be a refreshing supplement to any basic text. As suggested by the titles of the six parts, the reader should gain a clearer understanding of advertising, how the business works, how advertising is planned and managed, its role in society, its international dimensions, and various views both pro and con. Selections describing the operations of advertisers and advertising agencies are the most current and authoritative available. Detailed reports on government regulation, self-regulation, and the various regulatory agencies are valuable for reference purposes. Perhaps most unique are the selections reporting how the United States government, how agricultural organizations, and how labor unions use advertising. Once the widening scope of advertising becomes apparent it can be seen that the future of this form of communication is limited only by one's imagination.

PART 1

What
is
advertising?

Advertising is worth advertising

BY HERBERT STEIN
Chairman, Council of Economic Advisers

Ten years ago, in the first "World of Advertising" issue of ADVERTISING AGE, then Secretary of Commerce Luther Hodges observed: "In selling goods, Madison Ave. has no equal. Yet it has not been very successful in selling itself."

This observation seems every bit as true today as it was in 1963—at least with respect to this country, where the cons of advertising are more loudly and vehemently voiced than its pros. Why this is so is not entirely clear. But that it is so is also something of a comfort. If the magicians of advertising cannot charm us out of some skepticism about advertising, perhaps they don't have the malicious power ascribed to them in other respects.

Valid criticisms have been leveled against advertising by consumers and consumer groups, by the press, by the regulatory agencies—including your own American Assn. of Advertising Agencies—and even by economists. But advertising plays a useful economic and social role, and its good points deserve equal time with its bad.

We Can Sell Russians—Can We Sell U.S.?

Indeed, Madison Ave. appears to be selling itself abroad with greater success than it is at home. The advertising bandwagon is even being jumped on in Russia, where one would least expect it. Brand names are increasingly being used as an aid to both consumer and planner; advertising agencies are even being set up. This is ironic, but not, of course, conclusive. The Soviet endorsement of advertising does not certify its economic rationality.

In the mythical world of perfect competition, where economists like me learned our ABCs, there would be little need for advertising, since information would be costless and consumers would have full knowledge of all available alternatives. As we all know, these assumptions, like other assumptions underlying the perfect competi-

tion model, do not literally correspond to reality. And in the divergence between these assumptions and reality lies the key to the economic role of advertising—to provide information linking the consumer with the producer.

The price tag on this information is not insignificant; it has been estimated that advertising expenditures amounted to $23.1 billion—or around 2% of gross national product—in 1972. These costs are, of course, reflected in the prices paid by the consumer for advertised products. But it would be a mistake to conclude from this that the price of products would necessarily fall in the absence of advertising—just as it would be a mistake to conclude that the price of products that require skilled labor in their production would necessarily fall if unskilled labor were used instead.

Better Sales Tool than Ads? Where?

The price-reducing roles of advertising must be appraised by reference not only to the price of specified products, but also to the adaptation of the market-basket of products to the desires of consumers. To produce cheaply things consumers don't want, or don't even think they want, is not economical.

From the standpoint of the producer, advertising is clearly used because it is thought to be the most efficient marketing technique. If the advertiser knew of a selling tool that promised lower costs or greater returns, he'd be irrational to continue advertising.

This is not to say that there is no economic waste in advertising—that advertisers are perfectly rational and that advertising is invariably the most efficient marketing technique. Advertisers may misjudge how much should be spent on advertising—they may spend too much or they may even spend too little. Such inefficiencies are regretable, but by no means a unique property of the advertising industry.

There is yet another way in which advertising can affect prices and resource allocation, and that is through its impact on industrial structure. Advertising differentiates products and creates brand loyalties, thus reducing the consumer's responsiveness to the offer of a competing product, even at a lower price. As a result, new entrants may well have to spend substantially—and perhaps prohibitively—more on advertising than do the going companies to earn a "name" with the public. Advertising can, in other words, erect barriers to entry and thereby reduce competitive pressures. This impairment of competition could result in higher prices, lower quality products, and less efficient resource allocation.

Ads Can Help, Hinder Market Entry

Fortunately, though, such barriers to entry are, by and large, not insurmountable. Consumer buying habits are not chiseled in granite, at least not by advertising. They shift in response to price differentials, dissatisfaction with particular products, desire to experiment, and a host of other factors—not the least of which might be a persuasive advertising campaign by a competitor. This has been repeatedly attested by the successful introduction of new products and new brands, and the resultant changes in companies' market shares.

Advertising can, then, facilitate entry—or it can impede entry. In a similar fashion, advertising can perform an informational service to the consumer —or it can perform misinformational disservice.

Advertising can serve the consumer by providing useful and accurate information on the availability, characteristics, performance and safety of particular goods and services. In the absence of advertising, the consumer's search costs would be increased; he would have to spend time and money to gather information on which to base his purchasing decisions—or make his decisions on a less informed basis.

Regrettably, not all of this information provided through advertising can be taken at face value. Advertisements can be deceptive and misleading; they can create a false image for a product or company. Fortunately, there are safeguards against such types of advertising; and it is, I feel, a positive development that advertising claims are

Ad data round out today's picture

Total Advertising Expenditures as per cent of

	GNP	Consumer Expenditures
1950	2.00%	2.92%
1952	2.07	3.28
1954	2.26	3.45
1956	2.36	3.67
1958	2.32	3.51
1960	2.37	3.67
1961	2.21	3.51
1962	2.23	3.47
1963	2.22	3.50
1964	2.24	3.53
1965	2.23	3.52
1966	2.22	3.57
1967	2.13	3.43
1968	2.10	3.38
1969	2.10	3.36
1970	2.01	3.18
1971	1.98	3.13
1972	2.00	3.20

Advertising Expenditures by

	Local Advertisers	National Advertisers	Total All Advertisers
1950	2.4%	3.3%	5.7%
1951	2.7	3.7	6.4
1952	3.1	4.1	7.2
1953	3.2	4.5	7.7
1954	3.4	4.8	8.2
1955	3.8	5.4	9.2
1956	4.0	5.9	9.9
1957	4.1	6.2	10.3
1958	4.0	6.3	10.3
1959	4.4	6.8	11.2
1960	4.6	7.3	11.9
1961	4.6	7.2	11.8
1962	4.7	7.7	12.4
1963	5.0	8.1	13.1
1964	5.4	8.7	14.1
1965	5.8	9.4	15.2
1966	6.5	10.2	16.7
1967	6.6	10.3	16.9
1968	7.2	10.9	18.1
1969	7.9	11.5	19.4
1970	8.1	11.5	19.6
1971	8.8	12.0	20.8
1972	9.9	13.1	23.0

Local Advertising Expenditures as per cent of

	Retail Sales
1950	1.63%
1955	2.07
1960	2.09
1961	2.10
1962	2.00
1963	2.03
1964	2.07
1965	2.04
1966	2.14
1967	2.10
1968	2.11
1969	2.21
1970	1.98
1971	2.15
1972	2.21

National Advertising Expenditures as per cent of

	Pre Tax Profits
1950	1.31%
1955	0.90
1960	0.68
1961	0.69
1962	0.72
1963	0.73
1964	0.76
1965	0.83
1966	0.82
1967	0.79
1968	0.80
1969	0.74
1970	0.65
1971	0.70
1972	0.70

Source: Robert J. Coen, McCann-Erickson.

now being more closely watched, for that means that these safeguards are being made stronger.

Ads Can't Really Mesmerize You

The ultimate safeguard is, of course, the test of the marketplace. While advertising can persuade a consumer to try a new product or brand, it cannot mesmerize the consumer into continuing to buy an unsatisfactory product. Lincoln's maxim that "you can fool some of the people all of the time, and all of the people some of the time, but you cannot fool all of the people all of the time" is as applicable to advertising as it is to other forms of salesmanship.

Another safeguard is the corrective limelight that the media, consumer groups and others have thrown on advertisements. One ad, for example, proclaimed that the water running by a firm's plant "still runs clear." But the picture was, it turns out, taken 50 miles upstream from the plant. The water wasn't so clear where the plant was actually located, as a leading national newspaper pointed out.

Yet another safeguard is regulation of advertising—both by the government and by the advertising industry itself. Public regulatory agencies, such as the Federal Trade Commission and the Food & Drug Administration, can and should take action against unscrupulous advertisers; so can private regulatory agencies, such as the Advertising Review Board.

The advertising agencies themselves have a vital role to play in this regulatory process. The responsible agency would seek to substantiate producer claims, as well as its own claims, before they have an impact on consumer spending. It should be able to assert: "We stand by our advertisements." This would clearly be in the public interest. But it would also seem to be in the advertising agency's own interest. The ad agency could thereby enhance its reputation and copywriters could expound the virtues of the products they are selling with greater sincerity—and hence enthusiasm.

Artificial Wants vs. Genuine Needs

Above and beyond these criticisms leveled against advertising on grounds of deception are those that are leveled against it on anti-materialis-tic and anti-big business grounds. It is claimed that the inducements and seducements of advertising contrive "artificial" wants, as opposed to "genuine" needs, but they reflect not consumer sovereignty, but producer sovereignty.

The exponents of this line of reasoning apparently think less of the consumer than I do. The consumer is not passive and ignorant, as they make him out to be. True, consumer buying decisions are not based on functional criteria alone. The purchaser of an automobile wants more than just transportation; he also wants comfort, style and status. And he would probably want these things even in the absence of advertising. An operational distinction between "needs" and "wants," according to which only "genuine needs" would be satisfied, would require an economic and political system based on much greater central control than has traditionally been acceptable in this country.

This is not to deny that advertising is an instrument of persuasion that might itself create wants. But advertising is not the only "hidden persuader." Wants are created by a host of influences—Washington, the churches, university faculties, mass media, and Mother, to name but a few. And it is by no means clear that Madison Ave. is No. 1 in exaggerated claims.

Another dimension of advertising that deserves at least a passing mention is its entertainment value. As advertisers are fully aware, advertisements, like other forms of communication, exert an impact not simply by dint of what they say, but also by dint of how they say it. Advertisements can in some cases be unwelcome interruptions, but they can also provide the highlights of a tv or radio program. Not many shows can generate the suspense of the commercial in which the approval of a product by a demanding man in a white sombrero will determine whether the townspeople will celebrate or go on welfare.

Advertising has a significant role to play, both economically and socially. Just as its abuses should be curbed, its uses should be more fully recognized. Truth in advertising is essential, but so too, from your standpoint at least, is truth on advertising. And in promoting both of these goals, advertisers and advertising agencies can—like the rest of us—always try harder. #

Reprinted from "Advertising Age," Nov. 21, 1973, pp. 4-5

U.S. advertising
hits $23.1 billion

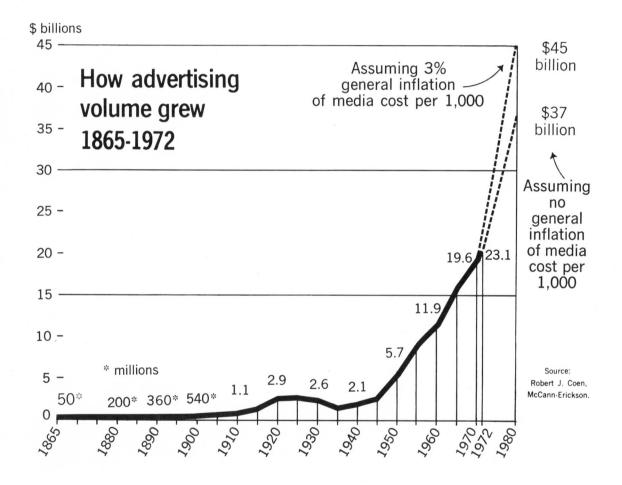

$ billions

How advertising volume grew 1865-1972

Assuming 3% general inflation of media cost per 1,000

$45 billion

$37 billion

Assuming no general inflation of media cost per 1,000

23.1

19.6

11.9

5.7

2.9   2.6   2.1

1.1

* millions

50*   200*   360*   540*

Source: Robert J. Coen, McCann-Erickson.

1865 1880 1890 1900 1910 1920 1930 1940 1950 1960 1970 1972 1980

Advertising is a $23.1 billion business.
It is a business that the U.S. Department of Commerce expects will climb to $26 billion by 1975 and to $36 billion by 1980. And these figures seem somewhat on the conservative side. For example, Robert J. Coen of McCann-Erickson, a recognized authority in such matters, anticipates total advertising spending of some $37 billion, and possibly as much as $45 billion, by 1980.

Advertising spending increased 10.7% last year alone, a faster rate than was enjoyed by the American economy. And the business is expected to grow faster than the economy again this year—a growth of perhaps $3 billion. As a matter of fact, advertising in this country has grown, in little more than 100 years, to a point about 460 times above what it was in the last Civil War year—and 150 times over that year's gross national product.

How did all this growth come about? Basically, it stemmed from the vast change that overtook the U.S.—from an agricultural country into an industrialized one, from a production to a marketing orientation. Mass production, made possible by new machinery, an expanding work force, and the proliferation of branded products, were all boons—if only sales could be dramatically increased. A way to stimulate demand for products

5

needed to be found, for manufacturers were no longer satisfied to sell their goods only in their home towns and were now becoming regional, even national advertisers.

Advertising: Low-Cost Sales Tool

In 1837, William Procter and James Gamble formed a company to make soap and candles, and thus was launched today's biggest advertiser. Four years later, in 1841, came the first advertising agents—actually, brokers of newspaper advertising space. These men brought manufacturers and newspapers together: They solicited business from advertisers, forwarded their copy to newspapers, collected the charge and kept 25% of the newspapers' bills as commission. They saved the manufacturer the time and effort needed to find available advertising space, and they eliminated the newspapers' need to solicit advertising, at some expense, far from their places of publication. As James Webb Young said in a study of advertising compensation, "Thus national advertising, the advertising agency and the publisher's commission to the agent appear to have come into existence together."

Since then, advertising in the U.S. has proved an indispensable and relatively inexpensive tool in the effort to sell the expanded output of a growing nation.

Since the Civil War

Between the end of the Civil War and 1900—years marked by growing mechanization, the advent of large-scale drug and patent medicine advertising, and the appearance of mass magazines as an important advertising medium (some 600 national advertisers were using the medium before the turn of the century)—advertising expenditures zoomed from $50,000,000 to $540,000,000. In 1900, the U.S. Census counted 12,000 "advertising agents and salesmen." And in 1917 appeared the first list of advertising agencies: 1,400 in all (in addition to their thousands of clients, there were another 2,600 "national" advertisers who used no agency's services).

After World War I, in the 1920s, business enjoyed a marked expansion; a mass market for automobiles came into being, and advertising saw million-dollar budgets become fairly commonplace. In 1923, National Carbon Co. sponsored the "Eveready Hour," the first regular series of radio entertainment and music "to be sponsored by an advertiser in this country or elsewhere." Radio networks came on the scene, and by 1929 radio sets were to be heard in more than a third of America's homes.

With the Depression, advertising volume slumped some 25%, falling back finally to about its 1915 level. But it started back up the ladder after 1935 and began a long-term trend that has not yet peaked. The ascent since World War II has been precipitous—from $2.8 billion in 1945 to $9.1 billion in 1955 to $15.2 billion in 1965 and to last year's $23.1 billion—figures aided handsomely since about 1949 by the new medium of television, which first became the No. 1 national advertising medium in 1955.

Ad Growth Soars in '50s and '60s

Despite a sag in the growth-rate lasting from 1966 through 1971, the 27 years since World War II saw advertising outlays grow more than eight times over. In the view of Robert J. Coen of McCann-Erickson, big corporations in the immediate post-World War II years went heavily into advertising as an investment in future growth and because advertising was above average in relation to pre-tax corporate profits.

"In the middle 1960s, however," he added, "large corporations ran into profit problems, and although their advertising budgets did not rise very much, their relationship to profits did not go up until, eventually, in the late '60s, the squeeze was put on advertising budgets. This was particularly true in 1970 when national advertising as a per cent of profits dropped to a 20-year low." But the trend, as we have seen, once again is upward.

Some reasons for the phenomenal growth of advertising expenditures from the 1950 level of $5.7 billion have been offered by Profs. Raymond A. Bauer and Stephen A. Greyser of Harvard Business School in "Advertising in America: The Consumer View":

"Growing consumer disposable income, greater propensity to spend on expensive appliances and the like, and greater willingness on the part of more people to spend more on services and pleasures were relevant personal consumer forces. With these were joined such institutional changes as rapid movement to self-service retailing, wider distribution of products in more varied outlets, and more extensive (and market segment-directed) product lines, with resulting modifications in the nature of our society.

"One key consequence was that advertising played a far more vital part for both consumer and manufacturer than had earlier been true. New and different media, such as television and specialized magazines, emerged as avenues of access to audiences both larger on the one hand, and more narrowly focused on the other, than heretofore."

As a matter of fact, the development of new media to transmit the advertising message from manufacturer to prospect has been an essential element in the growth of the advertising industry. In its early stages, advertising was a print media business, and advertising expenditures provided the financial resources for the proliferation of America's newspapers and magazines. Then, as now, advertising paid most of the costs of the communications media.

In 1922, radio became a reality in the U.S., and six years later American advertisers spent $10,000,000 in the medium. While over-all advertising volume declined during the Depression years, the new radio medium had small cause for complaint. Its revenues zoomed, and by 1935 radio was attracting $110,000,000 worth of advertising. By the end of World War II, the medium was getting more than $400,000,000 annually—15% of all advertising expenditures. By last year, when radio's share of total advertising expenditures receded to some 6.6%, its advertising revenues nevertheless attained the $15 billion level.

Enter Television—Hits $4.1 Billion

Television came on the media scene in 1947, and in 1950 it garnered $170,000,000 in advertising money. This performance was dwarfed by 1961's $1.6 billion and last year's $4.1 billion. (Network commercials brought in $1.8 billion, and spot commercials $1.4 billion, while local advertising accounted for the remainder.) No other medium in the history of advertising has enjoyed such spectacular growth in so short a period.

Another medium making notable gains has been direct mail. The volume of this medium in 1945 was $290,000,000. Last year it was at the $3.3 billion mark.

Meanwhile, the medium where it all began, the daily newspaper, continued as the No. 1 choice of advertisers through the years. Newspapers reached a revenue volume of $815,000,000 in 1940, advanced to $2 billion in 1950, to $3 billion in 1955, and last year reported $6.96 billion—30.2% of the $23.1 billion spent in all media. Local advertising, incidentally, accounted for $5.7 billion of newspapers' total in 1972.

As has been mentioned, advertising provides the financial wherewithal for America's unparalleled mass communications. John S. Wright, Daniel S. Warner and Willis L. Winter Jr. observe in the 1971 edition of their book, "Advertising" (McGraw-Hill), that: "Historically, mass communication media have been notably unsuccessful in attempting to survive on income received solely from readers, listeners or viewers. The critical financial support has come from political parties, from government or from advertisers. Unlike governments or political parties, advertisers are rarely interested in the editorial or entertainment policies of media except as they may affect the type or size of audience to whom the advertiser wishes to deliver his sales message. Moreover, the attitude or action sought by one advertiser is frequently the reverse of that sought by another, and the number of different advertisers is legion.

"Advertising support," they continued, "seems to promise greater freedom of the press than is possible through subsidy by government or political parties. The official history of the *London Times* credits advertising with freeing the press from political control, and observes: 'Such freedom as the press enjoys is dependent on commercial advertising'."

What the Future Holds

What does the future look like for advertising volume in the U.S.?

Robert Coen has predicted an upward trend lasting to 1980. With corporate profits improving in 1973, he said, advertising budgets can be expected to go up, "and, in fact, will continue to go up at a higher rate than profits because they had been depressed in the past (the late 1960s), and because new competition in this area is bound to become more intense. New brands will be introduced, new competitors will enter the marketplace, and corporate profit growth will permit higher budgets to expand and match competition." As a result, he anticipated that advertising volume will be somewhere in the neighborhood of $45 billion by 1980.

"This will occur," he added, "primarily because of an increased demand for advertising as the economy expands and corporate profits and profit margins improve. This will cause some degree of inflation in media rates of cost per thousands, partly because many prices were kept down from the middle 1960s until 1972. With demand going up, media rates will go up at a faster pace than circulation and audiences.

"However, if various pressures combine to prevent this anticipated general inflation, we may then expect that total advertising spending will be about $37 billion by 1980."

Advertising Has Its Critics

"Advertising is under fire. Its adverse critics come from many camps and their complaints tend to become increasingly vehement. Certain economists complain that its extensive use involves undue costs and is a bar to free competition, with a resultant adverse effect on the operation of the free price system. Home economics teachers charge it with being a poor guide to consumption. Students of ethics accuse it of showing frequent display of poor taste and misrepresentation. Business men themselves have not infrequently doubted its effectiveness for business purposes."

Sounds like 1973?

Yes, but those words were actually written in 1942 by Prof. Neil Borden of Harvard in the opening of his "Economic Effects of Advertising," a classic study. Advertising has been under the gun at least since 1759 when Samuel Johnson noted that "Advertisements are now so numerous that they are very negligently perused, and it is therefore become necessary to gain attention by magnificence of promises, and by eloquence sometimes sublime and sometimes pathetic. Promise, large promise, is the soul of an advertisement."

By 1971, the plethora of charges leveled against advertising could perhaps be isolated, with ten criticisms seeming to be "central" to them all. Kenneth A. Longman, former developmental research executive at Young & Rubicam, identified them in his book, "Advertising" (Harcourt Brace Jovanovich), as follows:

"Advertising sells people things they neither need nor want. People are not really influenced by advertising. Advertising imposes uniformity on the populace. Advertising generates senseless proliferation of variety in goods and services. Advertising results in higher prices. Advertising is false and misleading. Most advertising is irrelevant. Most advertising exhibits bad taste—or spon-

Medium	1971* Millions	1971* Per cent of total	1972 Millions	1972 Per cent of total	Per cent change
Newspapers					
Total	$6,250	30.0	$6,960	30.2	+11
National	1,140	5.5	1,240	5.4	+ 9
Local	5,110	24.5	5,720	24.8	+12
Magazines					
Total	1,399	6.7	1,480	6.4	+ 6
Weeklies	626	3.0	600	2.6	− 4
Women's	340	1.6	380	1.7	+12
Monthlies	404	2.0	470	2.0	+16
Farm National	29	0.1	30	0.1	+ 3
Television					
Total	3,590	17.2	4,110	17.9	+14
Network	1,593	7.6	1,780	7.7	+12
Spot	1,201	5.8	1,375	6.0	+14
Local	796	3.8	955	4.2	+20
Radio					
Total	1,440	6.9	1,530	6.6	+ 6
Network	63	0.3	75	0.3	+19
Spot	395	1.9	395	1.7	0
Local	982	4.7	1,060	4.6	+ 8
Farm Publications (Regional)	28	0.1	29	0.1	+ 3
**Total Farm Pubs.	(57)	(0.2)	(59)	(0.2)	(+ 3)
Direct Mail	3,050	14.6	3,350	14.5	+10
Business Papers	720	3.5	770	3.3	+ 7
Outdoor					
Total	261	1.3	290	1.3	+ 9
National	172	0.9	190	0.9	+ 9
Local	89	0.4	100	0.4	+10
Miscellaneous					
Total	4,102	19.7	4,541	19.7	+11
National	2,237	10.7	2,445	10.6	+ 9
Local	1,865	9.0	2,096	9.1	+12
Total					
National	11,970	57.4	13,100	56.8	+ 9
Local	8,870	42.6	9,960	43.2	+12
Grand Total	$20,840	100.0	$23,060	100.0	+10.7

Advertising volume in the United States in 1971 and 1972

*Revised   **Included in other media totals—not to be added.   Source: McCann-Erickson

sors it. Advertising is too intrusive. Advertising regulates discussion of public issues through its control of the news media."

Otto Kleppner, after making note of various criticisms of advertising, concludes in the 1966 edition of his "Advertising Procedure" (Prentice Hall) that:

" . . . Most consumers regard the standards of advertising today as higher than those of ten years ago. By and large they have found they can depend upon advertising to learn about the products that are available to them, and about ways of life they would like to attain. Advertising goads the producer to create better products. If he fails to do so, that fact will stand out in his advertising just as his success in offering better value is heralded by his advertising. Advertising helps create the volume of sales needed to get the advantages of mass production by telling about the product to the greatest number of people in the fastest time at the lowest cost per message.

"Advertising offers family entertainment, enlightenment and news on television and radio without any charge, and brings magazines and newspapers into millions of homes at a cost less than that of producing them.

"Because of its total service to society and to the economy, advertising has grown greatly both in volume and in importance, especially since World War II."

Reprinted from "Advertising Age," Nov. 21, 1973, pp. 6-7

What is advertising?

What does it do?

BY S. R. BERNSTEIN.
Chairman, Executive Committee, Crain Communications, Inc.

It is interesting that there has been very little effort devoted in the past 10 or 15 years to trying to define advertising—an endeavor which used to absorb a fair amount of the time of advertising people, scholars of language and its usage, and compilers of dictionaries. One gets the impression that everyone has been so busy denouncing or defending advertising, and feeling so sure of what it is, that no further definitions are necessary.

But this is not true. A great deal of the present criticism of advertising in educational and legislative circles is based on some serious misconceptions of what advertising is and how it is supposed to function.

Dictionary definitions of advertising, like dictionary definitions of so many words we use all the time, don't tell us too much about the modern uses or functions of this business tool. They tell you that *advertising* means *to make known, to publish, to inform, to attempt to persuade*, etc.

One definition, found in "The Reader's Digest Great Encyclopedic Dictionary," is one which many people would accept as simple and compact; but, in fact, it is too broad. Its principal definition says advertising is "the act or practice of attracting public notice so as to create interest or induce purchase; also, any system or method used for such purposes."

Advertising Identifies the Sponsor

Way back in 1948, the committee on definitions of the American Marketing Assn. agreed on a definition which considerably narrowed advertising to *any paid form of non-personal presentation and promotion of ideas, goods, or services by an identified sponsor.* And four years later, the International Chamber of Commerce issued a dictionary of marketing terms in which advertising was defined as a *non-personal, multiple presentation to the market of goods, services or commercial ideas by an identified sponsor who pays for the delivery of his message*

to the carrier (advertising medium); distinguished from **publicity**, *which does not pay the medium and does not necessarily identify the sponsor.*

The distinction made in these latter two definitions between advertising and public relations or publicity is most important. Because advertising, above all else, calls for an *identified* sponsor, so that the reader or viewer of advertising knows who is presenting the message, and is thereby equipped to weigh the advertiser's possible bias in the scale in which he judges the validity of the message.

Advertising Goes Beyond Presenting

(This matter of an *identified sponsor* is particularly important in non-commercial advertising—in political advertising and advertising for "causes" or points of view, where the identity of the person, company or group sponsoring the message is of vital importance. In the case of ordinary commercial product advertising, the identity of the sponsor is almost always self-evident).

The description of advertising as the "non-personal presentation *and promotion* of ideas, goods and services" is also vitally important, because advertising is more than *to make known, to publish, to inform.* Early advertising—the simplest kind of advertising—was designed to perform these simple functions, and much advertising still performs them. The sign outside a home industry or a modest store, identifying it as a grocery or a shoe repair shop or a vendor of drugs, does that. But modern advertising goes beyond the simple process of identification. It not only *presents* ideas, goods or services; it also *promotes* them.

In modern usage, that is the basic function of advertising: Not merely to catalog goods or services, nor to present them with a listing of their good points and bad, but to *promote* them so as to make them seem not only worth while but indispensable.

Advertising is not unbiased or objec-

tive with regard to the product or service or idea being advertised; it is a *special pleader*, hoping to surround its subject with a rose-colored aura of loveliness.

In short, advertising is, as it was defined before broadcasting was known, "salesmanship in print," a technique for *mass persuasion*—an extension and a multiplier of personal selling, and its usage and functions must be considered in this context.

Ad Is Substitute for Salesman

So, in essence, advertising is a substitute for the human salesman talking personally to an individual prospect or customer across a store counter or a desk or an open door. And, as a substitute for the human salesman, advertising has the same functions, abilities and attributes as the human salesman, although usually in less effective form.

It is less effective than personal selling, principally because it must be designed to appeal to a mass audience, in contrast with the personal salesman's ability to tailor his sales message to each individual prospect, and because, again unlike the personal salesman, it has no opportunity to "talk back," explain, or refute objections.

As a substitute and an extension of personal selling, advertising also has many of the same characteristics as the personal salesman. It can be hard-working and efficient, or lazy and wasteful. It can be upright and honest, or slick and shady. It can tell its story calmly and quietly and without hyperbole, or it can shout and posture and shriek menacingly in your ear. It can address you as though you were a rational, thoughtful human being, or it can assume you are a first-class boob and incapable of intelligent thought. It can be serious and thoughtful, or flip and humorous; it can reason with you, or entertain you, or flatter you.

It can be all these things, and do all these things, but no more. *Because in the end, its success or failure—and its value to the advertiser who pays all its costs—*

must rest on its ability to persuade a sufficient number of prospects to do what it says or buy what it sells ... without the use of any kind of force or coercion.

Leading You Down the Primrose Path?

This is advertising, no more and no less —a mechanized substitute for the personal salesman.

This is not the monster or the irresistible force so often portrayed in fiction. Most serious students of advertising are astounded at the image of advertising that seems to exist so widely in non-advertising minds. When they hear authors and legislators and educators and economists discoursing on the awesome, all-embracing power of advertising to hypnotize America's millions, to mesmerize the dollars out of their pockets, and to turn them from the road of economic virtue and sobriety into the primrose paths of overspending for useless, unneeded products, they shake their heads in wonderment. They know that advertising is not that good, not that powerful, not that influential.

Helping to Make the Sale

Actually, the great bulk of advertising is really more of a salesman's helper than it is a substitute for a salesman. In most instances, the advertising, hopefully, makes it easier for a sales person to sell you something at some future time, and at some place other than the place in which you see the advertisement. Thus, when your neighborhood supermarket advertises today's grocery bargains in the daily newspaper, it hopes to induce you to shop its aisles and pick the advertised (and maybe also some unadvertised) items off its shelves. The department store which advertises the appearance of the new season's clothing hopes for the same happy result—that you will come into the store and complete the buying pattern with the assistance of a sales person. And the national advertiser who tells you how delicious his soft drink is hopes, in the same manner, to make you think favorably about soft drinks, and to pick his, rather than some competitor's, off the grocery shelf when you actually make your purchase.

So it can be said that in relatively few instances is advertising designed to take the place of the salesman and actually make the sale. In far more instances, advertising is designed to smooth the salesman's path, to make it possible for him to get his order more easily and more quickly.

There is, of course, a substantial area in which advertising is expected to perform the entire selling job.

In the case of catalogs and other direct mail and direct marketing offers, and a very small amount of print and broadcast advertising, the reader or listener is asked for a direct response; he is urged to send in an order. In such cases, advertising is used as a substitute for personal selling. The sales proposition is stated in the advertisement, the catalog or the mailing piece, and the prospect is invited to complete the buying transaction without further discussion or negotiation.

We have all made purchases in this fashion. But direct-selling advertising, as this type of advertising is called, represents only a small (but growing) fraction of the total advertising scene. The big volume of advertising is designed to make the sale easier, but the actual sale must be consummated in some other place, and at some other time, than the time and place in which the advertising makes contact with the customer.

Retail Ad: Direct and Indirect Sell

Some common retail advertising illustrates both types quite clearly. In almost any metropolitan Sunday newspaper magazine section, or in the fashion and home magazines, advertising appears for specific items of female clothing, apparel, home furnishings, etc., which gives the sizes, color, price and description, and may conclude with some such language as this: "Linens, second floor. Phone 462-4747, Sunday, noon to 5; or write Carson's."

This advertising serves a double function. For those who elect to order by mail or phone, it completes the transaction, acting as a substitute for personal selling. For those who prefer to visit "linens, second floor," however, the advertising serves as a "salesman's helper." It induces the shopper to come to the store and actually shop the merchandise; but the sale is not completed until shopper and salesperson face each other in a typical personal selling situation.

■ The great majority of American advertising follows the latter pattern. The advertising on radio and television, the huge food pages in the newspapers, the copious advertising in magazines, and even a considerable volume of direct mail (which is considered largely a direct selling medium) are all designed not to make a sale, but to familiarize the prospect with the product or service being sold, to awaken interest, to develop desire, to establish superiority, to secure an inquiry or a "lead," etc., and thus to make it possible for the actual sale to be made at some other place and time.

It is true that in a great many buying transactions—notably in the purchase of food at retail—the actual salesman has disappeared, and self-service is the rule. Here advertising fills a relatively new role. It pre-informs and pre-sells the customer to such an extent that when she enters the place in which actual purchases are made—in this case the supermarket—the necessity for personal salesmanship has largely been replaced, and what was once a buying-selling situation now becomes a much simpler order-filling operation. Much spur-of-the-moment impulse buying still takes place, of course; but the essential elements of information about the product and confidence in its value have been developed as the customer or prospect has been exposed to advertising, and personal salesmanship is not required at the point of purchase.

Five Ways that Ads Work

In his book, "How to Become an Advertising Man," the late James Webb Young, a pioneer advertising man, said there are five basic ways in which advertising works:

"**1. By familiarizing**—that is, as the dictionary says, by 'making something well-known; bringing into common use.'" This is the absolutely basic value created by advertising, the one underlying all others.

"**2. By reminding**—a function that may alone, in some cases, make advertising pay.

"**3. By spreading news**—not only news in the newspaper sense, but a special kind of news that only advertising, in the commercial field, can most widely deal with.

"**4. By overcoming inertias**—the great drag on all human progress, economic or non-economic, as represented by the sociological term, 'cultural lag.'

"**5. By adding a value** not in the product —the most challenging field for creativeness in advertising."

■ We shall return to a discussion of some of these points later. At the moment, it is interesting to note that all of them lie in the "salesman's helper" area. They imply a preconditioning that will help consummate a sale later.

In similar fashion, McGraw-Hill, which publishes books and a host of specialized business publications, says there are six steps to successful selling to business and industry. They are:

1. Make contact.
2. Arouse interest.
3. Create preference.
4. Make proposal.
5. Close order.
6. Keep customer sold.

"The function of advertising," says McGraw-Hill, "is to reduce the cost of selling." And with the average cost of an industrial salesman's call estimated at more than $50, says McGraw-Hill, it is essential to use advertising to accomplish the largest part of steps 1, 2, 3 and 6, and thus allow the expensive salesman more time to concentrate on steps 4 and 5, which must be accomplished by the salesman and cannot be performed by advertising.

What has been said here about substituting for the salesman and acting as the salesman's helper has been principally couched in terms of the manufacturer or producer talking directly to the ultimate consumer. But in point of fact, most consumer goods and an important segment of capital goods do not move directly from producer to consumer. Instead, they move through a variety of intermediate channels of wholesalers, jobbers, distributors and retailers, which constitute the distributive channels for the particular product under discussion.

In most instances, advertising can be used in the various steps of the distributive process in much the same way it is used to reach consumers. Thus, advertising is "salesmanship in print" and salesman's helper in trying to make sales to distributors and dealers, as well as to consumers.

Advertising Is a Special Pleader

Advertising worth its salt to the advertiser has another attribute of the good salesman—an attribute sometimes thoughtlessly criticized. That attribute is enthusiasm.

No one likes to believe his actions or his buying habits are influenced to any important degree by the persuasion exerted by salesmanship, whether it is personal selling or advertising. We like to believe that all that is necessary is to uncover the wares, so to speak, and buyers will make their free-will choices without further ado. Any "salesmanship"—whether it be personal or impersonal—we tend to equate with undue or unfair influence.

■ The statement often attributed to Emerson that if someone built a better mousetrap, the world would beat a path to his door, is not even a half truth. Making a better mousetrap is not enough. Someone must explain that it *is* a better mousetrap, and *why* it is better. Someone must be enthusiastic about its merits and its advantages—enthusiastic and interested enough to sell others on its merits, and to overcome inertia and unwillingness to change.

This is the function of the salesman—and of advertising. By definition, salesmanship, of which advertising is one manifestation, is special pleading, not unbiased reporting. Yet this inspires one of the great general criticisms of advertising: That it induces people to buy things they don't really want and can't afford.

No one expects a good lawyer to present an unbiased resume of his client's position, nor a politician to outline dispassionately the advantages and disadvantages of the course he urges, nor a clergyman to explain the possibility that some other faith may have more to commend it than the one *he* advocates. But a good many intelligent people seem to feel that special pleading and enthusiastic selling in advertising are somehow immoral or anti-social.

More Jobs for Advertising

Thus far we have been discussing advertising quite literally as "salesmanship in print," or at least as the salesman's helper, making it easier for the salesman to consummate the buying-selling transaction. But the uses of advertising spread into many other areas, some of which are performed incidentally by the good salesman, and some of which cannot effectively be performed by salesmen at all, but which are general management activities.

The catalog of ways in which advertising may be used and the tasks it may be asked to perform are almost endless, but they may be categorized into three broad groups in addition to the principal one of selling, or helping to sell, the advertiser's products or services. These are:

1. *Reassuring and retaining present and former customers.*

2. *Bolstering and increasing the confidence, enthusiasm and eagerness of the advertiser's own personnel, and of non-advertiser personnel engaged in the distribution of the product, or involved in recommending or indorsing it.*

3. *Projecting a useful image to one or more of the advertiser's various publics.*

Ads Are Post-Purchase Reassurance

It is no accident that research into advertising has demonstrated conclusively that the buyer of a particular product or service, at the conscious level at least, is as avid a follower of that product's advertising *after* he has made the purchase as during the actual purchasing cycle, and this is particularly true with regard to major purchases, such as those of an automobile, a major household appliance, the purchase of a life insurance policy, etc.

Having made a major and important buying decision, the buyer is looking for reassurance that he has bought well, and he finds it most easily and most satisfactorily, in many cases, in the advertising of the product he has just bought. He finds it, first, in a reaffirmation of the product virtues and values which induced him to buy it in the first place, and he finds it, secondly, in the continued appearance of the advertising, for here is widespread public testimony to the buyer's wisdom. The more advertising there is, and the more persuasively it extolls the virtue of the product, the more the buyer is re-sold and reassured, and the

more likely he is to buy the same product under the same conditions the next time he is in the market.

Since practically no business can operate successfully without getting the vast bulk of its business from former customers who are satisfied enough to repeat their purchases, this reassurance of the buyer is the most important single thing an established business can do to insure success. And in most instances, even in the case of infrequent and expensive purchases, advertising can perform this function best.

Ads Are Impersonal, Massive

In this respect, advertising is more satisfactory than personal salesmanship for two simple reasons, aside from comparative cost.

First, because it is impersonal, it can "call on the buyer" far more frequently. Your automobile dealer, for example, can send you a monthly service reminder which also serves to bolster your pride in the car you bought. But a salesman who called you every month after he sold you a car would quickly get to be a pest.

Second, advertising is a mass, public operation. And the advertising of *your* car reaching your friends and neighbors and your business associates with the story of *your* car's virtues, automatically enhances your prestige.

It should be added that practically no advertising is bought by American business for this post-selling reassurance factor alone. This type of advertising benefit is normally a side effect of other advertising designed to perform a straightout selling or other function. But its value and importance cannot be ignored. And by itself, it goes a long way to explain why there is no practical point, in the lives of most businesses, when advertising can be stopped or sharply curtailed.

Back-Up for Sales, Dealer Force

The second "non-selling" value of advertising is its effect on the company's own employes, especially its sales force, as well as on those who do not work for the company but in one way or another handle the product or service in the chain of distribution which ultimately brings it to the point of sale. Here advertising can often help provide the indefinable difference between an enthusiastic, eager sales force, convinced of the value of its products and their intrinsic merit, and a lackadaisical, unsure organization which feels slightly on the defensive as it faces buyers and prospects.

Maintaining high morale among a company's own sales force and other personnel, and product preference among wholesalers, distributors, dealers and their sales personnel, is extremely important to most businesses, and a considerable amount of effort and thought is devoted to it. Again, relatively little advertising is run with the primary purpose of bolstering the morale of the advertiser's own employes, even though its value in this connection is not overlooked. But a considerable amount of advertising is addressed to non-advertiser personnel engaged in the distribution of the product—or involved in a collateral activity in which their endorsement or approval can be important in making the sale.

Thus distributors, wholesalers, dealers and others in the chain of distribution are reminded that the advertiser's product should be given active support at every distribution level, and that doing so will benefit the distributor, wholesaler and dealer, as well as the manufacturer, because the product gives satisfaction, is well known and easy to sell, and provides a reasonable profit margin, among other reasons.

■ In the case of many products, approval or endorsement by experts of one kind or another is of great importance. Approval of Crest toothpaste by the American Dental Assn. was of major importance in skyrocketing this brand into No. 1 position in its field. In the case of many health products and non-prescription remedies, endorsement or approval by individual doctors or dentists is of major importance. In the case of many building products, the architect's favor is almost basic. And consequently, a good deal of advertising is addressed to these and other "influentials," not to sell the product directly to them, but to familiarize them with it and to (hopefully) gain their approval or endorsement.

A very substantial volume of advertising—sometimes estimated as high as $3 billion annually—also goes into cooperative advertising, in which producer, distributor and dealer join in paying the cost of advertising addressed to the ultimate consumer. An important part of retail advertising featuring specific products or services is paid for in part or wholly by the producer of the products, who either underwrites part of the cost of advertising prepared by his retailers, or places advertising of his own to which retailers' names are signed or displayed.

Selling Your 'Image' or Reputation

The third broad category of additional jobs for advertising is that of projecting a useful image to one or more of the advertiser's various publics. Here we are in an area once comfortably known as "institutional advertising," which is now—after a period of relative eclipse—enjoying an important rebirth under the new title of "image" or "corporate image" advertising.

In broadest generality, it is possible to advertise one of two things: The goods or services you make or sell—or the company or people who make or sell them. It is this second category of advertising which embraces "institutional" or "corporate image" advertising. And although the term has largely been associated with the advertising of manufacturers and producers, its most important use probably continues to be in the retail field.

Every important retailer runs the two kinds of advertising we have just mentioned. He runs what the retail trade calls price-and-item advertising, to say that such-and-such a dress or chair or grocery special is on sale today, or will be on sale tomorrow, at such-and-such a price. Specific item advertising like this makes up the bulk of his advertising, in most cases.

Ads Push Store, Not Just Items

But he also runs other advertising, which talks in more general terms about his store's place in the community, its broad selection of merchandise, its position in the forefront of fashion, its stand on pricing and other matters. He is trying to project a favorable image of his store as the best place to shop, because he knows that such an over-all impression in the long run is more important to his success than the specific items he is able to promote.

Furthermore, it is impossible for a retailer to advertise everything he has to sell. One important department store executive estimates that 80% of daily sales are of items not advertised. Thus, a major function of the advertising is to attract traffic to the store.

Retail stores also have discovered that it is important for them to "position" themselves in the local buying spectrum, and they are careful, in the style and technique used in all promotions and advertising, to keep within the framework of the public image which suits them best. Some advertising says—more perhaps by its looks than by the words it uses—that the advertiser is an elegant, exclusive shop where one does not expect to find anything but the very best, at substantial prices; other advertising says, just as plainly, that the advertiser offers more modest merchandise at prices that have real appeal to people who must stretch their shopping dollars. The impression which the advertising gives must coincide closely with what the shopper senses when she enters the store.

Every retailer knows that his total image, the "look" and "feel" of his establishment as an institution, is his most important stock in trade. So everything he does in the way of promotion and advertising, as well as in pricing, fixturing, etc., is designed to enhance the image

he wants to project for his total establishment. He sells scores or hundreds or even thousands of different items, and the one thing that binds them together into an economic unit is his store name, his reputation, his "image."

Advertising Factory No Longer Works

The circumstances are different, however, for many manufacturers and producers. They sometimes make a single product, sometimes relatively few products, sometimes a wide range of diverse products, sold in many different ways and places. They do not come into direct contact with the ultimate buyer, who purchases their products in one or another retail store. Furthermore, the producer's enterprise is not normally a part (or at any rate an important part) of the local scene.

Initially, most products carried the owner's or the company's name. And much early advertising consisted of a picture of the factory or of the company's founder, and an "institutional" message that said, in one way or another, that the product had to be superior because the advertiser's great institution was responsible for turning it out.

But as the tempo of marketing increased, as products proliferated, as it became important for names to stand out clearly on self-service shelfs and to be easily and quickly pronounceable and identifiable, manufactured names replaced those of men or even companies. The great commercial names of America became not the names of individuals or companies, but the names of products. Everyone knew Ivory soap or Wheaties or Bon Ami or Camel cigarets without necessarily knowing—or caring about—the name of their makers.

■ During the 1930s in particular, when the Great Depression slashed away at established values and loyalties, many national advertisers abandoned their company names entirely in advertising (except for necessary copyright and other legal purposes) and promoted their products and brands with no attempt whatever to identify them with the company which produced them. Clearly, they felt that consumers cared nothing about the institution behind the product as long as the product itself was satisfactory.

This tendency toward corporate self-effacement in advertising was enhanced as such companies as Procter & Gamble developed lines of products which competed vigorously with each other, as well as with those of competitors.

But during the past 30 years there has been a reversal of thinking about the importance of the corporate image, and a very considerable growth in this type of advertising, as well as an increasing tendency to tie prominent brands to a corporate identity. Such advertising and promotional tag lines as, "Another good product of General Foods" are now appearing with increasing frequency. The initial impetus came during World War II, when producers who had withdrawn from the consumer market to make war material, or who could not supply normal demand for other reasons, sought to maintain their reputation in the marketplace.

Diversification Hikes Image Ads

The great growth of corporate image advertising, however, has resulted from the growth of great industrial complexes as businesses have sought diversification and have merged with and purchased other companies, and as advancing technology has resulted in fewer and fewer essential differences in the characteristics of competing products.

With products tending to become nearly identical in design, performance, price and other characteristics, many companies, particularly in the producer-goods field, have felt that the product itself is becoming a relatively minor factor in making a sale—that is to say, the buyer can get nearly identical products on nearly identical terms from half a dozen suppliers—and therefore factors outside the product itself, especially including the reputation and capability of its maker, may frequently be decisive in making the sale.

The federal government, as a tremendously important factor in the market for all kinds and types of industrial goods, including a great many experimental contracts in such fields as missiles and rocketry, has also been important in stimulating "image" advertising, because in many instances the "product" being ordered is a highly specialized thing which may never before have been produced, and in such circumstances, the company's "capabilities"—its size, depth of engineering and production skills, reputation, relations with labor—are often the controlling factors.

The development of the diversified super-corporation, often engaged in activities as far removed from each other as operating a shipping line, an outdoor advertising company and a petrochemical plant, has had a major influence on the reemergence of institutional advertising under its new name of corporate image advertising. Since all of these super-corporations are publicly owned, and since all have social and sociological problems because of their size and complexity which are not directly related to selling their products, they have a considerable need for projecting their image favorably

to various groups within the population—stockholders and investors, legislators, civic leaders, labor, college and high school students who may be induced to come to work for them, educators, engineers, and a host of others.

Ecology, Urban Woes Alter Ad Scene

Currently, the volume of "social consciousness" advertising is growing, as such national concerns as ecology, training and hiring of minorities, adequacy of private pension and insurance plans, and redevelopment of decaying inner-cities become more and more important.

Businesses are being weighed by government and the public in the scale of social value as well as in terms of purely economic value, and a very considerable volume of advertising is currently being addressed to attempts to bolster the individual business' image in the public mind as a good citizen as well as an efficient producer of goods or services.

Hiring practices, working conditions, anti-pollution measures, safety precautions and the like are the subjects of many corporate campaigns, and in the same way, business or corporate points of view are more and more frequently being promoted in advertising—both by business and by private or group interests which frequently oppose the business point of view. Ecological considerations, in such matters as development of atomic power plants, offshore drilling, the Alaskan pipeline, etc., tend to generate considerable advertising by proponents and opponents alike.

No Inherent Ad-Business Love Affair

There is a widespread belief, particularly in academic circles, that advertising *per se* is the darling of the business man, and many seem to believe that the institution of advertising is more precious, in itself, to business than the merchandise or services it sells, the general prosperity of society, or the over-all social climate.

Clearly, advertising has become a useful and many times an indispensable tool of modern business, but as we have just seen, it is no more than a tool, and usually no more than one of many tools a business uses to help make sales, to improve its corporate image, its standing and its long-term profitability. Most frequently, it is a substitute for or a teammate of personal selling.

Most businesses now advertise, in one way or another, in the same way that most retail stores have air conditioning and attractive lighting and fixturing. But it is still possible to run a retail store successfully without air conditioning or attractive lighting and fixturing, and it is equally possible to conduct a successful business without advertising.

The simple fact is that the business man—even the one who invests huge quantities of his company's money in it—has no inherent interest in advertising. He uses it because he believes it is a selling tool of greater value or less cost or faster performance than any other device of which he knows for making a sale. As long as it serves his purpose in these ways, he will continue to use it; the moment he loses faith in its efficacy or its value, or he discovers some cheaper, more effective way to accomplish his goals, he will cease advertising as quickly as he can get cancelation notices out.

To the average business man, advertising is one of an almost infinite number of influences that can be brought to bear—sometimes successfully, sometimes without success—on his central problem of getting orders and making sales. He can (within the limits of realism) improve his product, or reduce its price; he can package it more efficiently or more enticingly; he can try to secure wider distribution for it, or move contrariwise to restrict distribution, and thus make it more attractive for selected outlets to handle; he can enlarge his sales force, or offer larger discounts, or increase or extend his advertising. His choices are endless, and almost inevitably he must exercise them not in a single area, but in a whole complex of areas which together make up the "marketing mix" of his business.

Advertising agencies and their employes, those who provide materials and supplies used in advertising, and to a somewhat lesser but still important extent, those who work for or control mass media of communications which rely partly or wholly on advertising support, have an *inherent* interest in the size and the general state of health of the advertising business. If the total volume of advertising were to shrink greatly, their jobs and their businesses would be in jeopardy or would disappear.

But from the standpoint of those who pay the bills for advertising, the effectiveness of advertising and its efficiency as a selling tool are far more important than its total volume or the specific form it takes. Their view of advertising is a dispassionate and objective one; their interest in advertising is completely conditioned on its value or possible value to them as a tool to help sell automobiles or food or clothing or vacation trips or whatever they happen to be in the business of selling.

Controversy Over Advertising

In spite of—or perhaps because of—its great importance in the economic life of the U.S. and the entire free world, advertising is not universally loved and admired. Especially among certain schools of economists and social planners, advertising is viewed with displeasure and alarm, and frequently inveighed against as a social evil.

An excellent selection of points of view on the social and economic value of advertising—both pro and con—appears later in this volume, so here we shall attempt briefly merely to highlight the varied viewpoints, and, if possible, to narrow the area of debate.

Those who have no admiration for advertising attack it principally on the following grounds:

1. It promotes senseless materialism, and induces people to "buy what they don't need and can't afford."

2. In this process of promoting "artificially created wants," as one economist has phrased it, the nation's productive resources are wasted and "useful, even essential, public outlays" are prevented.

3. It distorts "normal" values and the "normal" supply-and-demand relationship in the marketplace by minimizing price competition and creating a largely fictitious competition based primarily on unreal psychological values attributed to products.

4. It promotes inordinate competition between brands and excessive switching of purchases, and thereby contributes to higher prices.

5. It is immoral or at least amoral, and it promotes activities and a manner of living which are inimical to the public welfare.

6. It degrades the general level of taste.

7. It is too shrill, too pervasive, too all-encompassing, too insistent.

Ads Can Sell Smut or Scriptures

In one very real sense, all of these criticisms (with the possible exception of the last) are based on the fallacy that "advertising" has substance and meaning by itself. Advertising, as we have seen it, is merely a tool and a technique, and attacks on advertising *per se* are therefore meaningless. It can equally well be used to promote materialism or asceticism; the purchase of cosmetics or U.S. bonds, the sale of smut or scriptures.

That is not to say that all the uses to which advertising is put, nor all the ways in which it is used, are above criticism. They are not. Many forms of advertising, and many uses to which advertising are put, are properly subject to question. But the important point to bear in mind is that over-all, indiscriminate opposition to "advertising" is no more sensible than opposition to "hammers" because they are occasionally used as bludgeons. Opposition to specific advertising or to specific forms or uses of advertising may be meaningful and sensible; opposition to "advertising" is not.

In its role as a substitute for and assistant to the salesman, advertising men say, advertising performs an essential part in an economy of abundance: It helps develop demand for the host of products and services which are available to and within the reach of, the vast majority, and by so doing it helps constantly to raise the standard of living and to keep the wheels of industry moving smoothly.

"Materialism" is not a nasty word—but simply the obverse of "high standard of living," they say, and it is advertising's assistance in spreading information about, and increasing demand for goods and services which helps prevent the society from stagnating, and instead makes it dynamic and forward-moving. As famed anthropologist Margaret Mead once put it: "Ours is an economy that is geared to a rising standard of living. We are geared to a notion that we could live better than we do—so no one has settled down very comfortably and is satisfied with the way he lives."

Blows at Ads Really Aim at System

Much opposition to advertising in general, advertising men believe, is in reality opposition to the operation of our social and economic system, rather than to advertising. Advertising gets the brunt of the opposition, they feel, because it operates in the full glare of public knowledge, but many of the criticisms aimed at it are in reality criticisms of the state of society, rather than of advertising as such.

Most current criticism of advertising falls in this category, or in the category of criticism of the products advertised. Laws prohibiting the advertising of cigarets on radio and television fall in this category. So do all the debates about advertising to children, especially on television, which not only proclaim that children require special protection against advertising claims, but also argue that "unwholesome" products or practices should be barred. Thus products like cookies or presweetened cereals, for example, are under fire because their advertising "promotes unhealthy dietary habits."

Even the most vocal critics of advertising, however, usually concede that some uses of it are proper. For example, advertising's basic function of disseminating news and information in a commercial sense is generally accepted. Advertising containing news of new products, of new sizes or prices, of sales, etc., is generally accepted as making economic as well as commercial sense.

Dump Ad Repetition? Can Be Suicide

On the other hand, "mere repetition" is criticized as an economic waste, resulting simply in transferring custom from one brand or producer to another. But advertising men insist that there is no such thing as "mere repetition" and can point out specific instances in which reduction or elimination of advertising—no matter how well known a product has been—has been the equivalent of commercial suicide. Furthermore, they say, while much advertising does result in switching the customer from one brand to another (a perfectly legitimate objective in a competitive society), the weight of the advertising for all brands almost invariably enlarges the total market for all products in that category.

Like everything else that goes into the production, distribution and sale of a product or service, advertising is a cost. And—as is the case with all costs—the consumer ultimately pays it. But advertising's sole reason for existence, from the standpoint of the advertiser, is that it performs an essential selling function more efficiently, and therefore at less cost, than any other known technique. Whether the cost of performing this service is acceptable in a broad socio-economic sense may be debatable; but it is not debatable in terms of the individual advertiser. Once the advertiser is convinced that his advertising is not helping him sell at less total cost than some alternative method of operating, he stops advertising immediately.

■ One other point deserves emphasis: By definition, advertising identifies the person or organization placing the advertising. Thus the person exposed to advertising always knows who is urging him to act in a particular way, and he can take this into account when he makes up his mind.

Some years ago there was much excitement over something called "subliminal advertising," by means of which mental impulses were supposed to be transmitted without identifying the transmitter or even making the "subject" aware that he was being influenced. Advertising men denounced the idea as unethical as well as ineffective. "Advertising" is always clearly identifiable as advertising; its self-interest and its bias are always clearly visible.

The Problems of Taste

Criticism of advertising in the area of good taste are the most disturbing and the most difficult to resolve of all questions facing advertisers. Good taste is an ephemeral, ever-changing, never too clearly defined concept. What is good taste here and now may be bad taste there and then. What seems perfectly proper to one person is extremely offensive to another—or to the same person under different circumstances.

The area is particularly difficult for advertisers because there seems to be an assumption in some quarters that users and producers of advertising are engaged in a deliberate attempt to lower the general level of taste. In fact, the opposite seems more nearly to be true, since producers of advertising are in the main inclined toward the artistic and the literate, with standards of taste which they like to believe are well above normal, and which they would normally delight to advance in advertising.

The fact is, however, that advertising, being designed to "sell" something to masses of people, cannot normally rise very much above the general level of public taste, nor fall very much below it. The most important job for advertising is to "make a sale" for a product or a service, and to do so it must clearly establish a rapport with its audience, which means that it must consciously stay within relatively narrow bounds of acceptability in terms of language, visualization, and general background and frame of reference. An approach which overestimates the general level of public taste, or one which underestimates it, is equally inappropriate for the advertiser, because it is unlikely to have the desired impact on the audience.

Do Ads Corrupt Public Taste?

There is a considerable body of evidence to indicate that, working within the rather narrow limits prescribed by practical commercial considerations, producers and sponsors of advertising have helped measurably to raise the general public taste in music, in art and in many other ways. But, like almost any assertion in the area of taste or culture, this is clearly subject to debate.

In general, advertisers are involved in matters of taste only incidentally, and they are unable to understand why they should be—as they sometimes are—accused of deliberately attempting to corrupt the public taste. The allegedly low state of television programing, for example, is frequently blamed on advertisers, but advertisers' responsibility is only by indirection.

Advertisers on television want only large audiences, which is understandable. But normally they are totally without preference as to the kind of fare which should be offered, just so it attracts a substantial audience. If westerns deliver large audiences, advertisers will eagerly sponsor westerns; if it is variety which produces large audiences, then advertisers want variety shows, and if grand opera or Shakespeare festivals mean big audiences, then advertisers will sponsor opera or Shakespeare. Their interest lies primarily in assembling a substantial audience to listen to their message, not in promoting one or another kind of program. They do not normally see it as their job to foster or promote any particular kind or level of taste, but rather to present that which is most pleasing to the greatest possible number of people in the audience they wish to reach. There is also, however, considerable evidence that many advertisers strive for programs and advertising that tend to elevate the standards of taste.

Reprinted from "Advertising Age," Nov. 21, 1973, pp. 8, 12, 14, 16, 18

PART 2 | How the Advertising Business Works

The advertiser—

how he operates

He is the basis of the advertising business, although primarily he's not in it so much as he is in the soap, or breakfast cereal, or automobile business. But to him, the advertising is vital.

A company is in business to do two things: To make a product—or provide a service—and sell it at a profit. In making the product, the company is a manufacturer; in selling it, it is a marketer. As a marketer, it uses advertising to inform people of the product's existence and availability, and to persuade them to buy it.

Advertising is a sales tool, a substitute for personal selling; a quick, and relatively inexpensive way to reach millions of people at one time. It is one element of something called the marketing mix, which also includes such activities as distribution and pricing. As a selling tool, advertising is used in one form or another by nearly every business establishment in the nation. The heavy and widespread use of advertising in the U.S. goes back 50 years or more, to the time of the rapid development of mass production, which reduced unit cost. As time went on, industry came more and more to the realization that mass production could be continued only if mass distribution was available. Marketing and advertising became the keys to mass distribution.

"The continuous flow of sales in large volume was essential to mass production," as was once pointed out by W. T. Holliday, then president of the Standard Oil Co. (Ohio). "The inevitable result, therefore, was that industry had to reach out past the middleman and appeal directly to the consumers: They had themselves to create the ultimate demand for their products. The natural way was the development of trade names and brands, and the advertising of them to the masses of consumers. Mass distribution required mass selling, and that required advertising of the brands."

Donald Kendall of PepsiCo Inc., which spends some $50,000,000 annually on advertising, has said that advertising "is an inseparable part of the total marketing function. Essentially, the marketing function is one of identifying consumer wants, moving to fill those wants by developing products with appropriate qualities, packaging them for attractiveness and convenience, pricing them right, and ultimately getting them into good distribution. Advertising's role in this function is to convey the news and the benefits of the products to consumers . . . This means selling the product."

National Advertisers Predominate

Everybody who advertised in 1972—manufacturing companies, service operations, retailers, wholesalers, distributors, associations, labor unions, schools, churches, governments, politicians, individuals placing want ads—spent an estimated $23.1 billion for the privilege.

Most of this enormous total—about $13.1 billion, or 57%—was expended by national advertisers. There are, in fact, more than 17,000 such advertisers in the U.S. The 100 largest of these companies (ranging from Procter & Gamble, with an expenditure of about $275,000,000, to the E. & J. Gallo Winery, with an outlay of $13,300,000) invested $5.27 billion alone in advertising media last year. Thus, fewer than 1% of all of America's national advertisers accounted for 40% of all national advertising dollars. Nine companies—P&G, American Home Products, Sears, Roebuck, General Foods, Ford Motor, General Motors, Colgate-Palmolive, Warner-Lambert and Bristol-Myers—spent more than $100,000,000 each, and their combined expenditures accounted for nearly 11% of all national advertising. Their combined sales added up to well over $70 billion in 1972.

■ While the 17,000 national advertisers have products that require 51 classifica-

tions for listing in "The Standard Advertising Register," a majority of leading national advertisers can be broken down into a handful of broad product categories:

Food—Of the 100 leading advertisers, 18 are food marketers.

Drugs and cosmetics—Another 22 of the 100 leaders have drugs and cosmetics lines.

Automotive—Six auto makers spent more than $459,000,000 on advertising last year.

Tobacco—Five cigaret manufacturers spent a total of more than $285,000,000.

Soap—The three leading soap and detergent marketers all ranked among the top 25 advertisers.

Beer and liquor—Two beers, three distillers and a winery are among the 100 leaders.

With the exception of automobiles, all the above categories contain "package products"—mass volume items sold daily everywhere in the U.S. These are products that depend heavily on repeat purchases: Food, drugs, soap, detergents, beer, cigarets are bought with great frequency by the same consumers. And most of these products are sold primarily in self-service outlets. For these reasons, the makers of these products use advertising to pre-sell consumers and to build preferences for their particular brands.

Drugs, Cosmetics Get High Ad Rates

For many of the companies in these fields, manufacturing costs are relatively low, so advertising becomes a major item in the corporate budget. For a number of drugs and cosmetics companies, advertising is the principal company expense. In 1972, Alberto-Culver put $62,000,000 into advertising, and its sales amounted to $181,681,258. Advertising thus amounted to 33.9% of its sales. Carter-Wallace put

$40,000,000 into advertising—30.7% of its sales of $130,120,000.

On the other hand, Exxon Corp., with sales of $22.4 billion, put $34,300,000 into advertising in 1972. Advertising as a percentage of sales amounted to 0.2%. General Motors had an advertising-to-sales percentage of four-tenths of 1% ($146,000,000 in advertising outlays, $30.4 billion in sales).

The proportion of sales to advertising will also vary within an industry by degree of success. For example, American Brands achieved sales of $2.99 billion in 1972 on $57,000,000 worth of advertising. Brown & Williamson, in the same field, spent $52,200,000 on advertising and got sales of only $876,267,795. Kraftco sales were $2.7 billion when advertising cost $64,500,000. But General Foods' sales amounted to $1.96 billion on an advertising investment of $170,000,000. "It's not the high advertising budget that produces the high sales level," says Kenneth Mason, Quaker Oats' advertising executive. "It's the high sales level that produces the high advertising budget. Or, to state it as a business principle: In most businesses, products which sell well tend to be advertised more than products which sell poorly."

How Much Should You Advertise?

But the practice of budgeting on an advertising-to-sales ratio, as has been pointed out by Benjamin Lipstein of SSC&B, "places the advertising function in a perpetually defensive position," where it is subject to budget-trimming to help make short-term profits. It is a posture that advertising will most likely retain, adds Mr. Lipstein, until such time as research comes up with the answer to the client's perennial question, "Am I getting my money's worth for my advertising dollars?"

Nobody really knows how much money should be invested in advertising. And if advertising money is spent to increase sales and profits, as it certainly is, nobody really knows how much advertising contributes to those dual goals. "I know half my advertising is wasted—but I don't know which half," goes the plaintive old saw.

Clarence Eldridge, former marketing boss of General Foods and later a management consultant, has said that two questions that plague advertisers are: How can we make our advertising more effective? How much advertising is enough? Not only can't we predict how much advertising it is going to take to produce a given result, we can't tell, when the advertising is finished, just what has been accomplished, he said.

Yet, *Forbes,* a few years ago, divined a "single characteristic shared by the lead-ing ten U.S. corporations whose money was best managed. The characteristic: "Each of these companies sells clearly identifiable, branded products with high reputations in their field and backed in every single case by an image of quality, the kind of image that can be created only by superior products backed by superior advertising and promotion."

Cut Advertising, and Sales Fall

Every national advertiser, however, is positive about one thing: Advertising is a cost of doing business, and for many, perhaps the single largest expense item. Some think it is too big a cost, although most of these might concede that large reductions in their advertising appropriations would surely result in a decline in sales volume. Prof. William Comanor of Stanford has contended that if advertising were limited to an expenditure of $50,000,000 for, say, the dairy products industry, which actually spends more than $84,000,000, its sales would fall 66.1% from their $4.25 billion level; if drug advertising were cut back from $207,400,000 to $50,000,000, sales of that industry would topple 78%.

General Motors, for one, would like to increase its advertising effectiveness without increasing its advertising budgets. Shelton Fisher, president of McGraw-Hill, has noted that, "The bigger advertisers, many of whom are manufacturers and industrialists at heart, are beginning (in 1971) to apply the same yardsticks to their advertising budgets, agencies and media that they apply to their factories and assembly lines. Out in the plant, these yardsticks are called 'value analysis' or 'value engineering.' Lawrence D. Miles, who pioneered this area for General Electric, defines the general concept as 'finding the lowest cost at which an essential function can reliably be provided.' What the advertiser wants is more efficiency without a reduction in quality. He figures that if he can achieve this goal in the manufacture of cars or groceries, why not in advertising?"

Advertisers do not have a vested interest in advertising per se, but they do have such an interest in selling more of the goods and services they offer to consumers. Advertising is an investment that they make to help them reach that goal. But 1972, a year when national advertisers spent $13.1 billion on advertising, this country's industrial corporations increased their sales by 13.2% and, according to *Fortune,* the 500 largest enjoyed a combined sales increase of 10.9%. National advertisers like Chrysler, Ford Motor, Eastman Kodak and Mobil Oil all made notable sales gains. As a matter of fact, the 100 leading national advertisers last year increased their advertising expenditures 7.5% over 1971 levels to $5.27 billion—but each of them showed a sales increase over 1971—an unprecedented sales record.

Stocks Do Better for Advertisers

It is, of course, somewhat misleading to relate advertising to sales on a cause-and-effect basis. To the advertiser, advertising is just one of any number of factors that help influence the sale of his products, including the product itself, its price, distribution, packaging and the competition.

In any event, a study by Robert A. Herzbrun for the ADVERTISING AGE Advertisers' Common Stock Index (measuring the price movement of common stocks of 30 leading national advertisers representing a broad range of consumer goods and services to see how well they perform compared with the rest of the market) showed that advertisers' stocks outpaced the market for four consecutive years, from 1969 through 1972. Six of the 30 stocks more than doubled during the four-year period—while the market as a whole grew by a shade less than 10%. The six: Philip Morris, up nearly 270% over the four years; Procter & Gamble, ahead nearly 159%; Norton Simon and Coca-Cola, up 108%; Distillers Corp.-Seagram, 104%; American Home Products, 103%.

1972 top ten in ad expenditures

1972 rank	1962 rank		1972 total	1962 total
1	2	Procter & Gamble	$275,000,000	$139,150,000
2	12	Sears, Roebuck	215,000,000	53,600,000
3	4	General Foods	170,000,000	101,000,000
4	1	General Motors	146,000,000	160,000,000
5	14	Warner-Lambert	134,000,000	46,000,000
6	3	Ford Motor Co.	132,500,000	106,000,000
7	8	American Home Products	116,000,000	65,500,000
8	9	Bristol-Myers	115,000,000	65,000,000
9	6	Colgate-Palmolive	105,000,000	70,000,000
10	11	Chrysler Corp.	95,415,400	54,062,000

"Advertisers' stocks," reported Mr. Herzbrun, "have been consistent performers, not only topping the New York Stock Exchange Index by a 5-to-1 margin over the last four years, but out-performing it in each of the years individually as well. During that period, we've seen a President inaugurated and reelected, a war wound down, and the economy bounce around like a yo-yo. Along with it all, the stock market moved from a state of bullishness to utter despair to the euphoria of breaking the 1,000 barrier. With four years like that, it would appear that the continued strength of advertisers' stocks is standing up to the test of time."

As pointed out by Profs. Albert W. Frey and Kenneth R. Davis in their landmark study of "The Advertising Industry" for the Assn. of National Advertisers in 1958, "The basic purposes of marketing do not change with the years (but) change does occur in markets, in the products and services to be marketed, in the prices of the products and services, and in marketing methods and tools."

Big Problems for Advertising

Their study identified a number of "major" problems in the advertising industry—all of which were still current in 1965 (as reported in "Management & Advertising Problems in the Advertiser-Agency Relationship," a study conducted for the ANA by Booz-Allen & Hamilton) and remain current in 1973. Among them: (1) "Evaluating the effectiveness of advertising efforts," (2) "persuading top management of the usefulness of advertising in meeting company profit objectives," (3) "inducing client management to establish specific marketing and advertising goals, recognize the importance of the marketing-mix concept, decide logically what services are needed and the proper sources for these services," (4) inducing client top management to recognize the importance of clear-cut, intelligent direction of advertising activities, and to give undivided authority and responsibility to competent personnel appointed for the task."

There is no uniformity in the way business uses advertising. Each industry, indeed, each company, develops its own approach. One advertiser will opt for the placement of most of his promotion budget in television, another company in the same field will want the money going into magazines and newspapers. Ethical drug advertiser "A" will depend heavily on direct mail advertising to reach physicians, while company "B" will use advertising in medical journals. A consumer products marketer will rely on advertising to do his major selling job and will employ perhaps only a handful of sales-

SALARIES PAID TO ADVERTISER PEOPLE

(Figures represent high and low averages.)

	LARGE (Over 200 million sales)	MEDIUM (Under 200 million sales)
DOMESTIC		
Marketing director	$40-60,000	$30-40,000
Advertising manager	25-35,000	20-35,000
Group brand/product manager	28-35,000	22-25,000
Brand/product manager	22-28,000	18-20,000
Assistant brand/product manager	14-18,000	10-14,000
Sales promotion manager	18-25,000	15-22,000
Market research director	30-38,000	22-25,000
Media director	20-35,000	18-25,000
Tv producer	20-30,000	15-23,000
Public relations manager	35-60,000	25-35,000
Personnel director	30-40,000	22-35,000
INTERNATIONAL		
Marketing manager worldwide	40-60,000	30-40,000
General manager regional	35-45,000	25-40,000
Area manager	25-40,000	20-24,000
Product/brand manager	25-28,000	22-25,000
Advertising manager	30-40,000	20-25,000
ART DEPARTMENT		
Executive art director	18-35,000	16-18,000
Promo designer	14-20,000	10-16,000
Packaging art director	13-25,000	15-20,000
Packaging designer	14-20,000	15-18,000
Editorial art director	25-35,000	14-25,000

NOTE: Figures above are based on 2,000 New York and Chicago job-search assignments undertaken by Jerry Fields Associates between September, 1971, and September, 1973. Figures do not include bonuses, stock, profit sharing, etc.

men. (McGraw-Hill studies have shown that the cost of a single visit by a salesman rose from $30.35 in 1961 to $57.71 in 1971.) An industrial advertiser, on the other hand, may use his advertising as a salesman's helper—while maintaining a large sales staff to sell his industrial products. This happens because his products are high-priced and technically complex, requiring personal demonstration of their operation, care and maintenance to spur the sale.

Today advertising by business to business is a multi-billion-dollar operation. There are 2,381 business publications in the U.S., and advertisers support them to the tune of more than $880,000,000 a year (and advertising sales of $925,000,000 are expected this year). These publications include titles in such areas as metalworking, engineering, product design and development.

Advertising of industrial products is not limited to the business press. A lot of it is also on television and in general magazines which are read by important business men and government officials.

Varied Users of Advertising

Orange growers, apple growers, commodity producers likewise are important users of advertising. The Florida Citrus Commission spends perhaps $7,000,000 a year advertising orange products and grapefruit. In California, growers of avocados, raisins, apricots and other food products together spend over $10,000,000 annually on advertising. In still another area, the American Iron & Steel Institute makes efforts to promote the use of those metals in commercial, industrial and institutional markets—and, indeed, these days it sponsors advertising depicting the steel industry as a good citizen, aware of its ecological responsibilities.

Industry groups of all kinds use advertising to create preferences for the materials they manufacture and which, in turn, become ingredients in other products. All of them realize they need not only to sell their customers, but their customers' customers as well. Makers of automobile tire components such as polyester and steel not only advertise the advantages of their materials to Detroit's auto makers, but to the general public as well.

New Products Are Big Ad Users

For America's national advertisers, new products have long been regarded as a source of sales and profit expansion. Last year 52 new items went on supermarket shelves in a typical week (although only 11 were accepted by shoppers). In 1971, the Kellogg Co. introduced some 64 new products (24 in North America, 40 overseas). Perhaps not so coincidentally, Kellogg's sales that year increased 10% and its net earnings advanced 11%.

Advertising is recognized by most large companies as a key factor in building demand for a new product. A 1972 ADVERTISING AGE survey of major national advertisers indicated that new products would constitute a major influence on the companies' 1973 advertising budgets, citing new products as the primary reason for increasing their advertising investments. New product introduction is costly. Procter & Gamble put $15,000,000 into the introduction of Gleem toothpaste; its introductory advertising for Crest took $16,000,000. When P&G makes up its mind to go with a new product, it may well decide to spend as much as $25,000,000—the amount it put behind Bold detergent in 1965. (By 1971, P&G's spending on Bold was down to $5,000,000.) Advertising investments behind new consumer packaged goods may run, at the start, to something like $1 for advertising for every $1 of sales.

Some new products that were introduced in the last few years were the Mazda car with its rotary engine; Gillette's Trac II razor; Procter & Gamble's Pampers; Eastman Kodak's Pocket Instamatic camera; General Mills' Hamburger Helper; Mennen E deodorant and Brown/-Forman's Frost 8/80 white whisky. The last two never made it, proving costly errors to their companies. But Trac II grabbed a 10% share of the blade market and a 40% piece of razor sales; Pampers got as much as 90% of a $200,000,000-plus market; Hamburger Helper had 1972 sales estimated at $60,000,000.

Ads Hasten Product Failure

New product failures can be extremely costly. The failure of the Edsel cost Ford Motor Co. $250,000,000. Last year the failure of its Raggedy Ann and Raggedy Andy disposable diapers reportedly cost Scott Paper Co. $12,000,000. General Foods, in the past, has had to withdraw a new baby food line, a gourmet food line and other products. In 1968, nearly 9,500 products were introduced in supermarkets, but only 20% of them met their sales goals. "A single product failure," commented T. L. Angelus of the New Products

Action Team Inc., "can cost from $75,000 in test market to $20,000,000 for a national introduction." Advertising, it has been pointed out, can actually speed up the demise of an inadequate product by sharply increasing the number of people who give the new product a trial. Good advertising cannot overcome a poor product.

Advertising is not only incapable of selling a poor product, it cannot sell a good product that the public does not want. General Mills once brought out a cereal called Clackers after research indicated that a graham-flavored cereal would do well. Test market advertising achieved good scores, and Clackers went into distribution. But the product had to be dropped when consumers declined to make repeat purchases. General Mills concluded, "The product can completely cancel advertising's potential."

The reasons for consumers' reaction to Clackers may be somewhat obscure. But one explanation may lie in what Prof. Theodore Levitt of Harvard has pointed out:

"The 'purpose' of the product is not what the engineer says it is, but what the consumer implicitly demands it shall be. Thus the consumer consumes not things, but expected benefits—not cosmetics, but the satisfactions of the allurements they promise; not quarter-inch drills, but quarter-inch holes; not stock in companies, but capital gains; not numerically-controlled milling machines, but trouble-free and accurately smooth metal parts; not low-cal whipped cream, but self-rewarding indulgence combined with sophisticated convenience. The significance of these distinctions is anything but trivial."

Advertisers Hone Ad Skills

Some significant changes have overtaken the advertising business as a whole in the last ten years, including changes in the ways national advertisers manage the advertising function. No advertising agency man would quarrel with the statement that more and more marketing and advertising expertise is now located at the client level.

In 1971, the Assn. of National Advertisers found advertisers to be diversifying, multiplying product lines and setting up venture teams. "Clients," reported the ANA, "are putting greater emphasis on the creation and placement of the advertising message. They are pressing for creative alternatives and better media efficiencies."

What specific trends in advertising management practices and agency relationships had been forming? The ANA listed them: New organizational concepts for handling new product assignments;

greater in-house capability and self-sufficiency on the part of many advertisers —managing the marketing function themselves and getting into activities previously left to advertising agencies to handle.

Also, the certainty that the advent and proliferation of independent media buying companies, creative boutiques and other specialized service firms gave clients resources which previously had been non-existent, and that a growing interest in controlling expenses had resulted in some clients contracting only for services they really needed from their full-service agencies.

Advertisers' Needs Are Changing

This experimentation with new advertising approaches—especially noticeable in packaged goods companies—visibly affected traditional, full-service advertising agencies, who got the message that "advertisers' needs are changing and that agencies should be prepared to meet these changing needs or the advertiser will find another way to solve his problems." It was apparent that the cost-crunch was forcing the client to save money by purchasing limited services from the new breed of independent specialist organization, by performing some advertising functions themselves—and by bypassing full-service agencies altogether.

One illustration of what was happening is provided by Norton Simon Inc., a $50,000,000 a year advertiser. In 1971 this company set up Norton Simon Communications, and its first assignment was handling about $6,000,000 in advertising billings from Hunt-Wesson Foods, a Simon subsidiary, an account resigned by full-service Young & Rubicam when it learned of the formation of Norton Simon Communications as a house agency. NSC named the William Esty Co. and SFM Media Buying Service Corp. to do media buying for products handled by NSC, and paid them less than the standard 2.25% of billings for media placement. It gave some creative assignments to DKG Inc., Lois Holland Callaway, and four other agencies, on a monthly fee basis.

How Advertisers Organize

Companies commonly use one of three ways of organizing their marketing activities: By function, by product, or by market. Functional departments (such as advertising, market research, sales promotion) may report to the company president or to a marketing vp. The advertising activity, over the years, was headed by an advertising manager or advertising director whose task it was to see that advertising made its maximum contribution to corporate profits and growth objectives of the company.

It was he who helped determine advertising policies and objectives, who built the company advertising program, prepared advertising budgets, interpreted his company to the advertising agency, who evaluated the agency's services, kept in touch with media representatives and outside suppliers, and who kept himself informed of competitors' advertising, and who checked out the results of his own advertising.

The position of advertising manager goes back only as far as the 1890s. At first he was not an important corporate official, and when a company did have such a man on its payroll, he customarily reported to the sales manager. However, as advertising budgets grew, the stature of the advertising manager increased, and eventually he became a member of the top management team in many leading corporations. His prominence stemmed in part from a profound change that occurred in corporate thinking: Where once the idea of business was to sell what could be *made*, now the idea was to make what could be *sold*.

This change in corporate thinking led to the development of the "marketing concept"—which held that marketing efficiency is the key to the success of a business and that the proper starting point for marketing is prospective customers. This, in turn, resulted in greater attention to the "marketing mix"—an integrated combination of marketing elements (one of which, obviously, is advertising).

Enter: The Brand Manager

The stature of the advertising manager or director in recent years, has, however, diminished; his authority has eroded; in some instances his title has been eliminated and he has been given other responsibilities. In still other situations, he has moved to a corporate level and has become an advisor on advertising matters.

The reason for this may be found in the advent of the brand or product manager. Brand managers are generally all-purpose business men who are responsible for the management of a particular brand, and they are not usually skilled *advertising* specialists. Brand managers customarily work with the company's advertising agency, a situation in which they get involved with advertising development and decision making—regardless of their degree of expertise in those areas.

According to a recent study made by the Assn. of National Advertisers, brand managers have come to the fore, particularly in packaged goods companies, as a result of:

● "A belief that a centralized advertising department cannot develop the products and market expertise desired for a large number of products (and product proliferation has been a characteristic of the industry, especially in the last decade), except by the costly practice of having a large staff of advertising specialists, each concentrating on one or a few products and markets."

● "The effort to shorten lines of communication by having the product manager deal directly with the agency without going through the advertising department."

● "The very fact that a professional advertising agency serves the company makes it possible for the product manager to deal with advertising matters irrespective of his degree of experience."

The product manager system has, nevertheless, evoked the criticism that the creative quality of advertising is unfavorably affected because of the brand manager's relative inexperience in evaluating an agency's creative work. Also, a result of the advertiser's ultimate recognition of this inexperience is that he then sets up a multi-layered approval process for proposed advertising—an arrangement that slows decision making and fosters safe, conservative, often ineffective, approaches to creative concepts.

But in companies organized by product, brand managers have come to the fore, and today many of these companies have marketing directors or vps in charge of marketing, who, in turn, have charge of a number of brand managers. They are likewise responsible for all marketing functions—marketing research, advertising, selling, sales promotion, publicity, distribution, package design, pricing, and so on. (In some instances, old-time advertising managers moved into these newer positions.)

The Ad Scene Changes

A 1971 ANA report, prepared by William M. Claggett of the Ralston Purina Co., noted that many changes had been made in recent years in the ways advertisers manage the advertising function. Organizational structures were overhauled in some companies; in others, decentralization along profit center lines took place. "More and more marketing and advertising expertise is now located at the client level.

"Companies are diversifying, product lines are multiplying and venture teams are being established," said Mr. Claggett. "Clients are putting greater emphasis on the creation and placement of the advertising message. They are pressing for creative alternatives and better media efficiencies. And, as if in response to chang-

ing company structures and resultant changes in advertiser requirements, a great number of new firms specializing in such things as creative, media and new product development have come into existence." The latter reference was to the emergence of creative boutiques, independent media buying companies, and independent venture groups whose arrival on the scene reduced the services which advertisers previously paid traditional-type advertising agencies to supply. (*See story on The Agency, Page 34* .)

It was as pointed out by Richard L. Gilbert of the Gilbert Grace & Stark advertising agency: The middle 1960s "witnessed the beginning of a marketing shift, and by 1970 the pendulum had swung (away from the traditional agency) to the client, who today is at the center of all marketing knowledge."

A national advertiser tries to persuade consumers to buy his product—anywhere he can. A retail advertiser urges consumers to buy the product from him—not elsewhere. Retail ads aim at selling specific items by giving information about brands, sizes, prices.

What Retail Ads Should Do

Frank Mayans, a vp of Federated Department Stores, which includes Shillito's in Cincinnati, Filene's in Boston, Sanger-Harris in Dallas, and 177 other outlets, has said that Federated advertising "should identify our store, reflect its character, help distinguish us from our competitors. It should tell customers and potential customers when the store is open, whether items can be ordered by mail or phone, if delivery, installation and service are available as part of the purchase price or as options, what credit terms are available, parking facilities, and the many other bits and pieces of information that go into each individual buying decision. Local retail advertising saves the customer time and money by providing information so he or she can make some decisions before the car leaves the garage."

The urgings of the national advertiser appear in media that go everywhere in the country. The messages of the retailer—department store, discount house, supermarket, specialty shop—appear in local media like the community newspaper.

Local Advertising Hits $10 Billion

While national advertising expenditures in the U.S. last year amounted to $13.1 billion, local advertising took nearly $10 billion. Local advertising at one time was largely confined to newspapers, but for some time now it has been a major factor also in such media as radio and television. Local advertising in newspapers last year reached $5.7 billion; national was at $1.2 billion. Television had $955,000,000 in local advertising revenues; radio over $1 billion.

J. C. Penney Co., the department store and catalog chain, last year had sales of about $5 billion. It spent over $15,000,000 on national advertising—and perhaps $88,000,000 in local newspapers, local television and local radio. Sears, Roebuck, with sales of over $10 billion, spends more than $200,000,000 on national advertising—and nearly $300,000,000 on local advertising. (Both Penney and Sears use advertising to build preferences for their own brands—thus coming into competition with the advertising done by manufacturers.)

Retailers customarily do not make use of the services of advertising agencies, relying on the services of their own advertising departments, which function, in effect, as an agency serving a single client. In a department store, for example, there may be a director of advertising and publicity of vp rank, and under him an advertising manager, who will make decisions on how much space or time each section of the store will get. Under him are copywriters and art directors, production people, radio and television specialists, and direct mail employes. The size of the advertising department, of course, varies with the retailer's annual sales volume and his advertising volume.

Big department stores have sizable ad departments, and their people turn out more advertisements in a year than most advertising agencies. A small retailer, on the other hand, may have one or two advertising people, and he will depend on creative help from the media he plans to use for his advertising.

Whatever the size of the retail outlet or its ad department, the main function of such a department is to bring people into the store with a desire to buy. To do this, the advertising department must work closely with other departments. Since a store is engaged in reselling the merchandise it has purchased, the store's buyers of that merchandise are in pivotal positions as far as the advertising of the merchandise is concerned. Thus, the ad department may be on a level with the merchandise buyers, or it may be inferior to them.

Reprinted from "Advertising Age," Nov., 21, 1973, pp. 20, 22, 24, 26, 28

Basic convictions

about advertising

Procter & Gamble, started in 1837 by William Procter and James Gamble and now the largest national advertiser with a 1972 outlay of $275,000,000 in all forms of advertising and sales promotion, offers the following convictions it has developed through years of successful marketing:

Advertising's chief role is that of selling the consumer.

Although there are other ways to do that job, Procter & Gamble believes that advertising is the most effective and efficient way to sell our types of products.

Advertising has told four generations of American consumers about Ivory soap. Year after year, Ivory advertising has mirrored the tastes and tempo of the times, and its techniques have paced the development of the advertiser's art. From its earliest days, Ivory advertising has struck a warm, human note; simple in style, it has spoken directly and convincingly to consumers about Ivory's purity and mildness. As the neighborhood store has evolved from the corner grocery of a more leisurely era to the bustling supermarket of today, advertising increasingly has served manufacturer, retailer and consumer alike through its ability to inform quickly and efficiently of Ivory's distinctive product features.

Advertising creates new markets.

Ivory's very first advertisement started to broaden the market by suggesting that the product be used for varied cleaning and laundry purposes as well as "for the bath, toilet or nursery." Later, Ivory was to be recommended for cleaning straw hats and washing ostrich plumes; for polishing rubber plants and cleaning oil paintings; for walls, furniture and silverware; for bathing both horse and harness; for embroideries, silk hose and knit shawls; for shaving and shampooing.

As technology permitted, specialized products were developed for many of these cleaning chores, and in each case advertising played an important part in introducing them to the market. By awakening interest in improved service, advertising not only creates new markets for products, but at the same time broadens the range of choices available to consumers.

Advertising lowers costs to consumers.

Although advertising is a part of the cost of marketing a product, properly used it brings about savings that may be expected to exceed substantially the cost of advertising.

By constantly broadening the market, advertising makes mass production of Ivory soap possible. Mass production and stability of volume bring about savings in the costs of manufacturing, distribution, and other business operations. These savings make it possible today for Ivory to be sold at prices that would be attractive even by the standards of days long past.

The wages and benefits of the people who make Ivory soap today are more than 30 times what they were when it went on the market in 1879. There was no corporate income tax in 1879; currently our company's total bill for income and other taxes is more than our net earnings [earnings, in 1972, were $276,310,000]. Expenses in every phase of our business have risen several hundred per cent. Yet, the same size bar of Ivory soap which housewives bought for a nickel in 1879 now sells for about 13¢. And improved many times, it's a far better product; penny for penny, it's a much better buy.

Ivory's record is dramatic because of the span of years it covers. But, as demonstrated time and again in our company, effective advertising brings about savings—in the costs of manufacturing, distribution, buying and other operations—that clearly result in lower prices to the consumer.

Advertising spurs continual product improvement.

Advertising cannot build an enduring business for a poor product; it cannot sell a product for very long in a competitive market if that product stands still in quality.

In 1891, a circular to the grocery trade made Procter & Gamble's position clear: "To advertise a poor thing is to make a losing investment. The careful housewife, who has been fighting dirt all her life with a cake of soap for her weapon, well knows its mettle; she does not try a poor soap twice."

Ivory's sales have grown and its advertising has been successful because Ivory soap has never stood still in quality. While still a fledgling product, Ivory was sent off to leading chemists for analysis and evaluation. Their reports testified to its quality and inspired Ivory's famous slogan—"99 44/100% pure."

In her struggle against dirt and in countless other ways, the housewife's life has been made easier over the years. But she still "knows the mettle" of the products she uses. And today, more than ever, "To advertise a poor thing is to make a losing investment."

Advertising forces competition.

Advertising will not work effectively if the product is not fully competitive in quality, or if the product, quality considered, is not fully competitive in price. Effective advertising demands that sales and other distributive functions be on their toes, forcing competition through vigorous selling and merchandising.

"It floats" described a strong performance advantage to people tired of groping for soap at the bottom of the bathtub; to Ivory's competitors, it posed a strong competitive challenge. Similarly, Ivory has faced continuing competition from an unending parade of new products for personal, laundry and dishwashing use.

To meet competition and to reinforce its bid for consumer acceptance, Ivory has used virtually every means of merchandising and every medium of advertising. Each in its way has helped Ivory to maintain its position of leadership over the years. More importantly, the competitive pressure of advertising has led to increasingly higher standards of quality that new products have had to meet. By sustaining this pressure for better products and lower prices, advertising contributes directly to better values for the consuming public.

Advertising and scientific research work hand in glove on a vast and amazingly productive scale.

When a company is confident of its ability to acquaint the public quickly with a product advance, it is more willing to invest dollars in research needed to bring that improvement from labora-tory to the consumer.

In 1939, after years of costly research and exploration, Procter & Gamble engineers perfected a completely new method of making Ivory soap. Replacing old processing equipment cost millions of dollars, but the new method made it possible for us to produce a bar of soap dramatically better in appearance and performance. The investment would have been difficult to justify if advertising were not available to tell housewives about Ivory's improved performance.

The success of Ivory has proved the wisdom of the changes that were made. But the story of how scientific research and advertising, working together, have resulted in successful new product innovations is far from unique. It has been duplicated in the introduction of detergents, in the development of the first decay-reducing toothpaste, in the setting of new standards of excellence for prepared baking mixes, in the perfection of an effective anti-dandruff shampoo, and in other improvements in Procter & Gamble's service to consumers.

In each case, effective advertising functioned as an essential, productive partner of research and product development; in each case, effective advertising contributed directly to Procter & Gamble's basic objective of bringing our consumers increasingly better products and a wider selection of products which are both fair in price and high in quality.

Reprinted from "Advertising Age," Nov. 21, 1973, pp. 26, 28

The advertising agency—

what it is and what it does

BY JAMES V. O'GARA
Editor-at-Large, "Advertising Age"

The advertising agency has been defined as an independent business composed of creative and business people who develop, prepare and place advertising in media for clients seeking to find customers for their goods and services.

The most important element in this definition is that advertising agencies *develop* and *prepare advertising*. These are what are customarily called the creative functions of an agency—the glamor areas of a business mythologized by Hollywood and novelists. But for success, advertising agencies must also depend heavily on media planning and placement as well as four other, perhaps less romantic, aspects: Account development, client contact, new-business-getting and financial know-how.

The creative process involves three steps. Tom Dillon, an outstanding copywriter now president of Batten, Barton, Durstine & Osborn, lists them as follows:

● To identify the prime prospects.

● To determine what problems the prime prospect has in the brand category under consideration.

● To examine the product or service in the light of what has been learned about the prime prospect and the problems involved in her decision-making process.

When these steps have been taken, a copy concept will have been developed—a statement of what it is hoped the prime prospect will carry in her memory about the brand.

If a copy concept is being developed for, say, a paper towel, the following ensues, according to Mr. Dillon:

Having examined the prime prospect's notions about the product field, you observe that a great number of prospects are concerned about the ability of the paper towel to sop up spilled liquids. This matches with the fact that, from a laboratory standpoint, your brand will absorb so many grams of water per square inch per second. But you also know that the prime prospect's experience suggests that in order to get absorbency, she may have

to put up with a towel that comes apart when it gets wet. Actually, the laboratory tests indicate that in this respect, you are materially better than your leading competitors.

If this is substantiated by testing the idea on prime prospects, your copy concept looks something like this: The advertising will communicate that the brand has a very high degree of absorbency and yet is strong when wet.

Now you have a pretty good idea of whom you are talking to and what idea you plan to leave in her head as a factor in influencing her brand decision.

It's Not Easy to Do

Then you have the problems of executing—in, say, a 30-second television commercial. The commercial must (1) get the attention of the prime prospect, (2) identify the domain of her decision, (3) register the memory of your brand in this domain, (4) register in her memory the content of the copy concept, and (5) link the concept to the brand.

"And all of this," says Mr. Dillon drily, "is not easy to do."

In addition to conducting research aimed at discovering how best to position or reposition a product in the consumer mind, and coming up with advertising calculated to give the client the best chance to improve his sales, the agency develops media proposals—and when all these have been approved by the client, the agency produces all the necessary materials, and these it sends along to the various media, checks to see if the advertisements appeared as per contract, bills the client, pays the media and pays its suppliers. The agency putting $1,000,000 of the client's money into advertising traditionally gets 15% from the media—in this case $150,000. (There are a variety of other methods of remuneration, but the arrangement under which the agency receives media commissions, plus a percentage on outside services [such as typogra-

phy], plus fees for some services performed by the agencies' own employes [such as art] still predominates.)

Ad Biz Is Small Biz

Besides all this, the agency may also take on many collateral functions on behalf of a client. It may handle merchandising for him, it may help to price, package or change a product, indeed it may develop a new product line for the client. The agency may also do sales promotion work, stage sales meetings, and exhibits, develop trademarks or outdoor signs and displays. Because it is in a service business, the agency, for example, often purchases Broadway play tickets and season boxes for baseball and football games and uses them to entertain clients.

While billings of advertising agencies, in the aggregate, make an impressive total, the agency business is, for the most part, a business that's on the smaller side. Early this year, ADVERTISING AGE reported that 652 agencies billed a combined $11.3 billion, less than half the advertising dollars that went into all media in 1972. Nearly 400 of those agencies individually billed less than $5,000,000—and, using the traditional 15% commission figure, those agencies averaged a gross income of about $263,650 (more than 60% of which, incidentally, was then applied to meeting payroll demands).

How does the agency get its income? An agency placing a page-size advertisement costing $5,000 at a publication's space rate receives a bill from the magazine for $4,250 ($5,000 less 15% commission). The magazine offers a 2% cash discount for prompt payment, which here amounts to $85 (2% of $4,250). The agency, in turn, bills its client for the full $5,000, less the $85 for prompt payment. In addition to the $750 commission the agency receives on the magazine space, it also charges the client for expenses connected with producing materials for the ad. This it usually bills at net cost—plus a service charge of 17.65% (equal to 15% on the gross figure).

The advertising agency business generally equates with nationally advertised products and services, and with the placement of national advertising in newspapers, television, magazines, radio and other media. The agency is not normally an important factor in retail advertising (although local advertising in all media increased at double the rate of national advertising in the five years ending in 1972), nor in classified advertising, and most of them do not figure in direct mail advertising, including the great bulk of the enormous catalog business.

Essentially a service business, with many overtones of professionalism, the agency field is nevertheless unlike medicine or law in that there are no legal requirements or tests of competence to meet before opening an advertising agency. No license is required before starting in business. There are countless one- and two-man operations in the field. But no matter its size, every agency must face at least one major hurdle: getting "recognition"—a status achieved mostly by meeting the financial requirements of a medium's credit department. Agencies involved in national advertising also apply for credit ratings to the American Newspaper Publishers Assn., the Periodical Publishers Assn., and so on.

At one time, media associations demanded that agencies seeking recognition agree not to rebate parts of their commissions to clients. But in 1956, following action by the U.S. Department of Justice, the associations signed a consent decree in which it was stipulated they would not intervene in any agreement between a client and an agency. (The American Assn. of Advertising Agencies, incidentally, agreed that it would not make a no-rebate clause part of its qualifications for membership.)

In addition to meeting media credit criteria, the new agency must also, obviously, have some business to place with the media, and employ people with the competence necessary to serve advertisers' needs.

For Agency, There's Many a Slip

Advertising agencies find themselves in a volatile field. It is a field perhaps less stable than many other kinds of businesses since the loss of a few accounts may cause the agency to disintegrate, or to retrench drastically. In 1971, when business men were generally cautious and tight-fisted, 189 advertisers moved accounts billing $349,941,000 to different agencies. In that year, 66 agencies billing over $25,000,000 each, cut their payrolls by 2,660 people. Last year, 213 major ad-

vertisers redistributed $455,295,000 in billings (including the year's biggest move of $23,000,000 in American Motors' billings) to other agencies. And 675 people were fired by agencies billing over $25,000,000.

Account changing of such magnitude is not an isolated phenomenon. Back in 1961, 260 major accounts—billing a total of $322,000,000—moved to different agencies. Between 1958 and 1961 about 1,000 important advertisers—whose business aggregated more than $1 billion—changed agencies.

There is generally no contract between an agency and a client (although the number of written contracts has grown in recent years). If there is one, it usually can be terminated at short notice, customarily 90 days. While many advertisers remain for years with the same agencies, account movement is a distinguishing characteristic of the agency business. Clients, with a number of notable exceptions, simply do not stay with agencies the way they do with lawyers. Jane Trahey, whose agency billed $6,000,000 last year, contends the reasons are two-fold: "A lot of shops don't give a cotton-pickin' damn for their responsibilities towards clients and their needs. But a lot of this is due to the fact that clients all too often don't give a cotton-pickin' damn about their agencies; most certainly they do not give them the sense of security and respect they automatically hand out to an attorney or an accountant."

Agency Trend: Fewer Employes

The biggest investment made by agencies is in their people. It is, very likely, the only business where, as pointed out by Fairfax Cone, "your inventory goes down in the elevator at night." The "inventory" includes writers, artists, researchers, media men, merchandisers, account people, administrators, sociologists, even musicians. Such people are customarily very well paid. Salaries take something like 61% of the agencies' gross income. (From management's standpoint, it used to be worse: In 1956, it was 64.7%.) The average number of employes per $1,000,000 in billings—for years after World War II—was 10; today it's down to 5.5 (and as billings increase, agencies tend to put fewer bodies against accounts).

Four A's member agencies reported that their profit levels fell to a ten-year low in 1971—2.87%, figured as a percentage of gross income. As a percentage of billings, the profit picture was nearly as drab—second lowest in a decade at 0.56%. (The picture brightened in 1972, when the percentages climbed to 3.62% and 0.75%, respectively.) Agencies that moved into the publicly-held area, however, apparently enjoyed substantially

higher profit percentages. For instance, Wells, Rich, Greene, which in 1971 was considered one of the biggest profit-makers in the agency world, enjoyed a 12.6% profit on gross, and 2.4% on billings of $109,967,659. McCaffrey & McCall, with 1971 billings of $51,222,036, had percentage profits of 8.4% and 1.28%, respectively.

Today's publicly-held agencies, for all practical purposes, date back to 1962, when Papert, Koenig, Lois offered 100,000 shares of its common stock. (In 1929, Albert Frank-Guenther Law made an offer of a public stock issue with the idea of applying the proceeds to finance an office building.) In 1963, Foote, Cone & Belding offered 40% of its common stock, and the 500,000 shares were "quickly over-subscribed" at $15.50 a share. The proceeds of $7,225,000 went to the individual agency employes selling their stock. In 1964, Doyle, Dane Bernbach offered 247,000 shares at $27 each. The shares represented nearly a 25% interest in the agency. Sold by 25 agency employes, the stock brought William Bernbach, president, $681,656; Ned Doyle, exec vp, $1,602,468, and Maxwell Dane, vp and general manager, $854,595, while other sellers realized lesser amounts.

Going Public—Pros and Cons

Since then, other major agencies going public have included Grey Advertising, the Interpublic Group of Cos., J. Walter Thompson Co., Ogilvy & Mather, Needham, Harper & Steers and Clinton E. Frank (although the latter agency has moved to buy its stock back from the public). At this writing, BBDO had decided to go ahead with a previously deferred stock offering. Carl Ally Inc. was still postponing a planned move to go public.

The incentives behind public stock offerings have been summarized by Edward Bond of Young & Rubicam. These include capital gains plus related tax advantages, a permanent and current public-value of the stock, stock availability for all employes, added working capital, stronger discipline on management (presumably from outside stockholders). Another incentive, obviously, is the huge payout accruing to stock-selling agency principals, who might otherwise have had to sell their share back to their agencies, thus putting strains on agency capital.

The shortcomings include the possibility of bad client reaction, resentment by lesser employes when they learn of the big money at the top, loss of privacy for confidential agency information—and the possibility that a poor stock market situation might be interpreted incorrectly as bad agency performance.

By February of this year—despite the

Agency costs, profits: A 10 year record

(Per cent of gross income unless otherwise stated)

	1963	1964	1965	1966	1967	1968	1969	1970	1971	1972
Number of agencies represented	238	234	226	239	246	216	209	220	215	240
Rent, light and depreciation	7.54%	7.22%	6.81%	6.80%	6.99%	6.93%	6.88%	7.30%	7.81%	7.74%
Taxes (other than U.S. income)	2.45	2.36	2.23	2.58	2.79	2.80	2.77	2.93	2.98	3.27
Other operating expense	14.32	14.29	14.41	14.28	15.06	14.56	15.09	15.40	15.86	15.95
Total payroll	67.99	67.01	67.14	66.05	67.06	66.16	65.79	66.67	65.26	64.53
Payments into pension or profit-sharing plans	1.63	1.98	1.93	2.00	1.79	2.29	2.21	1.67	1.87	1.96
Insurance for employe benefit	0.70	0.76	0.78	0.80	0.83	0.82	0.94	0.99	1.14	1.19
Total expenses	94.63	93.62	93.30	92.51	94.52	93.56	93.68	94.96	94.92	94.64
Profit before U.S. income tax* (as percentage of gross income)**	5.37	6.38	6.70	7.49	5.48	6.44	6.32	5.04	5.08	5.36
U.S. income taxes	1.67	1.62	1.77	2.00	1.49	2.11	2.13	1.58	1.76	1.60
Net profit (as percentage of gross income)**	3.70	4.76	4.93	5.49	3.99	4.33	4.19	3.46	3.32	3.76
Profit before U.S. income tax for incorporated agencies (as percentage of gross income)**	5.17	6.23	6.40	7.42	5.39	6.43	6.57	4.92	4.80	5.42
U.S. income tax for incorporated agencies	2.13	2.00	2.15	2.44	1.82	2.46	2.54	1.81	1.93	1.80
Net profit for incorporated agencies (as percentage of gross income)**	3.04	4.23	4.25	4.98	3.57	3.97	4.03	3.11	2.87	3.62
Net profit for incorporated agencies (as percentage of sales—i.e. billing)	0.55	0.83	0.81	0.98	0.69	0.76	0.80	0.66	0.56	0.75

Figures are for member agencies of American Assn. of Advertising Agencies.

*For all agencies—corporations, partnerships, proprietorships.

**Gross income comprises commissions, agencies' service charges, and fees. Source: Annual studies of advertising agencies' costs and profits conducted by American Assn. of Advertising Agencies. Figures are averages for agencies of all sizes.

---

profit-performances of such as Wells, Rich, Greene and McCaffrey & McCall— publicly-owned agencies were considering a joint effort to bolster their collective image on a generally sagging Wall St. This projected venture, of course, stemmed from collective unhappiness about the continuing price depression of agency stocks.

Ralph Nader, Boutiques and TV

If going public changed some of the character of the agency business, there were other developments that altered it more radically, for good or for ill. Since about 1963, there have been such developments as the advent of consumerism and such advocate champions as Ralph Nader; increasing government restrictions on the business; growing dominance of the media field by television (which helped hasten the demise of *Life* and *Look*); the introduction of the computer as a marketing tool, product proliferation, the rise of the

creative boutique, the independent media buying service, the a la carte operation, the client-sponsored house agency of varying kinds, and venture groups.

Off-Madison Ave. developments increasingly made their weight felt on that thoroughfare: The rise of discounting, the mushroom growth of private labels, the increasing merchandising clout of chain stores, the demand for new products, and insistent calls for an improved environment.

One of the most talked about topics in advertising circles in recent years has been the development of the "indies": The independent creative boutiques and media buying services.

Do Boutiques Save You Money?

Some admen trace the advent of the boutique to the proliferation of new products in the last ten years and to the traditional no-conflict rule: No single

agency should be allowed to handle competing accounts. Others say that clients fostered the boutique because, economy-minded, they wanted creative help without having to pay for other agency services, or because they were too small to get the attention they desired from large agencies. Some clients apparently were motivated by the belief that they could get their creative work done faster than at full-service shops, where layers of management often allegedly served to delay the completion of proposed campaigns.

And the outside creative help was certainly available. In the 1960s, the agency field experienced something of a creative revolution. George Lois claims in "George, Be Careful" that a "cluster of creative agencies sprang up" following the lead of Papert, Koenig, Lois and Carl Ally Inc. Many of these creative agencies were small operations whose principals were gambling that their creativity alone would attract large pieces of business away from old-line, full-service agencies.

By March, 1971, the Assn. of National Advertisers reported that a survey of 104 of its member companies indicated that 70% of them had indeed made one or more changes in their methods of managing advertising—including moving accounts to outside creative services and to independent media buying operations and new product-development companies, as well as to newly-formed in-house advertising capabilities.

Their reasons for these moves? "Greater economy"; disenchantment with the 15% commission system ("an advertiser is nuts if he pays 15% for everything"); "competitive account conflicts" in their existing agencies. They declared that the "independents" gave them "service tailored to specific needs"; "fewer layers of authority and approval"; "faster action"; "greater flexibility"—and services for which clients paid only for what they needed. Finally, they "saved money."

Agencies Must Change Ways

The Four A's took the stand in 1971 that it was clients' efforts to effect economies that resulted in efforts to buy copy from boutiques, and research and media assistance from various other sources, and assembling the end-product in-house. (Norton Simon Communications, for instance is a marketing, advertising and research subsidiary of Norton Simon Inc., an advertiser which last year spent perhaps $35,000,000 in various media. NSC does about 25% of its own advertising work, closely overseeing the remaining 75%, which is assigned to outside agencies and creative services. When NSC started in 1971, Young & Rubicam, a full-service agency, resigned Hunt-Wesson Foods, a Simon subsidiary, citing the new house agency as a reason for walking away from a $6,000,000 account.)

Meanwhile, according to the ANA survey, some advertisers were saying that agencies must change their ways to survive. These advertisers wanted a change in the commission system, a move to a fee system, specialized services, a curtailment of the full-service concept, and the ability to buy specific agency functions. In short, the old-line agencies would have to be competitive with outside services on a negotiated fee basis.

In any event, by the second half of 1971, the nation's boutiques were handling many millions of dollars in billings, and there was little doubt that full-service agencies were becoming more worried as substantial accounts moved out to the independents.

Nevertheless, the Four A's expressed confidence that departing clients would eventually return to the full-service shops.

because, it said, advertisers do not cost-account their marketing functions, because clients underrate the time and skill required to do the advertising job properly, and because they fail to appreciate the managerial disciplines brought to creative work. Besides, added a Four A's spokesman, the independents "are inefficient, inexperienced, unreliable."

By 1970 there were perhaps 50 independent media buying services, with a combined volume estimated at $100,000,000-plus. They came to the fore because advertisers then, as now, wanted more for their advertising dollar; traditional agencies were paying less attention to media buying than to their account and creative activities; broadcast time prices, and other media prices, were negotiable; and they offered to get the client a lower cost-per-1,000 and "quality."

Buying Services Ride Economy Wave

The attitude of clients was, in effect: We don't much care who does our media planning and buying so long as they're done well, and inexpensively and we get performance. The Assn. of National Advertisers, as a matter of fact, acknowledged in 1970 that the independent media services had been "a desirable development for advertisers" since more efficient buying practices had resulted from their advent. The ANA encouraged competition between agencies and independents, and a number of ANA members made it a three-cornered rivalry by setting up their own internal buying operations.

The independents, or some of them, received fees of 5% for spot tv buying for clients. The indies also got 5% for radio buys, 1.85% for network tv buys, 3% to 5% for newspaper transactions, 1.5% for magazine negotiations. For a total media job, the fee was about 3.75%.

Full-service agencies, alarmed at the inroads of the media buying services, insisted that what should be purchased was advertising, not discounts. "If the atmosphere around a tv spot isn't right, how much does the discount or the cost-per-1,000 mean?" They asserted that the independents could not deliver on their promises, they declared there were always some clients who tried to get something for nothing.

■ But in the end, the full-service agencies started improving their own media departments; they began copying the independents by offering buying services to non-clients; they used independent buying services themselves on behalf of clients. They conceded, finally, that the independents were likely to continue in existence, noting wryly that they would survive so long as media time and space rates were negotiable.

One of the problems of the agency business in the last few years has been "slow pay." One view of this situation held that, in a tight money market, some agencies were withholding payments to media for their time and space charges, and withholding for perhaps 30 to 90 days (instead of remitting within 10 days to get the 2% discount) and using the money to meet payrolls or banking the money to take advantage of fairly high interest rates. The agencies, in turn, blamed slow-paying clients and allegedly slipshod billing practices followed by the media, particularly broadcasting stations. One agency reported that it was placing 70,000 spot commercials each month and that only 0.6% of the bills it had received were more than 60 days overdue. (Bigger agencies use television heavily. Cunningham & Walsh, for instance, puts 68% of its $107,000,000 in billings into that medium—a not unusual situation.)

The controversy seemed to threaten the integrity of advertising for a time, especially after the high-billing Lennen & Newell agency went into bankruptcy, leaving some large media bills unpaid. But the publicity that attended the subject seemed to prompt corrective measures, and the issue seems much less touchy today than it was a year ago.

How Agencies Got Started

Advertising agencies these days are agents of advertisers. But it wasn't always thus. In the old days they were agents of the advertising media, representing newspapers and magazines in the sale of space to advertisers. Many early agencies became space brokers—buying space from newspapers and magazines at wholesale prices and reselling to advertisers at retail prices. Others took over the entire advertising space of publications for a lump sum and then sold it to advertisers. Still others first sold space to advertisers and then filled the orders with the desired newspapers and magazines. Rate-cutting abuses became widespread.

Order-taking put the agencies in the impossible situation of trying to serve both advertisers and media simultaneously. Then Francis Wayland Ayer, founder of N. W. Ayer & Son, announced his agency would no longer be an order-taker. In 1876 Ayer launched an open-contract-plus commission plan: Ayer would act for advertisers, trying to get them the lowest possible rates from media, then add a commission for its services. The commission ranged from 8% to 15%, later stabilizing at 16⅔%. In thus establishing the agency as a servant solely of advertisers, Ayer moved the business into the area of advertising preparation.

Commissions Move Up from 10%

But while Ayer's decision to ally itself with the advertiser became widely accepted and imitated, its compensation plan did not become standard. Media continued to grant commissions to agencies bringing them business. This was initially 10%, but it later moved up to 15%. The point is: *The agency worked for the advertiser but got its money from media.* And in 1893 the practice was formalized by the American Newspaper Publishing Assn. when it decided to pay commissions to recognized independent agencies and not to allow a discount to direct advertisers.

There are those who regard this situation as an anomaly of the business. Many challenges to the system have been made over the years. More than ten years ago, in an effort to clarify things, the then-president of the American Assn. of Advertising Agencies described the agencies' incentive as lying "in its ability, through commissions allowed by media, together with its own percentage charges and fees, to be paid for its creative work in proportion to the use made of it. If the results are successful for the advertiser, they are also successful for the agency. If they are not, the advertising stops and the agency is out of business on this account."

Continuing, he touched a vital point: "But it is the advertiser who pays the agency the total amount the agency receives. It is a mistake to say media pay agencies, because they do not. The money agencies deduct from advertisers' payments in the form of media commissions is never in the hands of any medium, and therefore cannot possibly be *paid* by a medium. The medium simply *allows* the agency to make the deduction."

Today, large numbers of agencies will work with clients on one kind of fee system or another. In 1960, Ogilvy & Mather and Shell Oil agreed on a fee permitting a 25% profit on estimated costs for a year; thereafter the fee was to be established by negotiation on a cost-plus basis. David Ogilvy insists advertisers "get the best results when they pay their agency a flat fee." In 1965, BBDO and SSC&B agreed with American Tobacco to a percentage of net profit on some $65,000,000 in billings, within a predetermined range, and to split "excess" profits (with the client getting the large share of the split). Some larger advertisers viewed the American Tobacco situation—which envisioned a substantial savings for the client vis-a-vis the 15% arrangement—as possibly the beginning of the end of the commission system, which had long been in disfavor as too costly.

But despite the willingness of agencies to do business in return for fees, the commission system remains dominant in the field today, though David Ogilvy, for one, holds it to be "unrealistic to expect an agency to be impartial when its vested interest lies wholly in the direction of increasing [the client's] commissionable advertising."

How Agencies Get Their Income

According to Four A's figures, larger agencies today receive a little more than 75% of their income in the form of commissions allowed by media, 20% from

SALARIES PAID TO AGENCY PEOPLE
(Figures represent high and low averages.)

CREATIVE	LARGE $50 million +	MEDIUM $10-50 million	SMALL $5-10 million
Creative director	$60-80,000	$40-65,000	$35-50,000
Associate creative director Creative supervisor Creative group head (supervises art, copy, tv production)	28-55,000	30-45,000	———
Copy group head Copy supervisor Copy chief (small agency only) (supervises copy only)	22-35,000	25-35,000	18-30,000
Copywriter	8-25,000	8-25,000	7-22,000
Executive art director	40-60,000	25-40,000	15-25,000
Group art director Art supervisor Associate creative director (supervises art, copy, tv production)	30-55,000	30-40,000	———
Art director TV producer	16-35,000	12-30,000	12-22,000
Assistant art director	8-10,000	8-12,000	———
Bull pen/board man	6.5-12,000	7.5-12,000	6.5-11,000
Promo art director	12-25,000	15-20,000	
Production manager-print	18-22,000	15-20,000	12-18,000
Production manager-tv	20-35,000	15-22,000	———
Traffic manager	14-22,000	12-18,000	10-14,000
Account management supervisor	55-70,000	40-55,000	
Account supervisor	28-50,000	28-40,000	25-35,000
Account executive	18-25,000	18-25,000	17-23,000
Assistant account executive	13-17,000	13-16,000	12-15,000
Personnel director	25-35,000	15-25,000	———
MEDIA			
Media director	35-60,000	25-35,000	15-25,000
Media supervisor	15-22,000	15-18,000	———
Broadcast supervisor	15-22,000	15-19,000	———
Media planner	10-18,000	10-15,000	8-12,000
Media buyer	10-15,000	8-12,000	7.5-10,000
Estimator	7- 8,500	7- 8,000	6.5- 7,500
RESEARCH			
Market research director	40-50,000	25-30,000	18-22,000
Associate research director	25-30,000	20-25,000	———
Research group head	20-22,000	16-18,000	———
Research supervisor	18-20,000	14-16,000	———
Project director	13-15,000	13-15,000	12-14,000
Research analyst	9-12,000	9-12,000	———

NOTE: Figures above are based on 2,000 New York and Chicago job-search assignments undertaken by Jerry Fields Associates between September, 1971, and September, 1973. Figures do not include bonuses, stock, profit sharing, etc.

29

the agency's own percentage charges made on purchases for clients, and 5% from fees. Among medium-size agencies, the corresponding figures are 60%, 20% and 20%. Among smaller agencies they are 55%, 25% and 20%, respectively.

The Four A's concedes that "the agency business is clearly in an era of commissions-plus. It is not a question of media commissions *or* fees—it seems to be more a question of commissions *and* fees. John Crichton, president of the Four A's, has said repeatedly: "We have been known as the citadel of the principle of media allowing a commission to agencies. We still are. However, we also believe that agencies should earn a reasonable profit. We do not believe in advocating the first to the exclusion of the second."

Ma and Pa Shops

Ten years ago there were perhaps 4,200 agencies in the U.S. They employed 60,000 persons and served more than 15,000 national and regional advertisers, plus thousands of local advertisers. Today there are an estimated 5,500 agencies in this country employing some 65,000 persons. They serve 17,000 companies which engage in national or regional advertising, plus many thousands of local advertisers. (Among Four A's agencies, the high-employment point came in 1968, when its members had 42,000 persons on their payrolls; today there are 38,000 people in 384 Four A's shops.)

The Top Ten agencies in billings last year employed 12,817 persons in their U.S. offices. The 63 agencies that billed more than $25,000,000 employed a total of 30,087 persons. In other words, the advertising agency business is one in which one- and two-man, and husband-and-wife operations are very common.

Nevertheless, the large agency has long been the major factor in the business, particularly in the handling of national advertising. The 63 agencies in the over-$25,000,000 classification last year accounted for a combined $8.5 billion in billings, and of this total, $4.6 billion·was billed by the Top Ten shops alone. Ten years ago, there were 42 agencies in the over-$25,000,000 bracket and they had combined billings of $3.6 billion. And of this figure, the ten largest agencies handled $2 billion.

Ten years ago, four giant agencies each billed more than $200,000,000. The same agencies today bill better than $370,000,000 each. The billings leader for the last 35 years has been the J. Walter Thompson Co., now with worldwide billing of $772,000,000 ($380,000,000 of which is billed abroad). Ten years ago, JWT was at the $400,000,000 level (one-third of which was billed overseas). In

second place is McCann-Erickson, which in 1972 billed $625,000,000. McCann is part of the Interpublic Group of Cos., whose agency units (including Campbell-Ewald, Erwin Wasey, and Marschalk) billed an estimated world aggregate of $893,099,000.

Madison Ave. Where It's at

The agency business is also highly concentrated geographically. While agencies are located in every major city in the U.S., they are most numerous in New York, Chicago, Los Angeles, Philadelphia, Detroit, Boston, Cleveland, San Francisco, Newark, Dallas, Miami, Minneapolis, St. Louis and Washington.

Most agencies operate out of one or two offices. It is only the larger shop that can afford to maintain a network of branch offices around the country, and only the largest have branches in various other parts of the world. However, many smaller agencies are able to offer their clients a kind of branch office service through their membership in agency networks. These networks include hundreds of geographically dispersed, independent agencies which are non-competitive with other members. Their reason for existence is that each member agrees to act as a branch office for every other member.

The rough rule-of-thumb in the agency business ten or more years ago was that 10 to 12 persons were required for every $1,000,000 in billing handled. Thus, if an agency billed $5,000,000, it needed 50 employees. But in recent years, because of increased attention to profitability and other factors, the figure has dropped to about 5.5 persons per million. The year 1970 was a difficult one for agencies, profitability declined and 2,860 people lost their jobs at the 196 agencies that billed $5,000,000 or better. And 1971 was worse: 3,442 employees were separated from agency payrolls at the 248 agencies that billed upwards of $5,000,000. In two years, the business separated 6,302 people. The paring process continued in 1972, but at a sharply reduced rate.

Standards for Service

Today's agency is vastly removed from the ones established in the last century. A fully-staffed advertising agency is now involved in many areas of marketing beyond the preparation and placement of advertising. For example, the American Assn. of Advertising Agencies has outlined the following set of standards for agency service, which "consists of interpreting to the public, or to that part of it which is desired to reach, the advantages of a product or service." Such "interpreting" is based on:

"1. A study of the client's product or service in order to determine the advantages and disadvantages inherent in the product itself, and in its relation to competition.

"2. An analysis of the present and potential market for which the product or service is adapted: as to location, as to extent of possible sale, as to season, as to trade and economic conditions, as to nature and amount of competition.

"3. A knowledge of the factors of distribution and sales and their methods of operation.

"4. A knowledge of all the available media and means which can profitably be used to carry the interpretation of the product or service to consumer, wholesaler, dealer, contractor, or other factor. This knowledge covers character, influence, circulation—quantity, quality and location, physical requirements, costs.

"Acting on the study, analysis and knowledge explained in the preceding paragraphs, recommendations are made and the following procedure ensues:

"5. Formulation of a definite plan and presentation of this plan to the client.

"6. Execution of the plan: (a) writing, designing, illustrating of advertisements, or other appropriate forms of the message; (b) contracting for space, time or other means of advertising; (c) the proper incorporation of the message in mechanical form and forwarding it with proper instructions for the fulfillment of the contract; (d) checking and verifying of insertions, display or other means used; (e) the auditing and billing for the service, space and preparation.

"7. Cooperation with the client's sales work, to insure the greatest effect from the advertising."

Agency Organization

Few agencies are organized exactly like others, but generally they all carry out their work for clients through the following people and departments:

1. Account supervisors and account executives. These people have the job of maintaining contact with the client. They are supposed to interpret the agency to the client and the client to the agency, an area involving detailing the client's problems to the agency and passing on to the advertiser the agency's recommendations and the advertisements the agency plans for his account. Once plans are approved by the client, the account people are responsible for seeing that the agency implements them. In a small agency, these functions are often assumed by the agency chief. In a large agency, where multi-million-dollar accounts are involved, there are customarily account groups headed by account supervisors, or management supervisors.

2. Copywriters. Skilled writers develop the ideas and write the advertisements. In addition, they often help to plan advertising layouts and illustrations. In larger agencies, there is a division between print writers and broadcast writers. With the domination of media by television, a generation of copywriters has come along whose members have never written a print ad. The production of television commercials, incidentally, is a joint effort of writers, art directors and broadcast producers.

3. Art directors and artists. These people supply the visual framework for the advertising message. They design layouts for print ads, the visuals for tv commercials; they create or supervise the creation of finished art and photography. Agency artists also work on designing booklets, packages and labels. While visual treatments are directed by the agency art department, much finished art for print and broadcast is purchased from outside specialists.

4. Media department. This department, under the media director, plans the use of media for agency accounts, and places the advertisements, commercials and other advertising messages developed by the "creative" departments. Department people advise on media use and strategy, then place the orders for space and time. In larger agencies, functions are usually divided by medium, so there are specialized print buyers, radio and television time buyers, and so on. Nowadays, the media director might work with an independent media service to plan media use and to place orders.

5. Research department. Since agencies rely on research to delineate copy and marketing goals for clients, they employ researchers who may be trained statisticians, psychologists, economists, etc., to provide "the solid floor of facts on which to practice the art of advertising." Researchers analyze markets, suggest copy themes, conduct consumer and dealer surveys, supervise pre-testing of advertisements, and recommend media to use.

6. Radio-television department. In radio's heyday, advertising agencies produced many radio programs for clients. Today, most television programs are produced by packagers and the networks. These days, the agency or the client buys packages of 30-second commercials, mostly, and spreads them over several shows, usually on several networks. Agencies are normally responsible for the creative work on the commercials, and this may include the selection of pro-

---

Big Budgeters

Procter & Gamble's very first advertising appropriation was $11,500. Sunkist oranges started with $6,800. Campbell soups were launched with a $4,000 budget; Armstrong Cork's line with $3,000; Borden with $500—and Wrigley Gum with a $30 budget.

---

duction houses to do the filming or taping of the advertisements.

7. Production department. People in production handle the mechanical production of ads—converting the art work and copy into their finished forms: Printing plates or other mechanical materials. Such materials are almost always purchased outside, under the supervision of a production manager.

8. Traffic department. The function of this department is to keep track of all agency work in progress and to see that it is completed on schedule and turned over for shipment.

9. Public relations. Many agencies do product publicity and other promotional chores for clients—usually on a fee basis. Some agencies also employ pr people to promote the agency itself. Such agencies sometimes have the pr man or woman on their own payrolls; sometimes they hire outside pr companies to do the job.

10. Merchandising. Many agencies are equipped to supply special services to a client, like promoting his advertising to his sales force, to wholesalers and to dealers; plan contests; help expand a client's distribution; and create point-of-sale materials and in-store promotions.

The areas just outlined cover the principal functions of an advertising agency operation. In a large agency there will be fully-staffed departments for each function. But since the majority of agencies are small businesses, several of these functions are handled simultaneously by one person.

Agencies Employ Many Specialists

In addition to developing and increasing the business of current clients (and thereby adding to their own growth), agencies depend heavily on the acquisition of new business. Sometimes they have new-business departments; sometimes they have a few people—customarily among top management—who are designated to attract new clients. In most instances, this is an additional duty. Agencies also have administrative heads who are concerned about financial and accounting matters, management of the

office and the people in it. Large agencies have plans boards whose job is to review new advertising campaigns prior to their submission to the client for approval. In smaller shops, the owner or the president assumes this task.

Within the departments outlined above—or outside them—frequently will be found a proliferation of specialists in one or another phase of marketing, advertising, distribution, research, psychology, sociology, medicine, music or whatever. The incidence of doctors of philosophy in America's agencies is high. Moreover, a large number of agencies have moved to the account team concept. These teams include specialists from all required areas who work as a coordinated group on one, or perhaps two or three specific accounts on the agency roster. Other teams perform the same functions for other accounts handled by the agency.

As has been said, the most important function of an agency, its reason for being, is to develop and prepare advertising. But advertising has become inextricably intertwined with all other aspects of marketing and selling and merchandising. So much so that today's agency is really a marketing specialist, and the designation "advertising agency" no longer covers the extent and scope of the services it offers. Advertising must be carefully coordinated with all aspects of the client's operation, even involving such considerations as financing, credit terms, labor problems, product development and improvement, product design, packaging, pricing, methods of distribution, and the organization of the client sales force.

The increment of such agency functions over the years has helped greatly to enlarge the agency business. However, it also created the field's biggest problem: declining profit margins and the need for obtaining fees outside the traditional 15% commission base to help pay for the constantly expanding list of services which clients seek.

Product Conflicts Are Big Problem

Over the years there has developed a set of standards covering agency relationships with clients and with media. These are not legal requirements—but they are followed by most agencies in this country.

Two of these standards may be expressed like this:

1. An agency will handle only one product in a field; say a toothpaste from Colgate; it will not also handle a toothpaste from Lever or Procter & Gamble. It is generally held by advertisers that an agency cannot do an effective job of advertising for two competing products. Advertisers also fear the possibility of the loss of product information confidentiality. (The Interpublic Group of Cos., with its various separate and independent agency units, was set up with the idea that those units could and would handle competing accounts, and do it effectively and with no product information disclosure.) But the tradition remains generally intact: no handling of competitive accounts. In this respect, agencies differ from legal, accounting and other professional service businesses.

2. Agencies are independent companies, free from both advertiser and media control. Agencies, in turn, generally do not control any medium (obviously because they must bring objective viewpoints to the media selection problems of their various clients). However, it is currently the rule of the American Assn. of Advertising Agencies that their member agencies (or employes of those agencies) may own an advertising medium, provided that disclosure of the fact is made to their clients, to other media and to the Four A's. Agencies controlled by advertisers are known as "house agencies." These have existed for many years and while they never amounted to much of a factor in the business, in recent years, as noted earlier, a number of clients have moved to this kind of operation for various reasons, thus posing new concern for full-service agencies.

No Price Competition

There is intense competition in the agency business for new accounts. It is not uncommon to find a dozen or more agencies making presentations to an advertiser when his account becomes open to solicitation. One of the characteristics of the agency business is that there is no obvious price competition. On the face of it, an advertiser with $1,000,000 to spend will find that one agency's service will not be cheaper than another's, except—importantly—in terms of one agency's ability to produce more effective advertising than another. But this is an important difference, making for actual price competition in the areas of the quality and number of services.

In 1955, as has been mentioned, the federal government, in an anti-trust action, challenged the recognition system (without recognition no agency could operate), and charged that the American Assn. of Advertising Agencies and the leading media associations were basically price-fixing in promulgating the 15% commission as a standard of the business. The associations' prohibition against rebating to clients was likewise challenged. The government view was

that agencies could rebate part of their media commissions to clients, and they could use this as a competitive price weapon.

While the associations agreed, in consent decrees, to suspend the practices, the actions affected only the associations as *groups*. Individual agencies were left free to do as they wished. But the practices complained about—stabilization of the media commission at 15%, no rebating, and no speculative presentations to prospective clients (showing suggested advertising campaigns in the hope of getting the advertising account)—continue to be practical operating principles of the agency business. But, on a not insignificant number of occasions, especially in the last dozen years, they have been completely ignored by individual agencies.

Reaching for Stability

The agency business is often viewed as unpredictable and sometimes frenzied, like "laying track ahead of a train moving 75 miles an hour." Nevertheless, it can be argued that stability and longevity are being melded into the business. Despite more than 200 account changes in 1972, the fact remains that the switches represent something on the order of 6% of the business.

A study by the Assn. of National Advertisers on the durability of client-agency relationships found that 81 companies among the Top 100 national advertisers using 393 agencies between 1958 and 1963 terminated 144 of those agencies. It also found that 15 of the client companies had terminated 79 agencies—55% of the total. (The 15 companies each terminated four or more agencies in the period.) As an observer on the agency side said of last year's account changes: "What you have to pay attention to is, what kind of business is that 6%? If it has a high proportion of repeaters, you know something you didn't know before." Moreover, a Four A's study shows that its average agency-member holds an account just short of nine years.

It requires somewhat more capital to open an agency's doors these days—and keep them open. This is not to say that success is impossible if one starts out with a small amount of capital. The agency business is one which, in the last ten years, has created more millionaires than in any preceding period. A truly entrepreneurial field, it is one in which the people who take risks may well reap very large rewards. But it would, nevertheless, require more than a little temerity these days to emulate David Ogilvy, whose initial capital was $6,000 when he

started shop in 1948. (Ogilvy, incidentally, ran through that sum fairly quickly and hung on only with the aid of a $100,000 loan negotiated by his partner, Anderson Hewitt.) In 1949, Ned Doyle, Maxwell Dane and William Bernbach launched their agency with $1,200 contributions from each of the trio.

Office space in recent years has been a big-ticket item. When Wells, Rich, Greene leased space in the new General Motors Bldg. in New York five years ago, the annual rental was $611,000. And Fax Cone to the contrary, not all the inventory any longer goes down in the elevators each night; much of it stays right there because it is physical equipment: costly computers, either bought or leased; expensive screening rooms with high-priced 35mm cameras and audio devices; Xerox machines, and so on. It all runs into an amount of money that tends to keep the agency together. A senior executive will give long thought before he moves elsewhere. "Whose computer can I hook into if I leave here?"

Increased stability in the agency field also stems from the practice, at least in privately-held shops, of restricting ownership to active workers. This practice has perhaps been carried to broader extents than elsewhere in the business world. Death or retirement sees the immediate transfer of that person's stock ownership to active employes. Agency ownership is often so diffused that no one person securely controls the reins.

Tax laws effective over the last 10 or 15 years have helped spur the movement of a number of agencies to publicly-owned status. As, indeed, did the fact most agency ownership agreements call for the transfer of stock at book value—a factor that often works against notable increases in the value of privately-held stock. Since 1962, as has been noted, about a dozen agencies have made public stock offerings—providing them with added working capital and other advantages, most of them calculated to add stability to their individual business.

Agency profit margins are not now what they were in 1952, when they averaged 6.25% on gross income. By 1961, the average had tailed off to 3.46%; and last year it was 3.76%. Net profit as a percentage of gross income in 1972 was the highest return since 1969, when the figure was 6.32%. The high point in the ten years from 1963 to 1972 came in 1966, according to the annual studies of costs and profits conducted by the Four A's. In 1966, the figure was 7.49%.

"Profit averages vary by agency size groups," reports the Four A's, "and tend, in most years, to run somewhat higher for larger agencies. In 1972, the average profit percentage ranged from a low of almost zero for agencies in one size group to a high of 7.30% of gross income for another group." And the agency business is one in which mergers have been not uncommon, creating larger and larger shops. Recent years have seen the amalgamation of D'Arcy Advertising with MacManus, John and Adams, and Needham, Louis & Brorby with Doherty, Clifford, Steers & Shenfield to form Needham, Harper & Steers, and the acquisition of Gardner Advertising by Wells, Rich, Greene, to name a few.

A study made by Rubel & Humphrey, management consultant, published last May, covered over 200 U.S. and Canadian agencies. It put the operating profit of the agencies (as a percentage of gross income) at 9.9%, compared with 10.5% in 1963 and 10.1% in 1969. Ranked by groups according to size of billings, the agencies in the over-$40,000,000 category last year enjoyed a profit of 16.8%; those between $10,000,000 and $20,000,000 got 10.3%; those in the $5,000,000 to $10,000,000 classification 10.1%; between $3,000,000 and $5,000,000 were at 8.8%, and under $1,000,000 at 7.7%.

Andrew Kershaw, president of Ogilvy & Mather, has referred to the "frenzy" of expansion by U.S. agencies to countries outside North America during the last half dozen or more years. This activity, he said, has increased the foreign billings of U.S. agencies to the point where they "now are equal to about one-third of domestic billings."

Underscoring this statement is the fact that in 1961, the Top Ten U.S. agencies in international billings had a combined volume overseas estimated at $372,200,000. By 1972, the Top Ten had increased their overseas volume to $1.9 billion. McCann-Erickson, the No. 1 agency in this area last year, alone billed $417,300,000 overseas—more than the combined billings of all Top Ten agencies 12 years ago. The 63 largest agencies in this country (billing over $25,000,000 each) handled a combined $8.55 billion in billings in 1972. Of this total, $2.36 billion was billed beyond U.S. shores.

As advertising volume mounted in Western Europe and in other parts of the free world—and as American advertisers expanded their operations to many corners of the world—U.S. agencies followed, initially making some rather loose affiliations with locally-based foreign shops, but later moving more and more to actual ownership of foreign operations and to starting up their own branch offices. Grey Advertising, to name one agency, today has offices in England, France, Belgium, Holland, Japan, Germany, Austria, Spain, Italy, Australia, Venezuela and Argentina. Compton Advertising not only has offices in many of those same countries, but also in Sweden, Finland, Norway, Denmark, Mexico, the Philippines, and other places as well. McCann-Erickson and J. Walter Thompson are the largest agencies in Argentina and Brazil; Benton & Bowles the biggest in Belgium; Ogilvy & Mather in Kenya; Leo Burnett in Rhodesia; Grant Advertising in Singapore and Zambia.

Whether the "frenzy" of expansion by agencies will continue in Europe is somewhat problematical. Now that the Common Market has been enlarged to nine nations with 250,000,000 consumers, it would seem that already-entrenched agencies (and American marketers) might stand to gain from increased trade. But as has been observed by Ramona Bechtos, international editor of ADVERTISING AGE, following talks with scores of marketing experts during a 1972 study trip through the European Economic Community, "U.S. agencies which don't yet have a foothold in Europe will find it increasingly difficult to take the step now. The days when U.S. agency expertise is sought by Europeans with the kind of fervor shown by prospectors in the California gold rush is coming to an end."

Reprinted from "Advertising Age," Nov. 21, 1973, pp. 34, 36, 38, 40

How admen see their business

BY MARTIN MAYER
Author of
"Madison Avenue, U.S.A."

With Ralph Nader, Betty Furness and Nicholas Johnson all in general agreement that advertising is crooked, with lawyers for the television networks insisting on rewriting everybody's commercials, with client corporations scheming to make the payments float benefit them rather than their agencies, and with the price of agency stocks down some manhole on Wall St., one might expect to find the advertising business in a state of somber if not suicidal contemplation. No such thing at all: With a handful of exceptions, everybody seems very cheerful. The adjective that best fits the mood is "complacent."

"Look, we've been through it all," said a man who runs a house agency. "If you tell me there's a great flood coming and in six days the whole world is going to be under six feet of water, I'll say, 'I've got six days? Good. I'll learn to live under water.'" Tom Dillon of BBDO says, "I recently told a man from *Forbes* that when I came to work here 38 years ago it seemed to me that five telephone calls would put the whole place out of business. But we've been perking along for 92 years. The record of stability in the agency business is quite remarkable. This business is like a ghost—hitting it with a bullet is difficult. Given the slightest competence in management, the agency business has a small downside risk."

There is general agreement that recent years have seen an increase in the stability of agencies. "We've gone from a feast-and-famine industry to a pretty controlled flow," says Warren Bahr of Young & Rubicam. "A lot of the risks have been taken out of the business." In part, the reason can be found in the great growth of expenditures by the largest clients. "You just don't change agencies any more," says a representative of one of the very largest; "it's too disruptive. When a sophisticated advertiser has trouble today, he goes to Mr. Bernbach or Mr. Foster and he says, 'I'm not happy'— and they restructure the agency for him."

A side effect of the increase in stability is a loss of glamor: "We are no longer advisers to presidents," Behr says, "we have become a service of supply." Jerry Della Femina, who at 37 says that people still consider him a kid (and who still, obviously, likes the idea of being considered a big, bearded, balding kid), feels that "the problem with the agency business is that they let some people escape. Most clients are represented now by guys who have been in agencies, which means the agencies have lost their mystique. At Ralston, my client comes from Gardner; at Bristol-Myers, he comes from Foote, Cone. I'm going to tell *him* I've got magic?"

Boutique? It's 'No Relationship'

The agency business has clearly weathered the worst of recent internal threats. Better accounting and internal control procedures (and hard-nosed approaches by clients) have ended the terrifying habit of relying for working capital on late billing by media and pre-payments by clients, which drove one big agency into bankruptcy and at least one other to the brink during the 1970-71 recession. Though there are more house agencies than ever before—Peter Allport of the Assn. of National Advertisers estimates that half of all large advertisers now have "at least a letterhead agency" on the premises—they are mostly not competitive for business the outside agencies would want. "The basics continue to be," Allport says, "that you cannot get a bunch of writers to work as well for General Motors—certainly not for a smaller manufacturer—as they will work when you summon them into an agency. But house agencies are tremendously valuable in the new-product field, where it may be too costly to go to an agency, or there's a product conflict at the agency, and you can go to a boutique or a moonlighter and do the preliminary work in-house."

A few years ago, many observers felt the full-service agency would split up into specialties, each charging a fee and nobody getting a commission. While the commission system is still under fierce attack, almost nobody now expects the agencies to crack apart. Being a boutique turned out to be unrewarding: "It's not a relationship," says Della Femina. "It's like the guy who meets the girl on Friday night at Maxwell's Plum and they go back to her place, and Monday morning they both go to work and they never see each other again. When you're an agency, they *love* you, they kiss you—it's a marriage."

Time buying services persist, but they have not delivered the miracles they once seemed to promise—and some of them have been caught out delivering shoddy goods. More important, probably, has been the improvement of performance in this area by the established agencies, even those which in past years couldn't have cared less about such mundane stuff. "We have an extraordinary young girl who came to us in that department about six months ago," says Norman B. Norman, who still prefers empathy to statistics, but lives in a competitive world, "and she has made an enormous difference. It's a tedious job that takes a great deal of talent—and executive talent, because you have to be sure that something you set up rigidly is in fact executed rigidly."

Pleased with Their Working World

The major source of good cheer, of course, is that almost everybody is making a whale of a lot of money. "Their complacency," says David J. Mahoney of Norton Simon Inc., who has ornamented all sides (and most corners) of the advertising business, "is directly proportionate to how business is this year." Carl Ally runs over to Marrakesh for four or five days "to get ready for the next ten-plus megaton meeting." The note pad on Bill Bernbach's table (he scorns a desk) is from the Plaza Athenee in Paris. At the agencies that have gone public, one can find a few hangdog stockholders. ("I can hire anybody I want," says the head of a house agency, denying allegations to the contrary; "sure, I don't pay the same salaries as the outside agencies, but when I give stock options, the stock goes up.") But most men, at least on the senior level, seem pleased with their working world as they find it on the desk when they arrive in the morning.

The old satisfactions survive, of course: "This is an emotional business," says Warren Bahr; "it's still a great ride on a great product." Bill Bernbach says, "I'm very lucky. I look at some work, I get a thought, and suddenly I'm enthusiastic again." George Lois illustrates the point: "The future for me is the work I'll do tomorrow: Am I really going to *love* it? I mean, I'm not Michaelangelo, but I'm not bad. Every time I do something, I like to think it's done with strength and vigor, and it's going to be *famous*. That's very important to me, personally . . ."

Consumerism's Ugly/Pretty Head

Admen's reactions to consumerism and to the new pressure from the Federal Trade Commission would make an interesting study in themselves, A. D. 1973. The official position is best stated by (naturally) Henry Schachte of J. Walter Thompson: "A lot of people think that if it's wisely done, it's going to be helpful; you know, honest men don't fear the law." Don Creamer of Creamer, Colarossi says, "On the assumption that it's being done by constructive people, it's going to do us a lot of good, create an attitude that the advertising must be truthful." Peter Geer of Geer, DuBois, who doesn't have any packaged goods accounts, says that "the tighter the restrictions, the more interesting it is. It's good to have a conscience imposed on us. I think it's a relief, and I think the industry finds it a relief."

George Lois argues (with himself) that "the FTC makes you think harder about the product." A number of agency people, none of whom would appreciate being identified, observe that it gives the conscientious copywriter a defense against an unconscionable client: "In the old days, you would say you wouldn't do it and you'd lose the account. Now you can say, there's this guy over there who won't let either of us do it, whether we want to or not."

Warren Bahr says, "Consumerism doesn't bother me in the least. I see nothing wrong with it. In fact, if what they say is right, I see a lot right with it. Sure, I think packages ought to be labeled

properly. We're sales people; puffery and showmanship were part of our bag, and if there's been deception it's got to be corrected." Then he adds, "But we ought to be able to present something in its best light . . ."

FTC No Worry to Mary

Mary Wells says, "The FTC is no problem. I've always found them a perfectly logical apparatus." Then she adds, "But the whole consumerism movement has passed from the hands of people who were intelligent and cared about things to people who are making short-term careers out of it. Reminds me of the McCarthy era."

After the early moments of conversation, concern does shine through even the most opaque confidence. "Of course," Henry Schachte says, "some people under the guise of consumerism are going to try to dictate to the public. It's the old split between advertising as informer and advertising as persuader. In the end, business doesn't succeed and the economy doesn't run unless people are persuaded." Peter Geer, young and serious-minded, a product of David Ogilvy's rather dignified shop, accepts the fundamental consumerist position: "In the last analysis, advertising is called upon to manufacture preference whether it's justified or not. We live in a society predicated on manufacturing more than anybody really needs, and something has to be done to follow through." Tom Dillon, starting with the statement that "consumerism is not entirely negative and not all that simple," moves on to the conclusion that "it has certain virtuous purposes, like the French Revolution, along about the time Danton and Robespierre got started, it's not as virtuous as it was."

Some of the younger men feel even more strongly. "The enemy is past being at the gates," says Jerry Della Femina; "he's writing our advertising for us. I don't think there's going to be an advertising business in 20 years. People are growing horribly cynical about advertising. It's the cynicism they used to have about bankers. Bankers were guys with white mustaches and funny hats who pushed girls onto the subway tracks because they couldn't pay the mortgage. But the banks survived because they convinced people they were vital. People don't think advertising is vital. You can tell it from the attitudes of the politicians; politicians can smell a cause two years ahead."

How much impact consumerism has had on the advertising itself is a matter for debate. Rosser Reeves, who pretends to have reached the age of 65 and keeps an eagle eye on the scene from a retirement perch on Gramercy Park, thinks

the results are ghastly: "And it's not the FTC, it's the NAB [National Assn. of Broadcasters]. They watch to see which ads sell goods, and then they make those illegal. I could hire a stenotypist and comment on a day's television commercials and triple the efficiency of 60% of them. Most people who write them don't know what they're doing; it's the inheritance of the boutique tendency."

Jim Shaw, who handles selling operations for ABC Television, feels some sympathy: "Code restrictions and copy clearance: They're *murder*." George Lois spells out what the new attitudes mean in practice: "First you gotta beat up your lawyer. That's not hard, because you're paying the bills. But if he's any good, he screams and yells back. Then you gotta battle the client's lawyers, and you compromise that one. *Then* you gotta battle through the networks, and you gotta change and twist. But if you've got a concept that's true, and you're honest, a good creative guy will find a way to do it. Guys who say you can't do good work because of the restraints never did good work. The real pro sits there and says, 'I'll outfox them.' Not that I want to do anything dishonest—I've never done anything dishonest in my life."

But Lois does not completely disagree with Reeves. "I hate most advertising," he says. "I go home as a consumer, and I want to put my foot through the screen." It would be interesting to organize a joint viewing, and to see whether Reeves began dictating to the stenotypist at the same moment that Lois put his foot through the screen. It might well happen that way; then again, it might not.

The Age of Computers

On the question of what the computer has meant and will mean to the advertising business, the experts go all over the lot. "I wrote in 1960," says William T. Moran, vp for marketing research at Lever Bros., "that the advent of the computer would shift the whole advertising business to direct mail. That way you can pick your customers. It hasn't happened yet, but that doesn't mean it never will. Where the influence is most visible right now is in the language, and the names. Research companies have become 'faceless—it isn't Politz or Hopper, it's Decision Data.' And 'resource allocation' has become the new buzz word."

"The computer hasn't yet changed the business at large all that much," says Tom Dillon. "It is being used for a lot of routine purposes, accounting and media; we run ours 24 hours a day, seven days a week—but before that we ran punch cards." Behind him, in our age of quartz crystals and tuning forks, a real ship's clock struck seven bells. "Then, on some different equipment, we have mathematical models of marketing, and these have been a very insightful thing. It's been a struggle. The number of agencies operating computers was not great enough to justify any investment by the software people, so we're all operating our home-brew systems. And sometimes you can get deceptive answers. The bane of all research, not just advertising research, is that the world works on a scoreboard. There's an athletic analogue. The score is 30-31, and that's a clear win for one side; but 30-31 really isn't a win at all."

Where the Agencies Goofed

Norman B. Norman thinks the logistics have been bungled: "Advertising agencies have made business very good for their suppliers. There could have been a single computer bank for the industry, but agencies which got theirs first thought they had some sort of advantage over the others, and they wouldn't cooperate. We're all duplicating this stuff all over the city, and we leave the door open for all sorts of obfuscation."

Computers have given both advertisers and their agencies control over vastly greater quantities of information. Today's advertiser can know in much greater detail where and to whom he is selling his product (this is the basis for Moran's prediction), and he can also know in much greater detail whom he is reaching with his advertising messages. In theory, the combination of these two can deliver much more accurate statements of the effectiveness of advertising—and in practice it has already begun to deliver a confidence that one knows what one is doing, which was unusual and not always wholly sane in years past.

This worries people like Lou Dorfsman of CBS, who puts together what is probably the largest single advertising campaign of every year. ("This year like last year . . ." His campaign never shows up that size in the figures, because the network pays nothing to itself, at least in external reporting, for promotional spots.) "Instinct and intuition," Dorfsman says, "all that goes into constructing a campaign, are getting a little too mathematical."

Biggest Change Is Fewer Employes

For David Mahoney, it's all a plus: "Do we know what things cost today? You bet your life we do. And we're more aware of spending the money wrong—not just in terms that you're going to waste $300,000, but that you're going to waste six months." Henry Schachte thinks widespread use of cost-effectiveness measurements in advertising is unlikely: "Really, nobody is that interested. The minute you introduce time spans there are too many

other factors that can enter." In fact, there is considerable reason to believe that a handful of the largest advertisers, led by General Foods, have gone a good distance down this road, and where it comes out, nobody knows. But for the time being, the impact of computers and control of information has been mostly on costs, and especially on personnel costs. Perhaps the greatest single change in the advertising business over the past 15 years has been a phenomenal reduction in the number of employes at each agency per million dollars of billings.

"When I went to work here," Tom Dillon says of BBDO, "we had 18 people per million, and now we're down to 4.3. Customers had difficulty measuring an agency, and the one question they always asked was, 'How many people do they have on my account?' They liked to see hordes of people. That's gone, and today we really don't have many juniors; the man to get the coffee isn't there any more. We've all come to understand that fewer people with more brains are better than more people with none."

■ Unfortunately, this coin has another side. With shrinkage in numbers inevitably has come a rise in the average age of the people in the business. One of the pains of being in the advertising business has always been the attitudes of one's own children; there may be no other occupation where so few sons (or daughters) follow the footsteps of their fathers (or mothers). "I wish I could convince my kids to come into this business," says Ben Colarossi, "but they won't be convinced; they believe we're a bunch of hucksters." Jerry Della Femina says unhappily, "We're not getting the kids; this isn't a kid's business anymore. The 18-year-olds who used to come in have been fed all this negative stuff about advertising by their teachers, their professors . . ."

Advertising was a victim of the (probably temporary) loss of entrepeneurship in the recent young, for part of its appeal always was the chance to measure one's performance as an individual against that of other individuals. "I meet a lot of young artists," Bill Bernbach says, "and I tell them, 'You're at a great disadvantage. Somebody comes to you and says something you've done doesn't work, you can say, You don't understand what I'm doing. I have a great advantage, because I'm in the real world, and the real world tells me if something works or it doesn't, and I can't argue about that'." That attitude does not attract a high proportion of our recent graduates, who want the real world to tell them only that they're wonderful, and keep quiet if by some aberration it thinks they aren't.

Some of the younger men feel that advertising has always been a game for the lean and hungry, and its lessened appeal simply reflects the general affluence. But the likeliest of all explanations is that there are fewer jobs, and occupations with limited numbers of jobs tend after a while to draw fewer applicants. What has been lost is something that may be very precious: The collection of surrogate children with whom one sympathized and quarreled and competed, to whom one gave ambiguous orders. Maybe you can't have that and stability, too.

Going Public Grows Dimmer

One wave of the future has receded: Advertising agencies have virtually stopped trying to sell their stock to the public, and even if the new issues market revives on Wall St., ad agencies are unlikely to be represented again to a significant degree. There are still some enthusiasts for public ownership, most notably Mary Wells. "Going public," she says, "is probably the best thing that's happened to the advertising business since it began. It opens up the agency. There used to be a small group of people up top who knew how much money was coming in and trucked most of it away themselves. Now everybody knows everything about everybody else. The honesty is very healthy. They know I make quite a lot of money; to keep from getting lynched in the halls, I have to work harder than anybody else, and always deliver. Then, you have to treat all your accounts equally, because Wall St. and the stockholders will take the loss of a $3,000,000 account as seriously as the loss of a $10,000,000 account. Having stockholders makes this a more serious business, with less fun-and-games, and the client gets more effort."

Nevertheless, the price of agency stock is still way down (including stock in Wells, Rich, Greene), and Wall St.'s disenchantment with Madison Ave. has come to be matched by the advertising industry's distaste for financial analysts. "Looking at the figures of any agency on a quarterly basis is utter nonsense," says Henry Schachte, whose agency is listed on the big board. "One year your big tv specials will fall in the first quarter, the next year in the second quarter. These financial people live on a quarterly basis, but agencies live—or should live—on a five-year moving average basis. I suppose the problem is that we don't really have a business: We have an accumulation of parts of a lot of different clients' business."

One of the first agencies to "go public" was Papert, Koenig, Lois. "In retrospect," says George Lois, who now has his own agency, "public ownership was the catalyst for destroying our partnership. People became rich quick and choked up. They started to think, 'We now have obligations to stockholders.' I always said, 'NO. My obligations are to myself and to my clients, to sell their merchandise.' When we first went public, we were saying, 'We're not just a service business: We have a product, called advertising'— and it was very exciting at the time. But what's wrong with the world is that 99% of the guys are worried about *holding* a job, not about *doing* a job, and that's too tough a decision when you have a publicly-held agency."

■ When agencies first began to sell stock in themselves, the public worry was that the business was so unstable, so dependent in each case on the services of a handful of people who might get killed or drunk or alienated, that the investment was unduly risky. This reasoning turned out to be false, but the statement that public ownership violated the essence of the business was probably true. Advertising was and is a business where a man can make a lot of money on a very small capital investment; public ownership is essentially a means of securing capital beyond what can be raised privately. The one necessity stock issuance was to meet —a way for senior people or their estates to realize the value of their share in the business—has turned out in many cases to be a mirage.

"We considered going public," says Norman B. Norman, "but we had clients who would have found it objectionable, so we couldn't. Looking back, of course, we're gratified. The guys who went public find that the price of their stock is down, they can't get out. If I wanted to quit, we could tighten our belts for six months and then buy me out from retained earnings. The great problem of going public is that somebody in the agency then has to be delegated to handling stockholders as a continuing problem. And if the top man does it, which will often be the case, you're *dead*."

Keep One Eye on the 'Street'

BBDO is going to try again, having been rebuffed a year ago in a first effort to sell its shares; there is no other way out for the insiders who bought then to sell later and are now carrying their holdings with borrowed money. But Tom Dillon agrees on the dangers of keeping "one eye on the 'Street.' Wall St. said, 'If you go public, you must show growth. You must cut dividends and retain earnings or people will think you're not going to grow.' But advertising is not a capital-intensive industry. You can double your business without changing your capital. This leads agencies into diversification schemes they are not qualified to manage. Like everyone else, advertising people, given a chance at omniscience, will grab for it, and then they're going to be in trouble."

If the market booms again, of course, there will be people who look longingly at what they are told their stock would be worth if they offered it. As of fall 1973, however, few agencies not already publicly-held seem to have the slightest interest in entering that arena. Too many lions; too much blood on the sand.

Overseas Is Where It's at

One development of the 1960s does continue to intrigue nearly everyone: Expansion abroad. As more and more of the largest clients become significantly multi-national, more and more agencies look wistfully at the prospect of handling their business all over the globe. Several agencies now do more than half their business—and more of them make half their profits—abroad.

"It's the best thing that ever happened to the advertising business," says Warren Bahr; Young & Rubicam now has 2,200 employes abroad. "An important psychic income has been delivered. And having molded ourselves into a more static situation here, a more guaranteed life, we find that a lot of our excitement comes from what is happening out on the edges. For people in this agency, experience overseas has become the necessary career path."

Maybe that's where the young people are: Abroad. Ben Colarossi thinks that abroad may also be where the next generation of leadership is hiding. "First we had the WASP, then the Irishman, the Italian, the Jew. Will the Puerto Rican make it? Or are we going to get our so-called leadership from Japan, or Colombia? And is it one of these guys," Colarossi adds, in a dreamy ex-boxer's way, "who will be smart enough to set up the first all-electronic agency?"

Reprinted from "Advertising Age," Nov. 21, 1973, pp. 48, 50-51

Advertising polices itself

in many ways

BY STANLEY COHEN
Washington Editor, "Advertising Age"

Over many decades, self-regulation has been a force for good in the marketplace, although sometimes the results left something to be desired. Now, as the business community—and the ad business in particular—seeks to respond to the challenge of modern consumerism, self-regulation has become a boom activity.

Like the marketplace itself, self-regulation in the past tended to be segmentized—a program to eliminate abuses in a particular community, product category or advertising medium. Sometimes the project represented little more than pious pledges, but at other times it might be as unyielding as the law permits.

With the creation of the National Advertising Review Board (NARB) in 1971, the entire ad industry united for the first time behind a mechanism pledged to deal effectively with deception and bad taste in national advertising wherever it occurs.

NARB not only responds to complaints by the public, but does its own monitoring. While the program is financed and administered by the industry, its actions are publicized, and its review panels always include representatives of the consuming public.

■ While NARB has been assuming a leadership role in the self-regulation of advertising, it is by no means in a monopoly position. Many of the more specialized programs, such as the code authority of the National Assn. of Broadcasters (NAB), are expanding their efforts. Local equivalents of the NARB are springing up to deal with local advertising problems. Hundreds of individual newspapers, periodicals and broadcast stations superimpose their own standards on top of the general standards.

And in the background is an entirely new development in the business world—the widespread experiment with self-regulation within individual companies to guard against practices which lead to public criticism.

Until relatively recently, self-regulation has consisted mostly of codes of conduct, with little attempt at enforcement, and the results inevitably have been spotty. There are legal and philosophical explanations for the shape of events.

■ Because anti-trust laws prohibit concerted action by competitors which could be regarded as suppressing competition, business men have hesitated to sit down with their peers to agree on selling practices which should be regarded as unfair or unethical. In fact, the legal archives are peppered with disasters, many of them involving well-intentioned self-regulators who confused "soft" competition with "ethical" behavior.

Moreover, self-regulation must overcome logistical problems unlike those which exist in less complicated societies. In Britain, where there are only a handful of national newspapers, periodicals and tv program producers, it is relatively easy for mass media to agree to reject any ad condemned by the self-regulation system. Here in the U.S., however, even in the absence of anti-trust inhibitions, an agreement of this kind would have to encompass thousands of newspapers and periodicals, as well as at least 7,000 hotly competitive radio-tv stations.

Association Efforts

The self-regulation question is further complicated by the question of what to regulate. One of the earliest and most productive systems—launched by the Better Business Bureaus—developed effective behind-the-scenes techniques for rooting out ads which bordered on fraud. Policing of this kind of problem is within the reach of government agencies, of course, but government action necessarily involves time-consuming legal procedures, while self-regulation can often move quickly and quietly to get the job done before too many people are hurt.

Self-regulation can also reach problems of taste which are harder to define and legislate against, such as the way women are portrayed in ads, or the use of visuals which project good safety habits—for example, the NAB code provision which requires the use of shoulder straps in commercials portraying a moving auto. So some of the momentum behind self-regulation currently reflects efforts of the industry to achieve standards of excellence beyond what government might require.

Even before self-regulation achieved greater visibility during the past decade, there was much more activity than the industry's critics acknowledged. Earl Kintner, a former chairman of the Federal Trade Commission, once explained: "Self-imposed restraints by individuals are tested in the privacy of offices. On the other hand, harmful actions by individuals who recognize no restraints inevitably command public attention."

Long before today's more dynamic efforts developed, advertisers who "recognized no restraints" were subject to policing and pressure from the industry. Locally, the Better Business Bureaus worked quietly to eliminate questionable claims from ads by their members, and provide authoritative information to newspapers and broadcast stations so they would act individually to cut off access to the public by any advertiser—member or otherwise—who insisted on using practices which the bureau considered illegal.

■ On the national level, dating from 1924, the American Assn. of Advertising Agencies (Four A's) called on its members to live up to a creative code which sought to spell out some of the ground rules for ethical behavior. While there was no public censure of those who deviated, it was more than a plaque on the wall. Through a joint copy interchange program, the Four A's, representing ad agencies, and the Assn. of National Advertisers (ANA), representing advertisers, pinpointed those advertisements which deviated from the creative code, and a process of moral suasion was undertaken to get the situation corrected.

The creative code covered some obvious points, such as price claims, unfair comparisons, unsupported claims, things offensive to public decency, and testimonials not reflective of the real choice of a competent witness.

As to good taste in advertising, the code states:

"We recognize that there are areas which are subject to honestly different interpretations and judgment. Taste is subjective and may even vary from time to time as well as from individual to individual. Frequency of seeing or hearing advertising messages will necessarily vary greatly from person to person.

"However, we agree not to recommend to an advertiser and to discourage the use of advertising which is in poor or questionable taste or which is deliberately irritating through content, presentation or excessive repetition."

For enforcement, the code provides that "clear and wilful violations of this code shall be referred to the board of directors of the Four A's for appropriate action, including possible annulment of membership."

■ The first major effort to enforce a mandatory code of behavior in the advertising world was set up in the broadcast industry in 1952 when the National Assn. of Broadcasters developed strict and comprehensive standards for radio and television, setting forth statements of good taste and acceptability in both advertising commercials and program content.

The code initially assumed that government and its agencies would keep watchful eyes on the honesty of advertising, so the industry effort could specialize on keeping programs and commercials in good taste and reasonable balance. With the passing of time, however, broadcasters discovered that criticism of advertising practices continued to increase and the industry's code authority gradually began to offer advice and preclearance of commercials in limited product classifications—toy ads, ads for personal hygiene products and proprietary drugs, and most recently, ads addressed to the child audience.

The code is administered by a staff employed by the broadcasters, operating from offices in New York, Washington and Hollywood. The staff provides advice to broadcasters who want to know whether a commercial or program meets industry standards. In addition, it negotiates with advertisers and advertising agencies which seek assurance that the scenario for a commercial will meet code standards.

Rulings by the staff can be appealed to a code board consisting of members of the National Assn. of Broadcasters. While there is no public participation in the administration of the code, there have been recent instances where representatives of the public have been permitted to appear before the code board to discuss specific problems.

■ The broadcasters were among the first to achieve some degree of enforcement in a code program. Under their procedure, stations which refuse to comply with rulings of the code board—and insist on carrying commercials which are rated as unsatisfactory—can be expelled from the program, and denied the privilege of displaying the code membership seal.

ADVERTISING EVALUATION POLICY STATEMENT

NATIONAL ADVERTISING REVIEW BOARD

The National Advertising Review Board is charged by business primarily to achieve and sustain high standards of truth and accuracy in national and regional advertising.

The principal means of carrying out this mandate of self-regulation shall be through the established procedures for panels convened to adjudicate cases of alleged abuse of truth and accuracy.

In the evaluation process advertising will be reviewed in terms of its technical and literal accuracy, and thorough consideration will be given to the question of whether it has the capacity to deceive, by commission or by material omission, the potential customer who would be exposed to the advertising in question.

The issues which come before NARB panels may take a variety of forms:

The adequacy of substantiation, including research data, to support an objective claim for a product or service.

A testimonial involving the competency of the testifier as a regular user reflecting average experience.

A claim with respect to bargain or price savings for a product or service.

The matter of fair and honest reference to a competitor or of a comparison of products.

Substantiation for guarantees and warranties and whether there is adequate disclosure of pertinent information about these.

Advertising directed to children where representations not misleading to the adult mind could have the capacity to confuse or mislead the immature and impressionable mind.

These are cited here for illustrative purposes only, and each case will be decided on its own merits.

The Review Board recognizes the existence of various codes and guidelines in advertising which may be currently in use by segments of industry, and which are based on their past experience in evaluating advertising acceptability. The Council of Better Business Bureaus has developed an extensive body of precedents in this area which is available to its National Advertising Division in carrying out its staff role of initial evaluation and review.

In cases submitted to panels of the Review Board, detailed standards utilized within industry, or government decisions may be viewed as precedents for an NAD decision in a given case. The panels will consider the applicability of such standards or decisions to these cases, but are not bound by them.

Further, the executive director shall make available to NARB panels decisions rendered by previous panels for the assistance and guidance that these previous decisions may provide.

In all cases, NARB panels will seek to arrive at a fair and speedy resolution of the issues.

Recognizing that from time to time NARB will be asked to consider content of advertising messages in controversy for reasons other than truth and accuracy, the Chairman shall appoint 5-member panels from the membership whose responsibility shall be to review broad areas of concern to the public and to business involving advertising, but not relating to specific cases involving truth and accuracy.

These Panels shall consider such matters as are referred to them by the Chairman, and shall report their conclusions to the Board in writing. The Chairman shall release reports based upon the judgments of these panels and which are approved for publication by majority vote of the Board.

This distinction in evaluating advertising complaints recognizes the educational and persuasive role of NARB with respect to advertising practices in general, while at the same time acknowledging that enforcement recommendations are limited to matters of truth and accuracy.

Adopted January 20, 1972

A policy statement of the National Advertising Review Board tells what issues come before the board and what it does about them.

There have been a number of expulsions, as well as situations in which stations preferred to resign rather than comply. The program has been denounced by critics as less than a total success, in the sense that non-participation or expulsion from the code has not represented a sufficient deterrent to make a significant difference.

One indirect factor which tends to escape public attention stems from the close tie-in between the code authority of the NAB and the copy clearance executives of the three tv networks. While the networks each act independently in reviewing and approving commercials, their top copy clearance officers serve on the code review board of the NAB, assuring an exchange of views which results in some uniformity in attitudes. Failure to get network approval of a commercial represents a serious impediment to an advertiser since it not only keeps him off the network, but also reduces his chances of getting acceptance from individual stations in the event the commercial is placed on a "spot" rather than a network basis.

■ Each network has its own staff of copy clearance experts working under the supervision of a vp who has the final say on what is acceptable for broadcast, both in programs and commercials.

The operations of these copy clearance offices are seldom discussed publicly because the networks say there is almost continuous confrontation with program producers and advertisers, requiring face-saving compromises which would be more difficult to secure if the discussions were known outside the room. Among advertising people, network clearance of a commercial is often the most difficult, and critical step, in getting a new campaign worked out in a form which assures access to the media.

The code authority of the NAB keeps liquor advertising off the air, and reacts quickly in situations where criticism pinpoints a particular problem. Through its code, for example, broadcasters successfully eliminated the "man in white" commercials, where simulated doctors extolled the purported merits of a health product.

Rulings of the code authority spell out in detail the themes considered wrong in promoting drugs and other sensitive products. There is particularly close scrutiny of ads for feminine hygiene products, for example, and there is a detailed list of "do's" and "don'ts" for stimulants, calma-

tives and sleeping aids. A companion statement, adopted by the Proprietary Assn. as a code of advertising practices for the non-prescription drug industry, resulted in a joint approach by broadcasters and advertisers, one designed to eliminate some of the extravagant claims and offensive methods which have prompted industry critics to rate over-the-counter drug ads as the most offensive on tv.

■ The NAB code authority became the first industry mechanism to confront the special problems that developed as a result of intensive advertising to children. As early as 1961 NAB developed, in cooperation with toy makers, a code which identified techniques which are rated as unfair in toy ads. Under this plan, toy ads were pre-cleared by NAB, and an approved list was issued for reference by stations which were scheduling ads that were offered to them on a "spot" basis.

As the subject of children's advertising became increasingly controversial, NAB issued special instructions on premium offers to children. It subsequently adopted a statement which reduces the amount of commercial time on network programs addressed to children. As the controversy surrounding children's advertising continued to boil, the Assn. of National Advertisers, which normally leaves self-regulation to others, displayed its concern by issuing its own children's television advertising guidelines. By late 1973, the NAB code authority began moving further into the area with a comprehensive set of guidelines pinpointing a broad spectrum of situations which it considered unacceptable in commercials directed to children.

■ Though the codes of the NAB provided some protection against the abuses that can arise in a highly competitive field like advertising, the rising criticism of the industry in the 1960s and early 1970s persuaded many industry leaders that a more concerted and visible response was needed.

Start of NARB

The call for action originated in the American Advertising Federation (AAF), a group representing many segments of the industry. It had long sponsored an "Advertising Code of American Business." But lacking any enforcement provision, this document offered small consolation to consumers who complained about advertising practices, or to in-

dustry leaders who looked for a solution short of massive government intervention.

The NARB was created in 1971 as a direct response of the ad business to consumerists and others who complained that the industry had no mechanism equipped to listen to the public and do something about deceptive and offensive ads.

The advocates of reform called for a program which would be visible to the public, and which would be responsive to public opinion. After extensive discussions within the industry, and between industry and government, all the major elements united behind a plan which:

● Provides a staff of experts to police advertising by reviewing complaints from the public and by operating its own monitoring program.

● Seeks to get voluntary compliance through negotiations with advertisers who are found to be doing something questionable.

● Provides for an appeal to panels consisting of sophisticated practitioners, as well as laymen.

As the plan for the NARB developed, the sponsoring group was enlarged to encompass the major advertising organizations—the AAF, Four A's, and ANA. At the same time, the goal was expanded. The industry would not only create a mechanism for regulating advertising, but it would also rejuvenate the Better Business Bureau movement to improve self-regulation over all aspects of merchandising, not only at the local level, but at the national level, too.

As the plan finally evolved, the reform involved the creation of a Council of Better Business Bureaus (CBBB), supported by national advertisers, to provide supervision of the national marketplace, and to provide leadership and supplemental funding so that local Better Business Bureaus could expand their staffs and improve their facilities.

At the same time, the basic staff work for the new NARB was assigned to a newly created National Advertising Division (NAD) administered by the CBBB. This NAD staff was positioned so that in addition to reviewing complaints from the public, it could work with the commodity specialists of the CBBB, who are continually monitoring ads and other selling practices which could become problems.

■ The NARB itself consists of 50 persons plus a chairman nominated by a parent body called the National Advertising Review

Council (NARC), which is run by the major ad associations—the AAF, the Four A's, ANA and CBBB. NARC picks the NARB members and provides logistical support, including financing. But NARB, in its substantive work, is autonomous, and is not subject to review by the parent groups.

The NARB is the first national self-regulation effort for advertising in the U.S. to include public participation. When the program was under discussion, industry critics contended at least half the appointees should be "public" people, from outside the industry. Finally, however, a decision was made that 40 would be from the industry, while the remaining 10, and the chairman, would be "public" members—educators, consumer leaders and others having no connection with advertising.

While the ultimate potentialities of NARB remain to be proven, the experience to date suggests that the percentage of public members is less significant than the caliber of the membership generally.

Out of a total of 477 complaints processed through July, 1973, 110 were sustained at the staff level and 175 dismissed. (Another 186 cases were closed, and 6 were up for panel review.) In most instances where a complaint was sustained, the advertisers voluntarily accepted the staff's findings. In about a dozen instances, the verdicts were appealed to the NARB, and in about half these cases, the findings were against the advertisers. In every instance the advertisers had already abandoned the challenged practices, or agreed to abandon them.

■ Under the NARB system, each disputed advertisement is appealed to a panel which consists of four from industry and one layman. In practice, industry people on panels are expected to function as citizens rather than business men, and a review of NARB panel decisions suggests that industry members are sometimes more demanding than the laymen. In fact, there seems to be no discernible pattern which suggests results would be any different if there were greater non-industry representation on the panels.

In its first years, the NARB has approached individual problems on an *ad hoc* basis. It has not adopted any codes or regulations of its own, but the staff and the review panels have, in each instance, considered disputed ads in terms of existing industry codes, such as the code of the

NAB, the creative code of the Four A's, the precedents established by earlier Better Business Bureau rulings, and the legal decisions of government regulatory agencies.

Among its first actions was the release of a policy statement which explained that the issues it expected to consider would take a variety of forms. Among them:

● "The adequacy of substantiation, including research data, to support an objective claim for a product or service.

● "A testimonial involving the competency of the testifier as a regular user reflecting average experience.

● "A claim with respect to a bargain price savings for a product or service.

● "The matter of fair or honest reference to a competitor or a comparison of products.

● "Substantiation for guarantees and warranties and whether there is adequate disclosure of pertinent information about these.

● "Advertising directed to children where misrepresentations not misleading to the adult mind could have the capacity to confuse or mislead the immature and impressionable mind."

Against this background, the Four A's and the ANA permitted their interchange program to

---

CREATIVE CODE

American Association of Advertising Agencies

The members of the American Association of Advertising Agencies recognize:

1. That advertising bears a dual responsibility in the American economic system and way of life.

To the public it is a primary way of knowing about the goods and services which are the products of American free enterprise, goods and services which can be freely chosen to suit the desires and needs of the individual. The public is entitled to expect that advertising will be reliable in content and honest in presentation.

To the advertiser it is a primary way of persuading people to buy his goods or services, within the framework of a highly competitive economic system. He is entitled to regard advertising as a dynamic means of building his business and his profits.

2. That advertising enjoys a particularly intimate relationship to the American family. It enters the home as an integral part of television and radio programs, to speak to the individual and often to the entire family. It shares the pages of favorite newspapers and magazines. It presents itself to travelers and to readers of the daily mails. In all these forms, it bears a special responsibility to respect the tastes and self-interest of the public.

3. That advertising is directed to sizable groups or to the public at large, which is made up of many interests and many tastes. As is the case with all public enterprises, ranging from sports to education and even to religion, it is almost impossible to speak without finding someone in disagreement. Nonetheless, advertising people recognize their obligation to operate within the traditional American limitations: to serve the interests of the majority and to respect the rights of the minority.

Therefore we, the members of the American Association of Advertising Agencies, in

addition to supporting and obeying the laws and legal regulations pertaining to advertising, undertake to extend and broaden the application of high ethical standards. Specifically, we will not knowingly produce advertising which contains:

a. False or misleading statements or exaggerations, visual or verbal.

b. Testimonials which do not reflect the real choice of a competent witness.

c. Price claims which are misleading.

d. Comparisons which unfairly disparage a competitive product or service.

e. Claims insufficiently supported, or which distort the true meaning or practicable application of statements made by professional or scientific authority.

f. Statements, suggestions or pictures offensive to public decency.

We recognize that there are areas which are subject to honestly different interpretations and judgment. Taste is subjective and may even vary from time to time as well as from individual to individual. Frequency of seeing or hearing advertising messages will necessarily vary greatly from person to person.

However, we agree not to recommend to an advertiser and to discourage the use of advertising which is in poor or questionable taste or which is deliberately irritating through content, presentation or excessive repetition.

Clear and willful violations of this Code shall be referred to the Board of Directors of the American Association of Advertising Agencies for appropriate action, including possible annulment of membership as provided in Article IV, Section 5, of the Constitution and By-Laws.

Conscientious adherence to the letter and the spirit of this Code will strengthen advertising and the free enterprise system of which it is part.   *Adopted April 26, 1962*

Endorsed by

Advertising Association of the West, Advertising Federation of America, Agricultural Publishers Association, Associated Business Publications, Association of Industrial Advertisers, Association of National Advertisers, Magazine Publishers Association, National Business Publications, Newspaper Advertising Executives Association, Radio Code Review Board (National Association of Broadcasters), Station Representatives Association, TV Code Review Board (NAB)

A foremost instrument of self-regulation is this detailed, painstaking creative code of the American Assn. of Advertising Agencies.

taper off, with NARB assuming the burden. Broadcasters, however, continued their independent programs, broadening the reach of their radio and tv codes, and expanding the authority of their staffs and review boards.

The NARB began under policies which indicated that it would confine itself mainly to issues of deception submitted by the public, and would share its decisions only with the persons who brought the complaints and with the advertisers directly involved.

Public-interest organizations soon began to test the potential of the NARB, submitting large numbers of complaints of varying validity. Many touched on taste, and on broad questions of policy which went beyond deception, and it soon became evident that the NARB would contribute little toward meeting the issues raised by industry critics unless it was also willing to go beyond truth and into more delicate subjects. The NARB decided it would commission special panels to evaluate broad problems, such as the way women are portrayed in ads, and the problems which ads can create in such areas as safety and environment.

■ Meanwhile, ADVERTISING AGE began to crusade for reversal of the secrecy policy. Through the cooperation of public interest lawyers, it secured copies of a number of NAD staff rulings and panel decisions which had been available only to the advertisers involved and the public interest groups which lodged the original complaints.

With the publication of these rulings, this newspaper pointed out that secrecy was depriving industry members of information they needed about what is permissible, and what isn't. Beyond that, it questioned whether the public or the industry could have confidence in a program with so little public visibility.

Late in 1972, the NARB voluntarily reversed its position and ruled that results of NAD staff and NARB panel decisions would all be on the public record.

■ While the NARB concerns itself exclusively with advertising, the revitalization of the CBBB represents a major commitment by industry to overcome some of the complaints about modern merchandising practices which have been raised by the consumerists.

CBBB has developed, for example, model programs of arbitration to assure the fair resolution of disputes between business men and their customers, and these pro-

grams have been introduced locally in nearly 100 communities by local Better Business Bureaus. The CBBB has provided funds which are enabling BBB units in many communities to expand their staffs, increase the adequacy of their facilities (including the number of phone lines available to consumers who call in), and make many other improvements.

The CBBB monitors advertising and other trade practices, and takes an increasingly active role in supporting various efforts to root out bad practices. The CBBB itself is achieving more public visibility through prime-time radio programs and tv spots, warning consumers about potential pitfalls, and calling attention to NARB and other programs which can help.

Moves by Local Groups

In addition to these national programs of self-regulation, many strong measures have been taken by local groups of admen, and by individual media owners.

As a result of a joint effort by the AAF and CBBB, advertising clubs and Better Business Bureaus in many cities are experimenting with local variations of the NARB. These local advertising review boards or similar bodies are already in operation in a number of cities, among them Phoenix, Seattle, Honolulu, Minneapolis, Dallas, Nashville, and Cleveland, and in Westchester County, N.Y. Plans for such bodies are in an advanced stage in Los Angeles, and at least half a dozen other cities. Most involve public participation, with the percentage of public members running as high as 50%, at least in one instance—Minneapolis.

Advertising problems tend to get particularly touchy at the local level where the issues may involve price misrepresentation and other high-pressure selling tactics. In Cleveland, the ad club and the Better Business Bureau assisted the city's office of consumer affairs in developing a stringent truth-in-advertising code covering some of the most blatant forms of deception, and local ad agencies agreed to volunteer time and talent to promote the code to the community. Advertisers who violate the Cleveland code could face fines under the city's consumer protection laws.

The Philadelphia Better Business Bureau, and the Poor Richard Club, which is the city's advertising club, have developed a retail advertising code which will encompass a region including eastern Pennsylvania, and parts of New Jersey and Delaware.

While this code is not legally binding, the Better Business Bureau plans to publicize instances where advertisers who violate the code fail to take corrective action.

■ Fully as comprehensive and energetic as advertiser and agency efforts at self-regulation have been the measures taken by media to detect fraudulent and offensive advertising and to reject it from use in print or on the air. Virtually every major U.S. daily newspaper has its own guide or statement of criteria, or uses one supplied by the Better Business Bureaus, setting forth what is acceptable and what is unacceptable in the newspapers' advertising columns. The public generally is probably unaware of this continual vigilance on its behalf.

Ad Copy Control

The American Newspaper Publishers Assn. surveyed its membership in August, 1973, and found itself engulfed with documents submitted by newspapers which had been updating and tightening their reviews of advertising copy. The *Detroit News*, *Milwaukee Journal* and *Louisville Courier-Journal* all reported elaborate copy review systems.

The *New York Times*, for example, maintains an advertising acceptability department, manned by several persons who read all advertising submitted for publication and screen out the objectionable.

■ The *Chicago Tribune*, like many other newspapers, distributes an "Advertising Acceptability Guide" through its space salesmen, explaining that the purpose of the program is to maintain integrity and good taste in its advertising columns, "thereby increasing the benefits which this advertising will bring to advertisers and readers of the newspaper."

Like the newspapers, magazines police their advertising pages to detect, whenever possible, and screen out objectionable advertising and see that the reader and consumer get a fair shake. Apart from altruism, the magazine's reputation is at stake, since any irregularities in an ad or product advertised reflects in part on the magazine itself.

Major publishers like Time Inc., *Reader's Digest* and *The New Yorker* have all been active leaders in enforcing rigorous advertising clearance standards, but these are merely better known examples. Most major magazines, aimed at high-level audiences, and determined to maintain tones of quality, have individual advertising acceptance standards which, though differing in detail, maintain an environment consistent with their concepts of editorial excellence.

■ At least two well known magazines go to outstanding lengths by maintaining programs of thoroughly testing their advertisers' products and making sure they meet advertising claims before the advertising is accepted. Advertisers that meet standards are permitted use of a seal.

Guaranty Seal

Oldest such program, with roots that go back to 1902, is that of *Good Housekeeping,* whose Consumer Guaranty Seal goes beyond all others in that it actually guarantees its advertisers' products, promising replacement or money back if product or performance is defective.

Products advertised in the magazine are tested in laboratories operated by the magazine and staffed by engineers, home economists, beauty and textile experts, chemists and technicians. When the product has been tested satisfactorily, the advertiser signs an agreement covering his use of the *Good Housekeeping* seal in ads in *Good Housekeeping* and elsewhere.

■ Another seal in which the magazine stakes its good name is the *Parents' Magazine* Guaranteed Seal, in which the magazine guarantees its advertisers' products and backs the seal with a testing program that rejects advertising of products that do not meet their advertised claims. Products are tested in the laboratories of the Nationwide Testing Co., Hoboken, N.J. The magazine also consults on products with physicians, engineers, architects, etc., makes use tests in the homes of consumers and sometimes inspects manufacturing plants to assure sanitary requirements.

The direct mail advertising industry, struggling to rebut the disparaging term "junk mail," operates a vigorous standards of practices and consumer satisfaction program through the Direct Mail/Marketing Assn. (DMMA), which speaks for about 1,600 of the biggest mail order sellers.

Every DMMA member is required to adhere to an "Ethical Business Standards Guideline" requiring, among other things, prompt acknowledgment and filling of orders, and immediate action on "satisfaction guaranteed or money-back" offers. The DMMA rules also cover such points as photos which faithfully picture the item being offered, and a ban on fictitious testimonials and prices. DMMA requires that on receipt of a request from a customer, an association member remove that customer's name from its mailing list.

■ Until recently, DMMA enforcement consisted of possible expulsion from the association on the recommendation of its standards of practices committee. More recently, DMMA has announced it will begin referring non-compliance situations to appropriate law enforcement agencies. The association has also announced it plans to take a more active role in supporting legislation dealing with such problems as deceptive fund raising by mail.

The DMMA effort goes beyond a code of behavior to include a redress procedure for consumers who feel they have been cheated. Through Mail Order Action Line, which operates from the association's New York headquarters, customers who deal with DMMA members are guaranteed satisfaction. The association contends such disputes between its members and the public generally arise unintentionally. It advises the consumer to contact the DMMA member company first. If after a reasonable time the problem remains unresolved, Mail Order Action Line promises to intervene on the consumer's behalf. The DMMA says it guarantees satisfaction if one of its members are involved, but it can often help with non-members, too.

All this direct self-regulation reflects a deep concern which has surfaced as business men became increasingly aware of the social consequences of the merchandising and marketing process.

Over the years, perhaps no other industry has had a trade press which has been more articulate and aggressive than the advertising press, which criticizes the industry as occasion warrants and campaigns for the betterment of advertising. The advertising press has articulated and harangued against advertising's faults with a "muscular candor" which sometimes made industry people wonder which side it is on.

■ ADVERTISING AGE and *Printers' Ink* (no longer published), the two national weeklies covering the general advertising field, have long records of aggressive effort to improve the quality of advertising and eliminate abuses. *Printers' Ink,* founded in 1888, developed and promoted a model "truth in advertising" law in 1911, which became the forerunner of most modern legislation outlawing un-truthful, deceptive or misleading advertising. ADVERTISING AGE, founded in 1930, became the industry leader in circulation and advertising volume, perhaps because it became known for news and for feature pages bristling with controversy and criticism.

Innovative Procedures

ADVERTISING AGE was among the first national publications to record the rise of the modern consumer movement, and to report its goals and achievements here and abroad. It crusaded for the creation of the NARB and publicized NARB activities at a time when the organization preferred secrecy. Its news and editorial features alerted the ad industry to the implications of contemporary social developments, including the equal employment opportunity program, women's lib, environmental problems and the energy crisis.

But self-criticism has become common not only in the trade press, but throughout the many organizations which have been created in advertising and other businesses, as companies and industries experiment with innovative procedures designed to anticipate consumer problems and correct them when they occur.

Much of the new thinking was collated in a series of nine reports by the National Business Council on Consumer Affairs, a group which consisted of over 100 leaders in business who were appointed by President Nixon to develop policy positions which would help the business community avert the kinds of situations which lead to demands for more government intervention in the merchandising and marketing system.

■ The council's reports deal with such subjects as "Responsive Approaches to Consumer Complaints and Remedies," "Product Warranties: Guidelines to Meet Consumer Needs," "Corporate Policies and Procedures on Advertising & Promotion," "Guiding Principles for Responsible Packaging and Labeling" and "Responsive Approaches to Consumer Complaints and Remedies."

The council worked under the supervision of an assistant Secretary of Commerce, and utilized the resources of the Commerce Department. Its reports carried the endorsement of leaders from all fields of business, and thousands of copies were distributed under the signature of the Secretary of Commerce to top level business decision makers.

■ One of its reports, for example, covers "Guidelines on Advertising Substantiation." It lists 13 precautions the advertiser should observe, and urges every company to have written instructions on product claim performance verification which will be fully understood by brand managers, advertising agencies and others involved in preparing and placing ads.

Safety, the use of ads to distort public issues, and the use of unfair appeals to children are among the most common issues raised about advertising, and they are all mentioned in the council's guidelines on ad substantiation. Ads should not suggest, depict or extol product uses or applications which present unreasonable safety risks to the consumer. Extra care should be taken in formulating and documenting claims related to controversial issues such as the environment. Special consideration must be given to eliminate confusion when communicating claims to special audiences, such as children, and every effort must be made to insure that the expectations of these consumers are not unintentionally raised above the product's ability to perform.

Others among the 13 points in the council's guidelines on substantiation include: Ad claims should be worded to communicate clearly and accurately the realis-tic scope of the claim; test information should be reasonably related to conditions of normal consumer use; performance demonstrations should be closely related to claimed consumer benefit; price claims which are exaggerated or incapable of reasonable verification should be avoided.

■ The council's work is consistent with the kinds of change that have been introduced by individual managements and industries on a large scale in recent years. The "consumer ombudsman" has become a new function in many companies, and industry-wide consumer redress programs have spread through many consumer product classifications.

The consumer "ombudsman" functions as a consumer voice within the company, positioned to have access to the ranking executive. The "ombudsman's" role is to reconcile consumer suggestions with company needs, and to help determine when complaints and suggestions require changes.

An early—and typical—"ombudsman" program operates at Giant Foods, a Washington-based chain of nearly 100 supermarkets, which employed Esther Peterson, who had been White House consumer advisor in the Kennedy and Johnson years. Working inside the company, she encouraged Giant to pioneer such projects as nutritional labeling of its private brand foods, unit pricing, open dating, ingredient labeling of drugs and beauty aids, and the introduction of environmentally-safe products.

■ The "ombudsman" process flourishes in various forms in most major food chains, and in manufacturing industries ranging from autos and soft drinks to appliances. In fact, the "ombudsmen" have become so numerous and omnipresent, that the CBBB assembled nearly 100 of them at a meeting in early 1973, where they moved to form their own professional organization.

The industry-wide redress system achieved widespread attention as a result of the efforts of the members of the home appliance industry, who created MPAC, an industry-sponsored conciliation group which received complaints from consumers who were unable to get satisfaction elsewhere. Through its contacts with individual companies, MPAC —which is operated by prominent laymen not beholden to the industry—effectively arranges redress in those situations where it finds the consumer has a valid case. Variations of MPAC have been attempted in other areas— auto repairs, carpets, furniture, optical goods, and so on.

Reprinted from "Advertising Age," Nov. 21, 1973, pp. 138, 141-142

Advertising: stepchild

of the first amendment

BY SAM J. ERVIN, JR.
Former U.S. Senator

There is no greater bulwark for freedom in our land than that provision in the First Amendment which reads, "Congress shall make no law . . . abridging the freedom of speech, or of the press . . ." Since its adoption in 1791 as part of the Bill of Rights, it has come to distinguish this country from almost every other in the world as a nation whose people are free to express their ideas and opinions without fear of government retaliation. It is the very heart of our system of government which depends upon an informed public and robust political debate. The First Amendment's protection of freedom of speech and freedom of press has given meaning to our traditional respect for the worth of the individual human being, and vitality to our belief in the possibility of mankind's continuing self-enlightenment.

In the final analysis, what the framers of the First Amendment did was to stake the very existence of America as a free society upon their faith that it has nothing to fear from the exercise of First Amendment freedoms, no matter how much they may be abused, as long as it leaves truth free to combat error.

■ In recent years, the First Amendment's guarantee of freedom of expression has come under considerable attack. All branches of government, at almost every level, have been tempted to interfere with the gathering, editing, publication, or distribution of information to the American public. Increased government subpoenaing of newsmen, the Justice Department's effort to enjoin publication of the so-called "Pentagon papers," and expanding government control and regulation of broadcasting are just a few of the reminders that government cannot be trusted to honor the commandments of the First Amendment.

One area of freedom of expression in which the government has become increasingly involved is with respect to commercial advertising. Two separate developments in the interpretation of the First Amendment have opened the doors for the considerable and increasing government regulation of advertising.

In the first instance, the courts have promulgated a theory of the First Amendment which distinguishes between "commercial speech" and other forms of speech, giving greater constitutional protection to the latter than the former.

The second important development which has led to increasing government regulation of "commercial speech" is the application of the First Amendment to broadcasting in a different manner than to the printed press. Government regulation of broadcasting, especially commercial advertising on the air, has been established by Congress, implemented by the Federal Communications Commission, and sustained by the courts in a manner which would be rejected out of hand as unconstitutional if applied to the printed press.

Rule 'Commercial Speech' Less Vital

In general, the courts have adopted and applied a First Amendment theory distinguishing between "commercial" speech and other speech on the basis of an asserted difference in the social purpose and value of these types of speech. They have determined that "commercial speech" is designed simply to entice consumers to purchase services or products, and that it does not serve the same high social purpose as does speech which advocates a certain political or religious position, presents general information, or involves the dissemination of culturally valuable matter.

In the case of *Valentine v. Christensen*, 316 U.S. 52 (1941), the Supreme Court first set forth explicitly this theory of discriminating against "commercial speech" in applying the First Amendment. This case involved a constitutional challenge to a New York City ordinance prohibiting the distribution of "commercial and business advertising matter" in public places. In dismissing the constitutional objections to the ordinance, the court said,

"This court has unequivocally held that the streets are proper places for the exercise of the freedom of communicating information and disseminating opinion, and that though the states and municipalities may appropriately regulate the privilege in the public interest, they may not unduly burden or proscribe its employment in these public thoroughfares. We are equally clear that the Constitution imposes no such restraint on government as respects purely commercial advertising."

■ The Supreme Court did not then, nor has it since, given us the benefit of the wisdom which underlies such a distinction. It simply asserted that "purely commercial advertising" was an inferior form of expression, a black sheep not embraced by the protective care of the First Amendment. Unfortunately, since this decision, state and federal courts alike have echoed almost in unison the same chorus, again without much explanation. Despite their uniform refrain that "commercial speech" is not entitled to First Amendment protection, they have not put to rest those few souls who still ask why.

Ads Are Step to Informed Consumer

The First Amendment was quite clearly adopted to protect the free communication and exchange of ideas. Nowhere in the Constitution is there any explicit limitation of the First Amendment's protection to a particular type of expression.

Private economic decisions made in a free enterprise economy by millions of individual consumers depend upon a wide dissemination of information to the consuming public about the various economic and financial choices available. Our society has an interest in encouraging its consumers to be knowledgeable consumers.

■ We all know that advertising has been an important source of new ideas about various possibilities of life styles available in our great country. Especially through the medium of television, advertising has brought to millions of Americans new ideas, not only about which soap to buy, but where to live, for which goals in life to aspire, what jobs to seek, and what to do with their increasing amounts of leisure time. Quite literally, advertising in America has been one of the most significant of all factors in altering our living habits, our social attitudes and our personal expectations. To dismiss advertising as we know it today in America as nothing more than an offer to sell or an offer to buy is not only to ignore its total impact, but it is to forget about our traditional belief in the importance of the communication of ideas—all kinds of ideas—to the advancement of civilization.

One perceptive critic of the courts' discriminatory application of the First Amendment to advertising has written, "Advertising is a medium of information and persuasion, providing much of the day-to-day 'education' of the American public, and facilitating the flexible allocation of resources necessary to a free enterprise economy. Neither profit motivation nor desire to influence private economic decisions necessarily distinguishes the peddler from the preacher, the publisher, or the politician."

Economic Interests Inferior?

Man is not only a political being. He is not only a spiritual being. Man has infinite dimensions to his being. His economic well-being, especially in an affluent country such as ours, constitutes a vital part of his life.

Our free enterprise system rests in part on the notion that a man should be just as free in making decisions affecting his economic well-being as he is free to assert his political judgment and his religious convictions. The better educated Americans become with respect to the innumerable possibilities available to them as workers and consumers, the richer our individual and corporate lives will become.

There are legitimate reasons in particular circumstances for treating advertising differently than other forms of expression. In my opinion, rather than accepting the difficult task of delineating these reasons and clarifying these circumstances, the courts have casually accepted the notion that man's interest in his economic well-being is constitutionally inferior to his other interests. This approach is not only judicially unsound, but destructive of First Amendment freedoms.

Another and especially serious threat to freedom in advertising is in the area of broadcasting.

Complexities of Broadcast Freedom

When they drafted and ratified the First Amendment, the founding fathers decreed that the freedoms it secures should extend into the future and apply to all activities falling within their scope, even though such activities were never envisaged by them. As a consequence, the First Amendment freedoms embodied in the phrase "freedom of speech or of the press" confer upon those who broadcast information or ideas by radio or television the constitutional right to do so, subject, however, to certain limitations which are not applicable to the press.

Those who wish to operate as radio or television broadcasters are required to apply for licenses to the FCC, which allocates available broadcast frequencies and compels each broadcaster to broadcast on the frequency alloted to it. These requirements are adjudged valid under the First Amendment simply because, in the present state of the science, scarcity of broadcast frequencies and unrestricted broadcasting would prevent intelligible communication of information or ideas on the airways.

Radio and television broadcasters are subjected by law to the fairness doctrine as authorized by Congress and expounded by the Supreme Court in *Red Lion Broadcasting Co. v. The Federal Communications Commission*, 395 U.S. 367, and other decisions. The avowed purpose of the fairness doctrine is to further the people's right to know the truth by requiring that discussion of public issues be presented on broadcast stations, and that all sides of the issues be given fair coverage.

Marginal Speech

To this end, the fairness doctrine obligates a radio or television station to give reply time to answer personal attacks and political editorials broadcast by it, and to extend time to a political candidate if it grants time to his opponent. The station must permit the use of its facilities for these purposes without compensation.

In 1968, the Court of Appeals for the District of Columbia sustained the Federal Communications Commission's decision to apply the fairness doctrine to cigaret advertising.

In its infamous opinion, the Court of Appeals relied in part on the theory enunciated in the Valentine case. It noted, "Promoting the sale of a product is not ordinarily associated with any of the interest which the First Amendment seeks to protect. As a rule, it does not affect the political process, it does not contribute to the exchange of ideas, does not provide information on matters of public importance, and is not, except perhaps for the admen, a form of individual self expression." The Court of Appeals ultimately dismissed cigaret advertising as "marginal speech."

Fairness Doctrine—for Everyone?

The court then dismissed the contention of the networks that the First Amendment protects broadcasters from government control of content just as it does the printed press. Merely suggesting that broadcasting was "different in kind" from the printed page, the court quickly brushed aside the networks' constitutional objections. It upheld the FCC's application of the fairness doctrine to cigaret advertising which required that any radio or television station which advertised cigarets must make available a substantial amount of time for "counter advertising."

■ Since this 1968 decision, an almost laughable turn of events has occurred. In order to apply the "fairness doctrine," there had to be a determination that the relationship of smoking to health constituted a "controversial issue of public importance" requiring that a licensee present with reasonable fairness both sides of the issue. That determination was made by the FCC and affirmed by the Court of Appeals. Subsequently and unfortunately, the Congress enacted a ban on all cigaret advertising on radio and television. This is another and particularly outrageous example of the "stepchild" treatment given to broadcasting with respect to First Amendment principles.

Some time after all cigaret advertising was removed from radio and television and while anti-smoking advertisements were still being put on the air, the tobacco industry requested the FCC to apply the "fairness doctrine" in such a way as to permit them to respond to these anti-smoking commercials. The tobacco companies did not seek to advertise any particular product or to encourage smoking generally. They simply asked that the FCC require licensees to give them an opportunity to respond to the claims that cigaret smoking is bad for one's health.

Is Final Truth in on Cigarets?

In an ironic and incredible decision, the FCC decided that the fairness doctrine could not apply in this case because, only three short years after the Banzhaf case, the relationship between smoking and health was no longer "a controversial issue of public importance." The FCC's holding was affirmed by the Court of Appeals for the Fourth Circuit and, upon appeal, affirmed in a *per curiam* decision by the Supreme Court. In effect, the FCC and the courts have determined that the final truth has been established with respect to the health hazards of cigaret smoking.

The impact of the government's intervention in the controversy over the relationship between cigaret smoking and health—first, in requiring counter advertising; secondly, in banning cigaret advertising from television and radio; and finally, in refusing to apply the fairness doctrine to the anti-smoking commercials—is worse than confusing. It represents in its total undertaking an effort by government to deny the public the fullest possible discussion of the particular issue involved. It results in anything but fairness. It undermines First Amendment principles.

Subsequent to the application of the fairness doctrine to cigaret advertising, many individuals and groups have petitioned the FCC to apply the doctrine to other advertising. A reading of several FCC decisions on this subject indicated that the commission is having a very difficult time explaining why counter advertising should not be required of broadcast licensees with respect to many other products than cigarets. Perhaps, ironically enough, in trying to apply the fairness doctrine, the commission will discover that there is a public and social value in commercial advertising, and sometimes even a "political question" attached to certain advertising. If so, the courts as well as the FCC will have to reexamine their assumption that "commercial speech" is devoid of content which the First Amendment was written to protect.

Reprinted from "Advertising Age," July 17, 1972, pp. 43-44

Markets are customer problems, not geography or demographics

BY TOM DILLON
President, Batten, Barton, Durstine
& Osborn, New York

Fortunately, there are a large number of areas in which man's desire to decorate his life and his desire to make functional tools do not come in severe conflict.

One does not usually complain about fine arts, novels, plays and music on the grounds that they do not work. On the other hand, one does not usually criticize crowbars, bulldozers and railroad ties because they lack meaningful emotional impact.

The problem only becomes severe when we have to create something that satisfies both of these needs. For creativity becomes very tricky, indeed, in those circumstances where it must effect a trade-off between emotion and function.

The creation of advertising falls right spang in the middle of this dilemma.

It is not alone. Architecture, industrial design, city planning and, indeed, many other activities produce the same kind of head-on collision. For example, some 65 years ago, we created in the middle of New York a full-size replica of a famous third-century Roman building whose architectural excellence has been universally acclaimed.

Railroad Station or Roman Baths?

The creative concept here was that it would make a fine railroad station. Thus we have the old Pennsylvania Station built on the Roman structure of the Baths of Caracalla. Now, meritorious as this Roman structure was, the original function was providing public bathing facilities for third-century Romans. It did not turn out to be the same function as getting tens of thousands of people on and off trains and subways. A few years ago, amid great outcries, the building was demolished and replaced by an edifice of no particular architectural significance.

The lesson here is more fundamental than that we should not select the Parthenon as our design in building the next New York international airport. I have nothing against the Parthenon personally, but I don't like getting wet on my way to the plane.

I feel that if the citizens of New York wanted to duplicate the Baths of Caracalla, it was certainly their privilege to do so. They then should have gone and built a railroad station. They would have ended up with a good piece of architecture and a good railroad station, but not at the same place.

Now to come just a little bit closer to home, let us consider the creative problems of a modern industrial designer. I had it put to me nicely a couple of weeks ago by a man whose job it is to style the outward appearance of automobiles. Being in a sympathetic mood, I suggested to him that it must be quite a problem to come up with new creative ideas in the field of automobile styling.

He said that, on the contrary, it was very easy to design beautiful automobiles of new, novel and striking appearance. There was, he said, only one problem—that was that the engine, the wheels and the room for the passengers made unsightly bumps on the design.

Hammer Must Relate to Shape of Nail

Now, of course, this is nothing more than the familiar dictum that in man's tool-making capacity, function dictates form. If you believe as I do that advertising is a tool which has a function to perform, then the creation of advertising should be consistent with the constraints of its function.

But here is where the industrial designers have it over us. Physical constraints in designing and building a car or a refrigerator are quite obvious. One is not going to spend much time designing a car with square or octagonal wheels or a refrigerator that won't keep things cold. But in the case of advertising, our functional restraints are not all that clear. We can readily realize the functional restraints of time and space in the physical production of advertising. But perhaps it is impossible to totally comprehend the functional constraints brought about by the human mind to which the advertising is directed. We are a little bit in the position of creating a screw driver, having only a fuzzy notion of what a screw looks like, or inventing a hammer without having any clear idea of the shape of a nail.

Alas, we cannot go to the museum and see a working model of a human brain. Yet, we are being paid to create a tool which will influence its function.

Now, at this point, we can take one of several roads. We can throw our aprons over our heads and deny the problem. We can, in fact, treat the creation of advertising as a form of personal expression, like finger painting. Advertising created in this concept almost invariably pleases the creator and not infrequently pleases the person who pays for the advertising.

This is where advertising has it over designing cars. If you manufacture a car with square wheels, the man who pays for it will certainly notice it in the first few miles. If you design advertising with square wheels, it may take a long time before it is noticeable. One can even be rich and retired before he is detected.

A second avenue is a lengthy collection of all-purpose creative principles. One does not have to be in this business very long to discover that there is a long list of mythological and pseudo-scientific truisms about the creation of advertising. Indeed, some of them are probably valid, especially in specific circumstances. But it is very easy, by picking and choosing among this welter of witchcraft and folklore, to construct an advertisement that does not fulfill its function.

Advertising—One-Way Communication

Which gets us back to the premise that advertising does have a function other than providing a living for those of us in it. At the risk of seeming pretentious, I would like to define what I think are the characteristics of this function:

First, I do believe that advertising is a purposeful form of communication. That purpose is usually to effect human decision. When it does not effect a human decision, it has failed in its function.

Advertising also is a form of communication with certain peculiar constraints. Ordinarily, an ad is communication with a single source to many receivers. Any single advertisement is also invariant in its content. It is rarely possible for it to be tailored to each and every receiver. Unlike person-to-person communication, it also has the defect that it is largely incapable of instantly reacting to the receiver's behavior. It operates as a one-way communication system, and what little feedback it gets cannot affect its content.

Ad Has to Be Remembered

Another constraint on advertising is that it most frequently, although not always, depends on retention in human memory. This means that its content is severely attenuated before the information is actually used in the receiver's decision process.

I say "most frequently" because there are outstanding cases where this is not true. Mail order catalogs, for example, do not rely to any appreciable extent upon the receiver's memory. Indeed, the entire pattern of direct response advertising is predicated on the assumption that memory is not a restraint. But virtually all advertising has the functional restraint that the receivers are not homogeneous. Unlike one-to-one communication, the one-to-many communication concept makes it a virtual mathematical certainty that there will be an enormous diversity among those who physically receive the advertising message.

To begin with, it is almost inevitable that a substantial number of individuals who physically receive an advertising message are not in a situation in which they are likely to make the decision which it purports to influence. No matter how finely tuned the media selection is, any mass communication is likely to be exposed to large numbers of individuals who are not making decisions in the area covered by the communication.

To make it more complicated, a good many of the individuals who may technically be involved in a decision process are economically insignificant. The volume or frequency of their decisions do not warrant the cost of trying to influence them.

This leads us to the position that the content of an advertising communication should be tailored closely to affect the minds of those who are an economically significant factor in the specific decision process involved.

From Demo to Psycho

You are all, of course, familiar with the notion of the prime prospect. In almost any universe there is a relatively small percentage of individuals who make a very high percentage of economically significant decisions in the category of goods or services or other consideration. In the past 20 years, there have been enormous efforts in the field of media selection to develop methods of defining these prime prospects. We have progressed from purely demographic considerations to attempts at psychographic identification, life style characteristics and other scientific or pseudo-scientific identifiers.

That these have virtues for purposes of media selection, I will not dispute. But as an aid to the communications content of advertising, they are woefully poor tools. It is not much help in creating the communications content of advertising to know that you are talking to an 18 to 49-year-old housewife living in A & B Counties with income in excess of $12,-000 a year. Granted, it is better to know this than to know nothing. Nor is it a great deal more helpful to have available a complex recitation of the probable psychological profile or life style of the prime prospect. The principal reason for this is that you are inevitably dealing with aggregates and averages. But our job is not communicating a message to an average person—we are communicating to an individual.

It's Not Life Styles, It's Problems

The primary link between you and individuals is not their demographics, their life style, or their psychographic profile. It is the problem that they have.

I do not think it likely in view of the multi-faceted character of every human being that a communication such as advertising is going to accommodate itself to the totality of their environment and personality. We cannot accommodate the entire human personality because we will be swamped by information which at present we have no idea how to handle.

So, for the sake of my argument, let us assume we create a kind of two-dimensional human being with the full knowledge that that is not a representation of totality. As I have said earlier, we cannot model the behavior of the human mind, but it may be possible to model some aspect of it.

The aspect that I propose to model is that the human being can be looked upon as a problem-solving organism. In simple terms, from the moment that we wake up in the morning, we begin a problem-solving routine. We brush our teeth to solve dental and social problems, shave to solve physical and social problems, shower to solve physical and social

problems. We make decisions about dressing to solve physical and social problems.

Indeed, throughout the day, from tying our shoes to signing checks and making telephone calls, we behave like a problem-solving mechanism. To be sure, we don't always do it too well. Sometimes we greatly reduce the amount of problem solving by the pattern known as habit. In effect, we are refusing to examine the problem anew every time and opting to repeat a previous solution.

What He Drinks Is Decoration, Too

I use the word "problem" here in more than its ordinary sense. We have, of course, physical problems which involve decisions about eating, sleeping, etc. Perhaps more importantly we have social problems. I have pointed out that man is a self-decorating animal. Solving the problem of decorating himself and his environment seems to be a deeply imbedded human instinct. In the concept of self decoration, I include not only his clothes, his jewelry, furnishings and the appearance of his home, but also the beverages he drinks, the cigarets he may smoke, the car that he may drive and the restaurant that he may frequent. For man's need to project his personality through decoration applies to a great number of things which are commonly regarded as purely utilitarian.

Now if we take this simplified model of man, in the full awareness that it is not a model of his entirety, it is a useful idea in the creation of advertising. It is useful because it gives us some idea of what we are to communicate.

It enables us to look at the idea of a market in a new sense. The word "market" is in many ways an unfortunate one for advertising. It is also a humpty dumpty word with a great many implications. It has geographical meaning and product meaning.

But if we take our simplified model of man, then a market for a product or service or an idea exists in all those individuals who have a common problem. If you accept the notion that a market is really an aggregation of problems which certain people have in common, then the function of advertising in respect to a market is very clear.

It becomes evident, then, that the function of advertising in any specific case is the communication of a solution to the problem.

West, Beer, Housewives—or Problems

I do not expect that this is a notion which will find instant acceptance. We have for a long time thought that there are such things as a West Coast market, a market for beer, a market for soap or a market of housewives. I am proposing to you that all of these notions are backward, that every market is not a market for products, but that a market is a group of individuals who share common problems. If there are enough people who share a problem that is frequent enough, big enough, and for which they are not aware of any solution, the communication of a solution by advertising can be extremely effective in modifying their decision process.

If this is true, then the most important ingredient in advertising communication is that it must answer the question of how the product or service answers the prime prospect's problem.

For if an advertisement does not communicate how the product or service answers the prime prospect's problem, it is like our automobile with the square wheels —it may be beautiful, entrancing, memorable and a triumph of creative skills. But it will not function! #

Reprinted from "Advertising Age," Sept. 2, 1974, pp. 29-30

The agency business in 1980

By PAUL C. HARPER JR.
Needham, Harper & Steers
New York

In 1980, advertising agencies will be doing the same thing they are doing in 1972. They will be trying to influence human behavior in ways favorable to the interests of their clients.

But there the resemblance will stop. Their services, methods, structure and economics will be different. They may not even be called advertising agencies—because that name may no longer fit.

Any service business is a reflection of the aggregate market for its services. By 1980, the market for agency services will have changed as follows:

By 1980, few parity products—products that offer no clearly defined advantage—will be advertised extensively.

It is in the parity product area in particular that private brands will take over. As distribution becomes more concentrated, and distributors more powerful, the squeeze on advertised me-too products will become unbearable. As shelf space, floor space and showroom space become more and more costly, more and more parity brands will be thrown out. The distributors' incentive to earn a double profit will become overpowering.

Consumers are accepting fungibility. For years they have suspected that all gasolines were alike. Now they are beginning to believe this about many other frequently purchased categories.

Parity Products Bow to Private Label

Furthermore, when they perceive that products are the same, they increasingly tire of being told that they are different. Advertising money spent this way will become less and less productive.

In addition, there are many in the government who think that the advertising of parity products is deceitful and wasteful. They may have their way.

By 1980, for the above reasons, many companies that are now heavy advertisers of parity products will cease to advertise them at all. They will manufacture parity products for private label.

And they will not advertise or market a brand of their own—unless it has a meaningful exclusive that can be clearly communicated in advertising.

Thus, large sectors of the current advertising arena will dry up, leaving the field to those advertisers who have something to say.

This will mean that in many product categories the *primary function* of the advertising agency will be strategic planning and conceptual input in the new product area. Because of the central importance of this function, it will require behavioral and business knowledge of a much higher order than is generally present now among agency "strategists."

In the advertising for service businesses, the same forces will work, but to a lesser degree. Advertising of parity services will decrease. The fungible airline hostesses and gas station attendants with their plastic smiles will disappear from advertising. But the major service industries—airlines, automotive service, fast food, insurance, small loans, banking, business machines, car rentals, hotels and travel and others are the most rapidly evolving sectors of the economy—and the new dimensions of service which they will bring forth will require heavy promotion.

Service Industry Ads Shift Emphasis

However, funds currently used to advertise mere parity service will be diverted to at least three other kinds of activity:

1. On-premise communications. More use will be made of the captive nature of the customer to both entertain and indoctrinate him as he waits, shops, eats, flies, etc. On-premise promotion will extend into a full range of video, audio, as well as print, media.

2. Behavioral training. In an increasingly crowded world, the service industries will spend more communications dollars to train their employes to be polite,

clear, prompt, accurate, etc. A dollar spent producing a smile on a real attendant's face will be worth far more in repeat business than an advertised smile that doesn't materialize at point of sale. This will require whole new dimensions in employe recruitment, training and continuing indoctrination.

3. In a society which finally recognizes that commercial success and the social good must be reconciled, there will be more communications which address these common interests. (Auto insurance—safe driving; life insurance—good health; oil industry—pollution reduction; fast food—good nutrition.)

Whether or not there is a net *reduction* in service industry advertising, the strategic emphasis will change, and the use of media will become more segmented and specialized. This will require more strategic guidance from the agency, and it will require the extension of agency service into all forms of communication. Because of this, the highest degree of sophistication will be required of those delivering service to accounts.

Three Kinds of Market in 1980

By 1980, the "national advertising market" as we know it, where most products and services are advertisable on a national basis, will not exist.

Instead, there will be three kinds of market:

A. The *"fungibles"* market, composed of product and service categories which are fundamentally satisfactory, and not susceptible to, or needful of, further refinement. This market will be:

• National and homogeneous.

• Dominated by store brands or captive services.

• Heavily price promoted.

• Virtually unadvertised on a national basis.

B. The *"improvables"* market. This market will be composed of products and services which cater to broad, but not

51

universal, markets, and where continued technological refinement is feasible or where fashion and style are important sales factors. This market also includes major new product and service forms, replacements for existing forms.

- Demographically and regionally segmented.

- Dominated by manufacturers' brands and independent services—or by the brands of the stronger national distributors.

- Heavily advertised in local and regional as well as national media—with presentations varied to meet different demographic tastes and needs.

C. The *"enclave"* market. This market can only be described as a three-dimensional grid—with the axes representing income, geography and life style, and representing, therefore, a wide degree of variation. This will be a diverse, volatile series of smaller markets where the premium is on individuality. Novelty will be a virtue with some, permanence with others, high style with some, homespun style with others. In current terms, it will be composed of a range of tastes and needs represented by *Vogue* on the one hand and the *Whole Earth Catalog* on the other.

Many of these "enclaves" will be viable markets for extensive advertising because of better education, the growing diversity in our society, and the increasing need to express individual identity.

This market will be characterized by:

- Products and services designed to serve specialized tastes.

- Boutique merchandising (within major distributive centers) and mail order merchandising.

- Highly focused advertising in terms of presentation and media. Media usage will take advantage of the new, highly focused forms, such as video cassettes, paperbacks, cable tv. Advertising language will reflect the mode of the submarket being addressed.

Again, because of these new dimensions, the agency of 1980 will be called on for strategic guidance in a complex marketplace, where the "broad strokes" of the past are no longer economical—and where highly focused communications with their efficiencies (and their risks) are required.

By 1980, the western world, as well as large parts of Asia, will be homogeneous as far as marketing techniques, product technology and demographic structure.

This means that not only will these markets be economically interdependent, but they will be technologically and culturally interdependent.

In 1980, the world market for product ideas, merchandising and advertising ideas will indeed be one.

The result of this is that, to survive, the advertising agency of 1980 must be international in its outlook, its input and its physical and human resources.

The Government as an Advertiser

By 1980, the government will be a major advertiser. As public corporations like the Postal Service and Amtrak prove themselves, others will be spun off. Wherever the government offers a discrete service of economic value to a definable customer group, it should be spun off and charged for. Some will, despite political pressure to the contrary. These services will be advertised.

The new volunteer armed services will require heavy advertising support, and so will recruiting for certain civilian activities.

Eventually, many of the causes now supported by the Advertising Council will become government funded, when the social cost of certain forms of behavior gets too high.

To compete effectively for government business agencies will have to have:

1. A highly developed sense of the difference between the commercial and bureaucratic worlds.

2. Ability to distinguish between the cruder forms of buying behavior and the more complex forms of social behavior which government will be trying to influence.

The Government as a Regulator

It is not necessary here to review the growing efforts of government to regulate advertising and marketing. Its net effect by 1980 will be:

1. To restrict competitive claims, which will reduce advertising effectiveness, which, in turn, will reduce dollars spent in many categories.

2. To eliminate advertising in some categories and impose ceilings on others.

3. To limit advertising as a per cent of content of certain media.

4. By applying increasingly higher clinical and technical standards, to greatly increase the cost and risks of introducing new products in certain fields.

In this climate, it will be essential that the advertising agency be equipped not only to avoid legal pitfalls, but to help develop corporate strategies that work, while still observing legal and regulatory guidelines.

In 1980, therefore, the advertising agency, if that is what it is still called, will be operating in a world where:

- Many major current categories of advertising will have dried up, due to (a) inroads of private brands, (b) government action, and (c) public skepticism and indifference.

- New major advertised categories will be generated only as real product or service innovations occur. The entire corporate strategy of today's "brand" manufacturers will revolve around meaningful innovation.

- Much service industry advertising will be diverted to on-premise promotion or employe training and indoctrination.

- Much advertising for certain service industries and for the government will address social issues involving complex facets of human behavior.

- The consumer market as a whole will become more complex and segmented.

- Dramatic evolution of audio-visual media as well as print media will allow highly focused attack on market segments that would today be inaccessible.

- The more highly developed world markets will be truly homogeneous.

In this environment, what kind of an advertising agency will be able to grow and prosper?

Any service business is a reflection of its aggregate market. As the market changes, so must the service business.

Today in 1973, it is already within the capability of many advertisers to perform many of the conventional agency services for themselves. The others they can buy outside piecemeal.

Self-sufficiency is already an option for any advertiser with a medium or large communications budget. By 1980, this option will have been exercised by a large number of today's major advertisers.

Agencies who do not prepare for this day will find themselves scratching for project assignments in the creative and media areas. They will become journeymen and little more. To escape this fate, our industry must redefine its product and structure.

The Customer and His Future Needs

Any agency function that can be performed by others *as well as* the agency is now doing it must be raised to a new level of excellence or scrapped. The *central* function, or product, of the agency (a) must address the basic needs of the marketer of 1980, and (b) must be something he cannot get from any other form of business organization.

Our customers in 1980 will include any type of organization that serves the social good (broadly defined). This will include manufacturers, distributors, service companies, government, other institutions, citizens groups, etc. Each of them will be competing for favorable attention and action in a diverse, complex, noisy and confused arena.

Yet client management then, as now, will continue to have two related problems that can potentially stifle success.

1. Any management must spend much of its time worrying about what goes on in the factory (the hangar, the kitchens, the garage). It must spend part of its time worrying about finance, material resources and logistics. The greater this internal focus becomes, the more apt the management is to make external mistakes.

2. Marketing departments were created to avoid the above problem. But marketing departments must focus on the problems at hand, and they, too, can develop tunnel vision.

They can be, and sometimes are, overwhelmed by the internal orientation of their own top management.

These are dangers now, and they will persist because they are founded in human nature. But in the market of the '80s, where corporate strategy must be fine-tuned to meet even more complex external realities, they will be no longer affordable.

Advertising agencies have always provided "the outside view" of the marketplace. Many times they have served to refocus basic client thinking—and have thus served as ad hoc management consultants. But this function has only been performed intermittently, usually as the result of some particularly close individual relationship—or the presence of some extraordinary creative talent. By and large (and more and more), agencies have performed routinized communications functions, and the bigger the agencies get, the more internally focused their own managements have become.

How Agencies Can Survive in '80s

To survive in the '80s, the advertising agency must rediscover its real exclusive over time; this real exclusive has become encrusted with administrative and structural barnacles. For future survival it must be scraped clean and remarketed.

The agency's exclusive service is precisely the service its customers will need to survive *themselves* in the '80s. This exclusive is strategic communications counsel on the highest level based on the broadest possible experience. Advertising agencies today possess an unparalleled aggregate of knowledge of what works and what doesn't work in the influencing of human behavior—across the entire spectrum of human activity—and in every medium.

Agencies are the *only* kind of business organization that:
• Works with clients in every sector of the social and economic structure.
• On a continuing basis.
• In ever medium of communications.
• Within a pragmatic framework, where work must show results.

The application of this unique insight in the development of product and communications strategy is our exclusive product. Specifically, the surviving agencies of 1980 will be offering:

1. Continuing predictive counsel on all aspects of the client's marketing arena. (Who is likely to do what, when, for what reasons, and with what impact.) This includes a prediction and analysis of government actions and attitudes. Since the world market is the arena, the counsel will be based on worldwide intelligence and input.

2. Basic product strategy. Continuing counsel in depth on what products and services to offer and to whom.

3. Continuing strategic counsel on every aspect of communications, external, internal and on-premise—including fundamental corporate positioning.

4. Implementation of any aspect of the above counsel (exclusive of manufacturing, finance, direct sales and logistics). (Implementation may even include location of supplementary or even primary research/development facilities, and would certainly include working closely with such facilities.)

The New Agency Professionalism

The basic product of this new kind of "advertising agency" will *not* be filmed commercials, although we will conceive and produce them; not corporate logos, although we will design them; not sales brochures, although we will write and design them. Our basic product will be *strategic counsel* relating to what values a client offers the public, and how it communicates these values. This new kind of company will comprise an objective strategic adjunct to the management of client organizations. It will offer, on a continuing basis, the authoritative "outside view" that all managements need and will need increasingly in the future.

The agency of the '80s will operate in an environment where:

• Most of its present services can be purchased from other sources, or performed by the client himself.

• Clients will be operating in an "idea arena" where the currents of change are far more swift, subtle, and fragmented than they are today.

• Clients will *not* pay high prices for journeyman media, research, creative and production work.

• Clients *will* pay high prices for continuing high level strategic input.

For survival in the '80s, the advertising agency must offer a new dimension of professionalism. And to do so, it must restructure.

To offer this kind of service to a large, diversified client list requires, in operating terms, a *partnership structure*. The management structure of the agency will be expanded horizontally, like that of a law firm, so that all clients will be able to deal with a partner at regular intervals—a partner sufficiently involved to be able to give thoughtful input on a continuing basis.

Steep pyramidal structures will disappear. They do not permit the intensive high level coverage required. They foster the loss of good ideas, because these ideas tend to be handled at too junior a level or at too many levels. They also foster the "bag handler" syndrome, with its deadening build-up of administrative layers.

The management structure of the agency will be simple. It will consist of several more or less horizontally aligned partners. These men and women will be "creative generalists." They will have a thorough grounding in marketing, communications, and business procedures, but they will have an essentially creative turn of mind.

The partners will have working for them, directly, a few highly trained specialists in the analytical disciplines. They will also be assisted by a few junior partners who are creative generalists by nature, and who are in training for full partnership.

Apart from the necessary business management and housekeeping functions this is all that will be left of the "advertising agency" *per se*.

The services of this new "agency" will be paid for by fee. The commission system is clearly irrelevant to this structure and will have largely disappeared.

Who Will Get the Ads Out?

The Account Executive: The agency of the future will seek some of its partners from among its account executive staff. But only those who have proven themselves as well-rounded, insightful counselors will be selected. The partnership concept requires a complete redefinition of the "contact" function. The partner is not a "contact man," "an account executive," or a conduit for someone else's thinking. He or she must be capable of generating and implementing whole product strategies, communications strategies. The partner should have enough professional stature and acumen to sit on a client's board of directors.

Creative: In the agency of the '80s the creative department as we now know it will have ceased to exist. Creative people as we now know them will (according to their talents and tastes) have chosen one of three careers:

1. Some, with broad talents, will have become full partners in the new structure.

2. Others will move to boutiques or house agencies.

3. Others will join to form the creative subsidiary of the new advertising agency.

The agency of the '80s will have one or more subsidiaries whose sole function will be the translation of strategy into finished communications material. The creative subsidiary will be a separate profit center whose fees will flow from partnership clients—or from business that it obtains on its own. The agency of the '80s may structure its creative function into more than one subsidiary, in order to avoid problems of conflict—or in order to provide a higher degree of specialization—by media, or by type of communications problem.

In any case, the partner of the "advertising agency" will have an interesting and varied choice of creative resources. This is because the partner will not be required to use the creative subsidiaries of the corporation if he thinks he can get the job done better somewhere else. It may well be that for a specific job of corporate design or an advertising campaign directed toward a specialized market he will go to an outside creative resource. Or, if a partner feels that he can get better continuing work off-premise, he may do so. In any case, the corporation's creative subsidiaries must compete against the field in terms of creative excellence and efficient operation.

Research: Much desk research will be performed by the analysts on the partner's staff. But all field research will be planned and performed by the corporation's research subsidiary—if that subsidiary can compete effectively for the partner's business. Here again the partner will have a choice of all available research houses, and he will pick the one best suited for the job. The corporation's research subsidiary, likewise, will seek and serve business not handled by the partners.

Media: As the marketplace becomes more fragmented and complex, the media function must become more precise, responsive, and fast moving. As more and more advertisers do their media planning and buying outside of the agency framework, it will become harder and harder for the *conventional* media department to compete.

The media function, too, will be transformed to meet the new conditions. It will become subsidiarized, automated, and centralized. It will compete for the partner's business. It will also seek outside business on its own. Like research, its survival as a function within the corporation's structure will depend on its ability to use all the science and technology available to it, as well as on the judgment and insight of its managers.

Other specialized functions: The corporation will offer other services on a subsidiary basis as those services offer a profit opportunity. This will include sales promotion, design, public relations, government relations, food science, product development and testing, and others further afield.

The partnership and the corporation: Above, the terms "partnership" and "corporation" are used. It is the function of the *partnership* to deliver the unique product of the corporation—counsel in product strategy and communications strategy. It will do this with a minimal staff of its own as described. It will draw on and pay for the services of subsidiaries (or others) as it needs them. It will receive high cost-ratio fees for its counseling work. It will receive cost-plus fees with a nominal mark-up for the implementing services it delivers from the subsidiaries. The subsidiaries are then paid appropriately. The partnership manages client relationships.

The "corporation" is the fiscal and legal entity which ties the partnership and the various subsidiaries together in some kind of business harmony. It will have over-all profit responsibility and will decide on what new ventures should be undertaken and which should be discarded.

When all is said and done, the advertising agencies which survive and grow in the '80s will do so because they performed realistically two fundamental business exercises:

1. They have identified what *they do best better than anyone else* against a knowledge of client needs. They will then restructure so that this service is rendered as effectively and profitably as possible.

2. They will have submitted each of their present functions to the profit test. If the function cannot compete profitably against other sources of the same service, it will be dropped. If it can compete it will receive further investment and developments—along with new profit opportunities the agency may identify.

Reprinted from "Advertising Age," Nov. 19, 1973, pp. 35-36, 40

How to become a millionaire

in the agency business

BY L. T. (TED) STEELE
Former Chairman, Executive Committee
Benton & Bowles, New York

My subject is, "How to become a millionaire in the agency business before you are 70," and I am qualified on at least half of this subject—because I have not yet reached 70.

I propose to give the younger people in our international family ten tips on how to get ahead and make important money in the agency business.

Each of these ten tips is something with which I have had personal experience—at some point in my extended career. And each of them worked. Each helped me to receive more attention, more advancement and more reward from my superiors. Most of them represent rules of conduct which I was fortunate enough to recognize quite early in my business life, certainly before I was 30 years old:

1. Attach yourself to someone who can really help you.

The larger your agency and the lower your position in it, the more difficult it is (at least in the beginning) for you to come to the attention of top management. Yet you *must* find a way to make top management aware of you, to make them believe in you, to cause them to take an interest in your advancement.

A good way to do this is to select *one* key principal in the management and try to cultivate him. It must be someone whom you genuinely admire and respect, someone on whose business life you would like to pattern your own. It must be someone who is, at the outset, much wiser than you are—and willing to impart some of his wisdom to you.

Select someone from whom you can really *learn* how to succeed.

I believe that the best education comes from a close, one-to-one relationship between teacher and student—not from lectures, manuals of procedure, or reading old marketing plans. It comes from the voice of experience exchanging views, considering questions, analyzing problems directly with a sincerely interested

scholar.

Find yourself a man in management (or in these days of liberation—a woman!) who can really be of help to you. This does not mean "going around" or "over the head of" the section chief or supervisor to whom you report. You must somehow manage it without giving your immediate boss, the next fellow up the line, any reason to suspect that you are undercutting him. Because you've got to learn from him, too.

But if you are diplomatic, if you are discreet, if you really have a talent for this business of human relationships, you will find a way to get someone who is close to the top personally interested in your progress.

He will be your "agent" with the management. He will take on the responsibility for seeing that you get a raise or a promotion when you deserve one. He will remind the top people of your abilities and will defend you against unjust criticism.

You cannot afford to wait for good things to happen. In the beginning, you need a champion. Get yourself one!

2. Listen—and learn.

The most offensive mistake young people in our business make is an unwillingness to listen, an unwillingness to consider other people's ideas. This is especially obnoxious to clients. If a client has an idea about his advertising, or his marketing, or his product—listen to it, and listen carefully!

At Benton & Bowles, we have always prided ourselves on how deeply our partnerships go with our clients. We like to think that our account teams are virtually interchangeable with the product managers whom they serve.

And yet I am convinced that no matter how much we know about a client's business, the client *always* knows more about it than we do. I have long believed that an agency's greatest successes come from marketing efforts and advertising

campaigns which have, in a very real sense, been co-architected by the client's people working in collaboration with the agency team.

The remarkably successful J. Paul Getty commercial for E. F. Hutton & Co. —which received more press publicity around the world than any other tv commercial in history—is a perfect example of client-agency teamwork. The Hutton people's ideas and participation were indispensable in the creation of this advertising.

I could give you many other examples to illustrate my point that *it pays to listen.* Young people today in the agency business frequently arrive from the Harvard Business School (or some equally distinguished institution) with an M.B.A. degree, boundless self confidence and unlimited ambition. But they are no damned good to us until they have listened attentively to what we and our clients have to say—and until they have learned on the job.

3. Have faith in the boss.

You really must believe that the man directing the business is determined and able to build up the agency and to build up your fortunes along with it. If you cannot have confidence in the leadership of your company and you are at too low a level to change it, you should resign.

The worst thing that can happen to a chief executive is to lose (or never to gain) the confidence and the support of the people under his direction. And it is equally devastating, if you are a young man or woman, to work for someone for whom you have no respect.

But I urge all young agency men and women to give the benefit of any doubt to the boss. Do not decide too quickly that he doesn't know what he's doing. Do not conclude prematurely that he doesn't know what *you* are doing—and just how well you are doing it.

As I said earlier, when agencies grow in size it is not easy to keep track, from the top, of all the people underneath. But you might be astonished at how often the managing directors of your companies, the chief executives, discuss the performance of every assistant account executive, junior writer, apprentice art director and assistant media clerk on the staff.

A good rule to remember is: The boss may very well be better informed about *your* strategy than you are about *his.*

At times, you must be very patient with bosses. They make decisions which may be difficult for you to understand. They appoint and promote people you would not have appointed or promoted. They may not know the details of your specific assignments as well as you'd like them to.

But I have found that if you believe in them and serve them well (assuming the bosses are any good in the first place), they will, over time, take very good care of you.

So, "Have faith in the boss" is the third commandment—and the fourth is like unto it.

4. Love your neighbor.

It is almost as important as having faith in your boss that you have faith in your co-workers.

Everybody knows that ours is a business of *people.* Everybody knows that an advertising agency, whatever its organization chart may look like, must work as a team: Account-man-with-creative-with-research-with-media and even into financial, billing and collection procedures.

Everybody knows these things and their implicit corollary that you must respect and cooperate with the others on your team. And in places where it is a pleasure to work, there *is* this atmosphere of mutual respect. People help one another to succeed. People go out of their way to say to the boss: "I don't know what I'd have done without George's great idea for a headline!" or, "Sam worked all weekend and came up with a brilliant new media strategy!" or, "Boy! This new creative team on my account is just wonderful!"

Places where people say things like that are happy places. They do good work. The boss appreciates your reports on how good your associates are. And he therefore appreciates *you* more.

I had a client once—a huge, world-wide organization, which is the second largest in a highly competitive industry. It is a terrible place to work. The people are always blaming one another for mistakes which shouldn't have been made (and wouldn't have been made if the team worked together).

In working with this company for several years, I never heard the advertising director say one complimentary word about the operations manager. I never heard the general manager say one kind word about the advertising director. I never heard the president of the company say anything really personally favorable to any of them!

And you know something? This company is not only second in its category—it is having a hard time keeping from being overtaken by No. 3. Its product performance is very uneven. Its billings systems became so bad the company invested millions to automate them. The chief executive himself told me that his biggest problem was in service across-the-counter to customers. Yet he spends at least 50% of his time bawling out his subordinates. And since that's the pattern he sets, they in turn bawl out their subordinates. Staff meetings become brawls. I'm glad I don't have to attend them, even as an outsider, any longer.

If you love your neighbor, help him. Respect his talent. Give recognition to how good he is—maybe he'll do the same for you. And then your own star will begin to rise.

5. If you like the place, stay there!

The advertising community in any capital, New York, Paris, London or wherever, is bound to be a relatively small scene—and a volatile one. The good young people who begin to emerge in this scene inevitably develop initial stages of a personal reputation, a personal "image" which sets them apart from others.

And as there is really never enough top-flight talent to go 'round in our highly competitive business, it is understandable that Agency "A" will hear about a hot young tiger over at competition Agency "B." If Agency "A" has a need for one more hot young tiger, they make this one an offer, promising him great things.

Agencies looking for hot young tigers (or even not looking) get a great deal of stimulation in cities like New York and London from very aggressive flesh-peddlers who are paid a fee each time they move a hot young tiger from one menagerie to another.

And so, in the formative years of your career, if you are a hot young tiger (or if people think you are), you receive lots of offers. As they usually carry more money, a fancier title or an office with one more window, many such offers are accepted. The young tigers try several different menageries, looking for increasingly bigger cages, cuter tigresses and extra portions of raw meat every payday.

This is how the agency business derived its reputation for a characteristic which is variously described as:

- "Upward mobility."
- "Personnel volatility."
- Or "Instability."

I think it's okay to try several menageries before you eventually settle in one where you have your heart set on becoming Lord of the Jungle. But not too often! Not too many! Not across too many years! "Upward mobility" is not a substitute for capital gains.

Of course, I have one friend who, at age 50, has worked in executive capacities for Procter & Gamble, for one of the world's most powerful broadcasting stations, for three different advertising agencies, two motion picture studios and a pharmaceutical company—and who has made almost a million dollars just in settlements of unexpired employment contracts as he was fired from one job after another.

But he is exceptional—and although he is a charming fellow, his name is mud in our business. Contrast him with the following agency top executives and their tenure of employment with the companies they now direct:

Vic Bloede at Benton & Bowles for 24 years.

Ed Ney at Young & Rubicam 23 years.

Tom Dillon at BBDO 36 years.

Jock Elliott at Ogilvy & Mather 29 years.

Dan Seymour at J. Walter Thompson 29 years.

Bart Cummings at Compton 24 years.
And many more like them.

There is a great deal of risk in jumping from one job to another. If you are still a very *young* tiger, you can probably afford the risk, for a while. But there is much to be said for working your way gradually up through a company where you are happy, where you are respected and—let's face it—where you are protected.

The longer you keep making valuable contributions to your company, the stronger your franchise in that company will become, the more they will have invested in you—and the more encouragement and authority they will give you.

We're half way through the list.

6. Put yourself in the client's shoes.

One fact of life which it took me some time to learn when I was starting in our business is that "what is good for the client is good for the agency."

The client is not your adversary. You must never permit him to become that. You must recognize that the agency's success is a mirror-image of however much success its clients achieve.

The agency business is a fiduciary business. Clients entrust to us huge sums of money—millions and millions. We must be very careful how we invest that money for them. I hate to hear advertising appropriations spoken of as "how much the client spends." I prefer to think of how much he *invests* in advertising.

If you believe a client's business will benefit from putting money into trade or consumer promotions—instead of media advertising—tell him so! Of course, it may reduce the commissionable billing and your agency's income. But the reduction will probably be only temporary. Such deals are generally aimed at solving some specific problem: Consumer trial, distribution, shelf-stocking or some similar special circumstance.

If you help the client solve such a short-term problem, at the expense of some of your media commissions, that client is going to give you credit for being as concerned with *his* best interests as with lining your own pockets.

The majority of enlightened advertisers recognize that in today's world of supermarkets and self-service retailing, the most potent sales force is *consumer demand.* Consumer demand is developed by strong selling copy—not by deals. And thus, once his short-term crisis is over, your client is very likely to restore his media budget—accompanied by a new respect for your valuable counsel.

And by the way, nowhere is it more important to put yourself in the client's shoes than in a new business presentation. Although advertisers come to such presentations honestly believing that they want to hear about your agency, what they really want to hear is a discussion of their business, their products, their problems.

Learn to read a client's mind. Say to him, "I guess if I were you, these are the questions I'd like my agency to answer."

Try saying to a client sometime (if you believe it), "Maybe you should *reduce* your advertising budget, or eliminate advertising, on these items in your line. They appear to be going nowhere. The money saved might better be invested in research and development of one of your new product ideas."

Always remind yourself that what is good for the client's business will almost invariably be good for the agency, even if you have to sacrifice some short-term income in order to achieve long-term gains.

One of the nicest things a client can say about your agency is, "They certainly take an interest in our business. Their advice is entirely objective. They act like they really are working for *us!*"

7. Behave like a proprietor—and try to become one.

One of the founders of Benton & Bowles, the late Atherton Hobler, was talking to me once about an ambitious young account executive. This young fellow had two very conspicuous characteristics. He was extremely ambitious, and he enjoyed widespread personal popularity with his peers, the other young account executives.

"That young man," Mr. Hobler said, "is terribly eager to become a vice-president of our company. But he spends more time being one-of-the-boys than he does in thinking about Benton & Bowles. If he wants to become a vice-president, first he's got to act like one!"

It is very important that you handle yourself, the people with whom you work, your expense account, your travel and entertainment allowances—and everything you touch in your agency as though it were in fact "your" agency.

Do not fall into the trap of thinking, "It's *their* problem. *They* can worry about whether the company makes a profit or not. It's up to *them* to hold the clients—that's not my responsibility." If you are to succeed in the agency business, you must not separate yourself from "they" or "them." You must *become* "they."

Start thinking as though you owned the agency.

And if you are offered the opportunity to acquire shares, and thus to become a co-owner, seize that opportunity! Be a capitalist!

There are still too many people in our business (especially in Europe, where share ownership by employes is less widespread than in the U.S.) who limit their ambitions to a larger and larger *salary.* They do not seem to realize that the money that stays with you is the incremental money you make on your shares as an owner—not the money you are paid every week as an employe. Many countries as yet do not even levy capital gains taxes. And even where they are institutionalized to the extent that exists in the U.S., the capital gains rate ceiling of 35% is well below the 50% ceilings on earned income and 70% on other current income.

So—think like a proprietor! Act like one. And do not pass up any chance to become one.

8. Insist on 100% perfection in everything.

I know this sounds ridiculous, but I mean it. It is impossible to attain 100% perfection in everything. But it is perfectly reasonable to demand it. If you ask it—of yourself in your own work and of your associates in theirs—you may actually come out with 75% or 80%, which is very high, indeed.

If a piece of copy or a layout isn't right (and you *know* it isn't right), send it back! If one of your account associates comes to you with a poorly prepared plan-document, reject it! If you have made ten takes on a certain tv commercial sequence and it still doesn't look right, no matter if you're running into overtime—shoot an 11th. Get it as close to perfect as you can.

Years ago, I handled the French Tourist Office account for America. In one ad, the artist painted the French flag red, white and blue. We should have stopped the ad—but it was already engraved in four-color plates for a whole list of magazines. So we took a chance and ran it. The Tourist Office received many comments from outraged Frenchmen. The French tricolor is blue, white and red—in that order!

Had we lost the account in consequence of this carelessness, it would have been no more than we deserved.

I am appalled at the sloppy writing in many agency documents. Just because 80% of our billing is in television, we are not entitled to abdicate our responsibilities as communicators in print, as well as pictures.

Way back more than 2,000 years ago, the great Roman poet Horace wrote: *"Littera scripta manet"*—"The written word remains." He was right.

Do not let yourself become permissive. Permissiveness is the parent of laxity. Laxity means that one of these days you lose the account!

9. Learn all you can about managing money.

This may seem like a strange one. But I consider it very important, if you wish to succeed in the agency business.

Ours is a small-margin business. Many clients make a higher percentage of profit on net sales than we do. Cash-flow in the agency business needs to be watched very carefully. Managing it well can increase earnings dramatically. Doing it badly is a ticket to bankruptcy.

Your agency should not become a banker for your clients—carrying their accounts as "receivable" for weeks or months past due. The rule you should fix in your mind is that: "Accounts receivable should never exceed the billings for one average month."

Another and related rule would be: "Working capital should always equate with one average month's gross revenue."

You should find out and understand why these two rules are so important. You should learn how to manage your own agency's cash-flow (if you were the boss) so as to fulfill these requirements.

You should understand why your agency must not rely upon media volume-rebates to make a profit. Some agencies do just that. Media volume-rebates are still given to (and retained by) agencies in some European countries and in South America. They are an ephemeral source of agency income which I believe will sooner or later evaporate.

Why? Because as time goes by and advertisers become more sophisticated, it will be the clients who will object to these media volume inducements to agencies. The clients will say that such rebates exert too much influence upon agency recommendations. And that will be the beginning of the end.

Financially-minded men in advertising agencies in the U.S.A. and the U.K. have come into their own in recent years. They are increasingly important in agencies everywhere. An essential part of your executive equipment should be at least a working knowledge of agency finance.

And if you are serious about becoming a millionaire, you will need to learn all you can about the investment and management of your personal funds.

So experiment with different types of personal investment: Equities, bonds, real estate, mutual funds, tax shelters—the whole spectrum. Get some experience. Make your mistakes while you're young—at low levels!

Don't wait until you have a substantial corpus of capital to begin finding out how to manage it. It's a trying experience. There must be a dozen of us in this room who wish we'd studied money management more carefully—and sooner!

10. Believe in the business!

If the preceding suggestions seem to you to ring true but sound trite, then this is the most trite and true of them all.

There is very little room for self doubt in our highly competitive activity. People who wonder whether this is "really the right business" for them generally induce top management to decide it is not. People who accept their salaries but scorn the business are contemptible.

I suppose we have all known commercial writers who explain to their friends that "I'm just writing this junk for a living. What I really care about is this great movie I have in mind ..."

Such writers are taking money under false pretenses. They are fakes, and the advertising they produce usually looks, sounds and reads fakey.

Account executives with Hamlet syndromes are equally bad. Should they *really* be in "the ad game?" It is *not* a game. And they should not be in it.

As we all know, the advertising agency business is enough to try men's souls. It taxes a wide variety of skills. It burns up people. The average death age is still under 62—although it's been getting higher, thank God!

It is a demanding business. It has broken up some marriages. It has induced considerable alcoholism. It once led my wife's stepfather (a management supervisor at Erwin Wasey) to reach across a client's desk, grab him by the necktie and punch him in the mouth. (This helped my wife to understand our business.)

But the rewards are very great, too. Not just money. Where else can you bring together all the arts: Painting, writing, photography, music, film-making, acting, directing—and use them to give young girls self confidence as they wear your cosmetics—to make dishwashing (as P&G's Joy did) "almost nice"—to convince people in 100 countries and as many languages that "we try harder" is an adequate moral justification for renting a car that's been both used and abused?

It is a great feeling to observe the success of a product which you have helped to launch. Watching those share-of-market percentages go up can be a heady and euphoric experience.

And the money is there, too. Believe me, I did not *inherit* the chestnut gelding at Belmont, or the Ferrari Berlinetta, or the house in Acapulco. Each of these items is directly derived from services rendered to Benton & Bowles Inc.

And there are many more—including the 9% annuity with which I am dedicated in my retirement to beating the Metropolitan Life Insurance Co. at its own game.

You can do as well. Probably much better. I believe you *will* do so if you will heed my suggestions.

Reprinted from "Advertising Age," Feb. 18, 1974, pp. 49-50, 52

PART

Planning and Manage- ment of Advertising

The deadly quest for safety

BY DAVID J. MAHONEY
Chairman, Norton Simon Inc., New York

I was back in 1862. Bruce Catton had just put me there. And I was watching to see what Gen. McClellan would do.

McClellan had 126,000 men, and one overriding responsibility. He must protect the city of Washington. If Washington fell, even for the briefest of periods, the British would have the excuse they wanted to recognize the Confederacy.

But, McClellan also had a great opportunity. If he could push forward successfully, he might greatly hasten the end of the war by taking Richmond.

Like any prudent man, McClellan sought more information. He called in the head of his Intelligence Service, Allan J. Pinkerton, and impressed upon him again and again the terrible importance of safeguarding Washington.

If McClellan were to move his army forward, what chance did he have to win? Exactly how many men did Lee have confronting him?

Now Pinkerton was also a prudent man. If the boss wanted safety, he was going to give it to him. So, when Pinkerton's agents sent in their figures, Pinkerton prudently tripled those figures. And McClellan sat paralyzed, afraid to move against Lee's supposed horde of 280,000, while Lee—with about 90,000—wondered why on earth McClellan wasn't attacking?

Risk, Partner of Opportunity

In a sense, at this moment, we too are in McClellan's position. And so is every chief executive, and every rising executive, of every company that has successfully driven up the figures on the bottom line through the last two decades of almost relentless expansion.

For all of us, now, the stakes are high. Now, we too have large investments to protect. Large commitments. Large responsibilities. Like McClellan, we too now have much to safeguard. Like McClellan, we too have our Washingtons.

And, like McClellan, we too are faced by immediate risks. If we are to move forward, we shall have to assess and confront the ripening population explosion. The growing power of consumerism. The increasing pace of technological change. The changing character of the work force and the patterns of supply, including the emerging new structures of advertising. The snow-balling costs of new-product introduction. And the ever-accelerating revolution in consumer needs and wants that is constantly redefining our markets, both yours and mine.

But the very factors that pose the greatest risks are also offering us the greatest opportunities. The population explosion, for example, presents us with the problem of creating thousands of new jobs. But it is also expected to present us with a market so huge that the consumption of foods and beverages alone will nearly double by 1980. Moreover, consumerism—which has sometimes been criticized as a threat to the future of our economic system—will, I believe, become our best as well as our most dangerous friend. Risk is the inevitable partner of opportunity.

Standing Pat Won't Hack It

And so, like McClellan, we too face a choice. We can choose to stand pat. We can play not to lose.

Or we can play to win.

Now I, too, am a prudent man. I am very aware of the size of the stakes. And I, like McClellan, am personally accountable—to my shareholders, my board of directors, my staff, and myself. Yet all of my experience and judgment present me with one inescapable equation: Forward movement equals unavoidable risks, but inertia equals certain failure. In our volatile consumer market, the company that stands pat must drop dead sooner or later.

Therefore, I intend to play to win. I intend to take Richmond.

But, in order to take Richmond, we shall have to so manage, and so control, communications that our actions and ideas are constantly fed by an adequate and reliable supply of information. If we are to achieve this, we shall have to first outwit the problem that stalemated McClellan.

It is easy to think of this problem as the Pinkerton problem. Easy, but inaccurate.

In fact, Pinkerton's behavior was merely a symptom. The problem was really McClellan's. And, in a larger sense, it is the central problem of all management.

The Deadly Quest for Safety

I believe that the causes and effects of this problem go to the very root of most of the difficulties that plague all large and successful endeavors. I further believe that they have an added and particular relevance to advertising, since communications are your product as well as your most vital management tool.

And I am fully convinced that the No. 1 cause of this problem—the cause from which most of the other causes spring—is the misguided and deadly quest for safety.

Now it is probably self-evident that the desire for safety is basic to the human condition. And it seems equally clear that this desire increases as the stakes increase.

It is therefore not surprising that companies with the least to lose—companies whose only chances for success are still ahead of them—are often most willing to take risks and produce innovations. And so are their people. With nothing to lose but the specter of unemployment—and fame, wealth, and the hope of safety ahead if their new and insecure company becomes successful—such people may well dare to think for themselves. To talk straight to the boss. To offer the best ideas of which they are capable. Nevertheless, many such companies will, of course, fail.

Do It Like Xerox, Polaroid, VW

But when their ideas and their attitudes are compelling enough to attract the right people—people who will take an informed gamble on a large uncertain future in preference to a smaller, more secure, but more frustrating present—and when they have sufficient capital to adequately produce and promote their innovations, a new giant may arise and stride rapidly toward the top. Such, of course, was the case with Volkswagen as it entered the U.S. market. And with Xerox. And with Polaroid.

And it is not at all surprising that these companies ran outstandingly innovative advertising. They had to. Their advertising was an intrinsic part of the better mousetrap that made it possible for them to compete with established companies. Indeed, throughout the history of advertising, many of the most daring, memorable, and successful campaigns represented companies—or were produced by agencies—making their first entry into major markets.

But as such innovative companies grow famous, large, and successful—and I speak as the chairman of such a company—they run head on into the problem that their very success has created for them: The difficulty of maintaining effective communications. For success tends to breed bigness, which increases the stakes. And increased stakes breed the quest for safety, which fosters overspecialization, overstaffing, and long lines of communication. And long communication lines breed separation of authority from responsibility, which breeds second-guessing, stand-pattism, and corporate empire building. And all of these dilute and pervert communication.

Great Ads that Never Ran

Everyone in the advertising community has heard bitter stories of wasted work misdirected by second-guessing and misinformation. And of great marketing concepts that were never executed because of fear on the account side. And great campaigns that never appeared because someone was afraid to sell them. And great ads that were presented only at the eleventh hour because the client himself had come up with the same central idea after it had been shot down by agency people or by the client's own second-guessing subordinates.

I am quite sure that many of these stories are true and that their truth is one of the explanations for the emergence of some of the best new creative shops and services. After all, for many years I was in—and, in a way that seems increasingly useful and necessary to me, I still am in —the advertising business.

But I am equally sure that all of us in management, no matter what sort of endeavor we manage, can remember some point along the line when we were suddenly surprised by some complex and costly problem—a problem that could have been prevented or unsnarled earlier

if our own subordinates had had the guts and the knowledge to tell us what we must hear, instead of what they thought we wanted to hear.

How can we make sure that our subordinates do have the guts and the knowledge? How can we avoid breeding Pinkerton behavior? How do we assure ourselves of a constant two-way flow of innovative ideas and accurate information? I think we can begin to find the answers by looking at a situation where communication often functions most effectively: The new business situation.

Lean Staffing, Motivation

First of all, I think we will find lean staffs. New businesses can rarely afford much fat in their staffing. And lean staffs tend to prevent overspecialization and long communication lines. When there are few people, it is simply more necessary for each of them to be able to do many jobs. When there are few people, it is simply faster for them to gain access to one another.

At Norton Simon Inc. we have deliberately sought to create a corporate management structure that parallels the leanness of the new-business situation. Although total employes number 35,000 people, our total corporate staff numbers only 70 persons, including the switchboard operators.

Second, I think we will find that new companies live with challenge, because most of their history and their rewards still lie ahead of them. The motivation for success, therefore, becomes a daily, personal goal for new-company management, both for corporate and personal satisfaction. This, too, fosters honest communication.

We try to maintain this challenging new company environment at Norton Simon Inc. By paying excellent salaries, we try to attract the best people available. Then, in addition to salary, we reward each of our key management people with an incentive bonus that is directly related to his contribution toward meeting annual profit goals.

Our Managers Talk Back

With personal income tied directly to company profits, our people have a vital stake in seeking the truth, telling it straight, and no second-guessing. If a key manager foresees a problem, he doesn't bury it. He tells me about it before it gets bigger. And when our people have ideas, they fight for them. They talk up. And they talk back.

There is, however, a special place to which our key people may turn to be sure that all internal and external communications are fast, clear, cost-efficient, and effective. Here, too, they may tap a special pipeline to the consumer to get

fast, accurate information on which to base marketing, new product, and acquisition decisions. That place is the office of Norton Simon Communications Inc.

NSC is a unique communications facility—and facilitator—which we designed to meet our special needs. It may not be right for everyone. But its very existence indicates the central importance we give to communications as a critical management tool. NSC has already significantly altered our relationships with the advertising industry and enabled us to take flexible advantage of emerging structural trends.

Not a House Agency

NSC has frequently—and erroneously —been called a house agency. However, one of its functions is to prevent the very docility and second-guessing for which house agencies have often been criticized. In terms of its current and projected staff, it is smaller than many house agencies. In terms of its responsibilities and capabilities, we think it is very much larger.

NSC is a separate company within Norton Simon Inc., and its president is a peer with the presidents of all our other operating subsidiaries. The services he offers to those other companies both complement and compete with the outside advertising organizations that they are entirely free to employ.

Let me give you a few examples. Even if NSC is not their advertising agency, our operating companies may, at any time, ask NSC for support on critical marketing or advertising problems. Or to provide additional conceptual input. Or to run their proposed advertising through one of our NSC information-gathering research tools. Or to take on a new product advertising assignment. Or to give both our companies and their agencies a clearer fix on the consumer market through the Norton Simon Inc. National Consumer Tracking Survey.

Our main purpose in establishing NSC was not to cut our advertising costs, or to reduce the 15%. Our objective is to make the 85% work more effectively, because nothing is ultimately more costly than an ineffective campaign or a fundamentally unsound marketing concept.

Jefferson Had Some Words for It

Almost 200 years ago, Thomas Jefferson wrote that "all experience has shown that mankind are more disposed to suffer evils . . . than to right themselves by abolishing the forms to which they are accustomed." He meant those words to apply to government. But throughout most of our history, they have seemed to apply with equal profoundness to almost all the vital roles and institutions of life:

Sexual roles, marriage, living patterns, work patterns, management patterns, extending right down to the choices and uses of products.

But now much of this is changing. Even Jefferson's use of the word "mankind" might now be challenged by the militant leadership of the strong and growing women's liberation movement. And all these changes are having a significant effect on the life expectancy of consumer products and services and the corporations that provide them.

In our principal marketing area of foods and beverages, for example, approximately one out of six products now on retailers' shelves was not there last year. Moreover, when we consider items of all kinds now being sold in U.S. food stores, we estimate that half of these products were not in the stores five years ago. As a result of increasing emphasis on new products, product line extensions, new flavors and more convenient and economical packaging forms, it is estimated that about two-thirds of the products now being sold in supermarkets were not there ten years ago.

Obviously, these new items took an existing or potential share of market from older products. So it is not a surprising estimate that at least two out of five products that were on grocery store shelves a decade ago have now disappeared. And so, apparently, have some of the companies that produced them; many of the products introduced within the last ten years are produced and marketed by companies that either didn't exist at all or were not in these product categories ten years ago.

It seems reasonable to conclude from these facts that standing still is apt to be either directly deadly or deadly expensive. And this conclusion alone would tend to impel me to advance on Richmond.

But there are also some extraordinary, compelling, positive reasons.

The Rewards of Taking Richmond

For one thing, Richmond—and by that, of course, we mean our consumer market—is bigger and potentially richer in opportunity than any market that faced any previous generation.

By 1980, economists predict that the gross national product will reach $1.443 trillion, for a ten-year growth of 54%. That's as though we were to add to our current gross national product the national economies of Japan, France, Great Britain, Canada, and Belgium.

One-half of this projected growth in our economy will come from increased consumer spending. The market for food and beverages—our most significant market and the largest single category of consumer spending—is projected to grow at a rate nearly twice that of the national economy. In fact, although it has taken nearly 200 years for this category to reach $132 billion, it is expected to nearly double again by 1980.

Based on these projections, it would appear that, as a marketer of consumer foods and beverages, we might expect no less than a doubling of our business over the next ten years. However, the rapid projected changes in the market—constantly defined by accurate information—suggest that we will be able to grow even faster.

By 1980, there will be three young adults in the 18-34 age group for every two in 1970. They will form households at a rate of nearly five times that of population growth, and these units are the consumers of many of Norton Simon Inc.'s basic products. Moreover, these households will be affluent, their incomes often significantly increased by the working wife. By 1980, there will be a 22% increase in the number of working wives, so that approximately 40% of all wives will have a job outside the home. These working wives will create a growing demand for convenience food products and services.

Surely, there has never before been so great an opportunity for the resourceful and well capitalized marketer.

New Products Face Big Risk

However, lest I make the case for advancing appear too safe and too rosy, I am well aware of the difficulties of achieving new product success. And of the high odds against us. Over the past ten years—even among those better new product possibilities that survived to test market—from 40-60%, depending upon product category, died in test market.

During the same decade, the average cost of developing, testing, and introducing a new consumer product has risen dramatically.

Therefore, much of our effort in the area of communications management has been focused upon reducing both the risks and the costs inherent in new product development. We expect the increasing flow of information from our Tracking Survey and other information channels to give us an even more accurate fix on new product needs and desires by telling us not only where the consumer is, but where the consumer will be.

Moreover, armed with this knowledge—and with an honest supply of critical and innovative ideas facilitated by our growing control of communications—we expect to be effectively guided and helped by the powerful new force of consumerism.

Consumerism Can Be Advertiser Ally

Consumerism has been posed as a threat. We see it as potentially our strongest ally. For the informed consumer will not base her purchases on loyalty to brand monuments. She will choose on the basis of reason, not sentimentality. Therefore, a company that can give consumers what they want and need, at a price they can afford, will grow, and grow profitably, because its products will thrive even in the face of long-established competition.

We believe that companies will be able to give consumers what they want and need, at prices they can afford, if those companies—like consumers—prove themselves able to alter and abandon the forms to which they are accustomed. Such companies will find efficient new ways to produce competitively-priced products that offer legitimate benefits, not simply appeals to impulse buying. And, since they will offer legitimate benefits, such products should enjoy relatively long life, thereby proving that it is good business to heed George Washington's pertinent question: "If, to please the people, we offer what we ourselves disapprove, how can we afterwards defend our work?"

Hopefully, more and more companies will produce work that will need no defending. And we will all benefit.

After all, we, too, are all consumers.

Reprinted from "Advertising Age," Nov. 21, 1973, pp. 28, 32

How an agency uses

consumer research

BY CHARLES E. OVERHOLSER
Partner, Haley, Overholser & Associates

There are three basic steps in shaping advertising strategy, and consumer research is essential in helping us to make intelligent decisions at each. The three key steps are:

1. Product class definition.
2. Prospect group selection.
3. Message element selection.

I think the terms "Prospect group selection" and "Message element selection" are pretty self-evident. Clearly the advertiser must decide whom he wishes to communicate with and what he wishes to communicate before he can write the copy and buy the media time and space. But first a word in explanation of the first step, "Product Class Definition."

Why should the definition of our brand's product class be any problem? Isn't it perfectly obvious? A cigar competes with cigars. Everybody knows what a cigar is. But do Tiparillos compete only with other cigars, or do they compete in the consumer's mind with cigarets as well? Do White Owls compete with all other cigars, or are they seen as an appropriate alternative only to the smokers of *certain* other cigars—a discrete subsegment of the cigar market?

The answers to these kinds of questions are by no means self-evident and they are of fundamental importance to the advertising planners.

Traditional definitions of product classes as used in the trade are often arbitrary or obsolete, dictated only by custom or by availability of trade reports and bearing little relationship to the alternatives consumers face up to in their own minds when making a purchase decision. Increasingly as new products proliferate, brands compete *across* traditional product class lines or are specialized to compete primarily in a narrow *segment* of a traditional product class.

Problem: How to Compete

The first decision our advertising strategist must make is whether to compete broadly within the conventional product class, to compete only with some segment of the conventional product class, or whether to attempt to expand demand for the brand as an alternative for some other product class. This so-called "positioning" decision guides the selection of prospect groups and the selection of message elements to be communicated in advertising.

How does research help us to position a brand in the most relevant competitive frame? Measurement of consumer attitudes and behavior are directed at answering two key questions:

1. Is the "conventional" product class expandable?
2. Is the "conventional" product class segmented? Or segmentable?

For example, in the case of a product class like beer, a survey might indicate (I say might, because I am only hypothesizing here, not reporting findings) that most consumers seldom consider beer as a good substitute for other beverages, that on what they perceive to be coffee or whisky drinking occasions, beer is simply not perceived as appropriate. Moreover, analysis of cultural trends and long-term beverage drinking trend data might indicate what appears to be a gradual secular decline in beer drinking. We would conclude then that the "conventional" product class for beer was not readily expandable.

A study of dessert consumption behavior, on the other hand, might indicate that flavored gelatin desserts were considered appropriate for many occasions when some other dessert was actually served, implying an obvious possible opportunity to expand the conventional product class—by suggesting increased usage.

Beer is similar to gelatin desserts on our other key criterion, however. In both cases, there is not very important segmentation within the product class. Every beer is different, and consumers perceive difference in quality; but with a few fairly minor exceptions, beers are not seen as being different in character. By and large, most beer drinkers expect the same benefits and seek to satisfy the same general wants, regardless of which beer they prefer. We have the same situation with gelatin desserts. We call this an unsegmented market.

Cigarets, however, are an example of a segmented product class, a phenomenon which has become increasingly common in recent years. Twenty years ago all major brands of American cigarets were 87mm long, without filters, made of nearly identical blends of Kentucky burley tobacco without special flavor additives, and packed in soft, paper packets of 20. Each was designed to appeal to masculine tastes. Today the following distinctly different segments of the cigaret market can be listed.

- Non-filter straight (the 1930s standard).
- Flavor filters.
- Hi-filtration filters.
- Menthol flavored.
- 100 millimeter.
- Feminine design.

And, of course, there are all sorts of degrees and combinations of the above as various differentiated brands have been developed to satisfy the spectrum of wants which has evolved in this market. At the same time, for obvious reasons, there is no role for advertising in expanding the demand for cigarets.

The most complex of our cases is represented by the electric shaver market. There research might indicate that the product class is both expandable (as men may be converted from wet shaving) and segmented as men have developed varying value systems in respect to the relative benefits of closeness versus comfort or preferences for various features. The shaver may symbolize both segmentation and expandability. Each of these represents a prototype, although none of the actual examples fit that prototype precisely. Each of these prototypical market situations raises a different set of questions.

In situation 1, the beer case, we must decide whether to:

1. Compete broadly in the conventional class, or

2. Try to perceive an opportunity segment in the conventional class. (As might be done in the case of beer, for example, by estimating the opportunity for increasing the number of that small minority who prefer a dark beer.)

In situation 2, typified by gelatin desserts, we have a different choice. Whether to:

• Compete broadly in the conventional class,

• Try to perceive an opportunity segment in the conventional class, or

• Try to expand the class.

For markets of the third type, segmented but not expandable, the problem is more simply stated: Which segment to compete in.

Finally, the most complex situation, a market which is both expandable and segmented. Here we must answer a series of questions:

• Shall we compete within the conventional class?

• If so, in which segment?

• Shall we try to expand the class?

• Or, adopt a combination strategy?

The 'Best Opportunity' Concept

Sometimes the answers to these questions come easily. Many answers are dictated by the physical and objective characteristics of the brand in question. But in many instances, particularly, of course, during the development stages of a new product, a very careful evaluation based on the best possible research of consumer value systems, perceptions and behavior is required, if we are to decide wisely.

We use consumer research to help us select among alternative product class definitions on the basis of what we call the "best opportunity" concept. It is a very simple formulation, but it guides our strategic decisions not only at the stage of product class definition, but at every step in the development of an advertising plan.

We define the best opportunity as the product of "the number of chances for advertising to induce" behavior or attitudes favorable to our clients' objectives *times* the ease with which such behavior or attitudes can be induced. In other words, how many people may be interested in what we have to say, and what are our chances of inducing a change among these people?

Advertising is designed to induce change in behavior or attitude through the communication of information. The opportunity for success of any advertising strategy then depends on how many people might conceivably respond to the advertising and the ease with which such a group can be induced to respond.

What Research Can and Can't Do

Now, unfortunately, research cannot provide us neat, precise numbers to substitute into our equation. In particular, estimating the ease with which prospects can be induced to respond to an advertising strategy is a judgmental process.

But research *can* tell us a lot about the current state of consumer behavior and attitudes. It can tell us how many people eat dessert and how often. It can tell us what satisfactions beer drinkers seek. It can tell us how many people are primarily interested in closeness in shaving versus those who value comfort more, or speed and convenience. These kinds of data are critical in helping us to estimate the number of chances various product class positioning strategies will provide.

Secondly, research is used to provide help in estimating the ease-to-induce factor. For example, we can measure the relative extent of dissatisfaction with various competitive brands or products indicating where trial of our brand might be relatively easy to induce. We can estimate the degree to which consumers consider our brand to be an appropriate substitute for other products. We can analyze basic trends to estimate the expandability of a product class. Do cultural trends favor a growth in primary demand or not?

Each alternative positioning is reviewed—in the light of such research—and a choice is made on the basis of our research-based judgment as to which alternative will yield the largest multiplied product of numbers and ease.

Who Are Our Best Prospects?

Having made a tentative decision on the nature of the competitive frame or product class, we move on to consider a more precise definition of who will be the best prospects for our advertising.

We use research to define prospects more specifically. Not all users of our product class are equally good prospects for our advertising.

There are four major orders of classification which are widely used to help pinpoint the targets of advertising.

First, we are, for obvious reasons, always interested in knowing how product usage patterns vary within the population. It may seem equally obvious that we would select heavy users as our best

prospects since they, by definition, represent the largest number of chances we have to induce a purchase. But this is not always the case. Often heavy users are the most *difficult* to induce. They tend to be already well informed. They are likely to have very strong opinions based on extensive product experimentation, and they are likely to be very habituated in their purchase behavior. Hence many advertisers may choose the lighter user as the best prospect for an advertising effort—although it must be admitted that heavy users are the more common choice. Obviously, research is needed here to "count the numbers and to estimate the ease."

Who's Tried the Brand, When?

We also pay close attention to brand experience and attitude groups. We want to know how many people are aware of our brand, how many have tried it, on what occasions do they use it, what are their satisfactions, dissatisfactions with our brand and with competitive brands. All of this sort of information is used to help guide us as to whether to direct our advertising, for example, at consumers who have already tried us in the hopes of increasing their frequency of use, or to concentrate on inducing trial among those who have not tried us.

We seek through research to find opportunity groups. We often find through attitude research that a significant number of consumers have a badly mistaken opinion about our product. For example, many people believe that decaffeinated coffee has inferior flavor, and yet in blind product test after blind product test this myth is disproved. Clearly there is a good opportunity to induce trial of a decaffeinated coffee if we can persuasively inform this group that decaffeinated coffee is equal in flavor to other brands. Thus, we may choose a specific "attitude group" as our prime advertising prospects.

Suppose that research discloses that many users of competitive brands perceive it as weak in some important attribute—certain hair grooming preparations may be seen as too greasy, or too stiff by some of their users. If we can determine how many and what sorts of consumers hold this attitude, they may become the prime prospect group for a brand which is, indeed, superior in the attribute in question, for example, a grease-free hair grooming product.

The most important research in-put to the process of defining prospect groups is the study of "wants groups." Recent computer-aided advances in consumer research methodology have enabled advertisers to gain a much clearer idea in many product categories of the configuration of consumer wants within the total population. That is to say, considerable progress has been made in classifying consumers according to the relative value they place on specific benefits which a product may offer.

What Does the Consumer Want?

An over-simplified example: Dentifrice users tend to fall into several distinct benefit-seeking segments. Group I seek maximum cavity prevention. Group II seek maximum whitening and brightening. Group III seek maximum mouth and breath freshening. Group IV seek maximum flavor satisfaction. Actually the groups are bound to be more subtly defined involving combinations and gradations of these values. Nevertheless, if research can distinguish such benefit-seeking segments, characterize them in terms of their dominant wants, count their members, provide a detailed account of their characteristics, and finally tell us how our brand is rated by each of the groups, if we then match our knowledge of the true attributes of our brand to our knowledge of the consumer want structure, it should be clear, I think, that we have a very powerful tool by which to judge the best relative opportunity presented by each of these segments.

Such analysis is also, of course, of great value in guiding new product development. It helps tell us what wants are not being satisfied by currently available products.

For the jargon collector, this type of research is known as multi-variate benefit segmentation analysis.

Be All for All People?

Working with one or more of the orders of classification I have discussed, employing our "best opportunity" index, we develop a prospect group definition. The decisions involved are seldom easy. In the first place, the research base is never as complete as we wish it were. Often major factors have to be estimated because they have not or cannot, without great expense, be measured. But great progress has been made in both the quantity and quality of research available to the advertising planner.

A more intractable problem remains, however, for the advertising strategist. There is a tendency which might even be dubbed the "iron law of market segmentation" for research to present us not with a pat solution but with a dilemma. As size of opportunity goes up, ease to induce goes down.

The logic is fairly obvious: If wants are diverse, and they seem to be getting more so every day, the larger the number of people one tries to satisfy with a single appeal, the poorer the fit will be. Conversely, if one attempts to "be all things to all people" by stressing a broad spectrum of product benefits, one may wind up being everyone's second choice. Moreover, the larger the prospect group, the more likely it is that competition is already strongly entrenched with good products designed to fill that segment's wants structure. Thus, when we look at the larger prospect groups, they almost invariably look harder to induce than the smaller ones. Research illuminates this problem, provides the key evidence for the planner, but a lot of entrepreneurial business judgment is required for the final decisions.

Brand Performance in Lab, in Use

To make the final set of strategic decisions, those in respect to the content of the advertising message itself, we first of all need to study the technical product research which tells us how the product performs in the laboratory. Secondly, we need to know how our product and competitive products perform in natural use when tested among consumers under blind conditions, i.e., under conditions where it is not possible for the consumer to know what brand she is using, hence it is not possible that she be influenced by reputation or imputation of quality from price, package, etc. Third, we need to know what users and non-users of various brands think of those brands when they are identified, that is, when all imputed virtues or faults are allowed to play their role in affecting attitude.

Finally, of course, we need once again to study the expressed wants of various groups of consumers. All of this information, much of which I have already discussed in connection with prospect group selection, must then be evaluated once again to help us to select message elements which will give us the best opportunity to induce response.

This process starts by identifying and selecting for address a consumer want which is extensive and important in the sense that it is reasonably intense and hopefully is crucial in causing a purchase to be made. We are back, of course, to using research to count the number of chances to induce . . . that is, measuring the extent to which the wants exist among our prospect groups. We will want to address wants which are perceived as important; then the prospects will be relatively easy to induce.

That is, they will be easy to induce if we can select an attribute of our brand to stress which is (1) responsive to that want, and (2) is true and believable.

To find such an attribute, we need to study laboratory research, also blind product consumer product test data, and finally, so-called image data, that is, the opinions people have of our brand based on casual experience and reputation.

We try also to select an attribute to stress in which our brand has an advantage over competition. Ideally, an attribute which is not only important, but unique. To do this, of course, we need laboratory and consumer research on our competition as well as on our brand.

Hard to Have Product Advantage

Now, of course, this again generally raises the problem I discussed earlier, a corollary of the iron law of marketing segmentation. The more important an attribute is to a large number of consumers, the less likely it is that any brand in a highly competitive free economy will have a unique advantage. The strategist must often face a difficult choice between emphasis on an important but generic quality or on a somewhat less important but differentiating quality. Research can help by measuring the degree to which various attributes are perceived as important and differentiating and the degree to which our brand is perceived by consumers as strong or weak in the various attributes.

The last is of key importance because advertising is most effective when it communicates new information, so long as that information is likely to be persuasive. Thus, we try to select an attribute for stress in our message which is not only responsive to an important want, true and unique, but one which is not fully realized by the consumer. We conduct a great deal of research to measure the level of information and the perceptions which consumers have about brands, and we search for opportunities to correct falsely-based, negative opinions about our brands or to inform people of positive virtues which have not previously been well communicated.

We concentrate, of course, on information which we have reason to believe will be of real interest to our prospects. A 30-second commercial is not a patent application or even a catalog specifications sheet. If we are to succeed in communicating any information within that time frame, we have to limit ourselves

She Buys What She Likes

The consumer will pay attention or not, gain information or not, be persuaded or not, depending upon her particular sets of wants and the prior level of her information and, of course, depending on our skill in communicating. In the long run, she will choose the brand whose good points and bad points best conform to her personal value system.

It is the job of consumer research in an advertising agency to help the advertiser to understand how the value systems of consumers vary in the population and to understand the extent and nature of consumer information and attitudes about the brand we advertise, in the hope that such knowledge will increase our efficiency as communicators.

Reprinted from "Advertising Age," No. 21, 1973, pp. 56, 58-59

How much do you spend on advertising?

BY KENNETH MASON
Group Vice-President—Grocery Products, Quaker Oats Co., Chicago

With all the talk we've heard about advertising these last few years, it's hard to believe the world needs yet another dissertation on the subject of the theory and practice of advertising in America today.

And yet, presumptuous though it may sound, I am afraid it does. Not necessarily from me, I grant you. But if not from me, then from someone *like* me, who is not an economist, not a professor, not a lawyer, not a member of the government, but rather a working line manager, whose company is a major user of advertising, and who is perhaps even more concerned than advertising's social critics with some of the directions advertising and marketing have taken in this country during my own business lifetime.

Because, despite all the expert testimony on how advertising works from the professors, the economists, the government lawyers and a host of other critics, I have yet to hear anyone satisfactorily answer the three most basic and probably most important functional questions being asked about advertising today, namely:

● What is the relationship between advertising and sales?

● What is the relationship between advertising and prices?

● What is the relationship between advertising and competition?

The first of these functional questions —the relationship between advertising expenditures and sales—is such a central issue in our concern over advertising's role in our economy and society, one would think someone like John Kenneth Galbraith, who has been such a perceptive critic of business, would have answered it years ago. But if he has, I have not been able to find it in his writings.

Sales Level Sets Ad Budget

One would have thought that Stephen Greyser would have brought this point out in one of the excellent models of advertising he presented to the Federal Trade Commission's advertising hearings. But if he did, I missed it.

Even Yale Brozen, in his now-famous vindication of advertising as an economic force, has not really nailed down the basic relationship between advertising expenditures and sales as clearly as I think it ought to be nailed down. Because it seems to me absolutely essential that before the professors and the economists and the lawyers set out to change advertising, they understand this simple truth: It's not the high advertising budget that produces the high sales level. It's the high sales level that produces the high advertising budget.

Or, to state it as a business principle: In most businesses, products which sell well tend to be advertised more than products which sell poorly.

The idea that Procter & Gamble, to use America's most famous marketing company as an example, has more success with their new product introductions than the rest of us because they spend more advertising money than the rest of us is not true. What's true is that P&G has historically spent more advertising money than ordinary companies because they have historically come up with more successful products than ordinary companies.

How much a company spends to introduce a product does not determine how well that product will sell. It can only affect how well the consumer understands the product and how rapidly the product reaches its sales potential. At the Quaker Oats Co., our eight most recent new product, first year advertising budgets ranged from $6,000,000 for Product A to $1,100,000 for Product G. As you can see from this chart,

Product	First Year Budget (in millions)	Annual Sales Level (in millions)
A	$6.0	$ 8
B	4.0	28
C	3.9	20
D	3.7	20
E	3.5	11
F	2.5	11
G	1.1	11

our largest advertising budget happened to produce the lowest selling product of the group. Similarly, three products that ended up achieving almost an identical annual sales level of approximately $11,000,000 each used introductory advertising budgets that varied as much as 250%.

Obviously, in our society, all companies need some form of communication with the consumer to create awareness of the existence of a new product. But, as this one small example suggests, there is no consistent correlation between the level of advertising spending used to introduce the products and the real level of consumer purchases the products will actually be able to achieve on a continuing basis.

Private Labels Get Big Ad Budgets

Perhaps other companies have had different experiences, but I doubt it. While companies differ greatly in how they use advertising to launch new products, very few companies continue to advertise products that don't sell. Very few companies stop advertising products that do. And that's the relationship between advertising and sales.

Why advertising theorists have found this relationship so hard to understand, I don't know. Any more than I can understand why theorists have failed to answer satisfactorily the recurring suspicion that high advertising budgets are somehow related to high prices, which is functional point No. 2.

The idea that advertising inflates the price of a product probably originated with the common experience of most of us that products with unusually low prices frequently turn out to be unfamiliar brands made by companies we never heard of.

Private label food products in the supermarket are an example. It just seems logical to think that the difference between the price of the private label and the price of the national brand is simply the difference in their budgets.

But logical or not, let's remember two things about private label. During the week of April 24, food retailers in Chicago ran approximately 39,000 lines of advertising devoted to packaged food products in the four major Chicago newspapers. 37.1% of this linage was devoted to their private labels. Project this nationally and you get an annual expenditure in newspapers for private label food products of around $36,000,000 per year. Private label brands are not totally unadvertised brands by any means.

Private Label Food Advertising

Chicago—Four major newspapers
Week of April 24-30, 1972

Total packaged food linage in retail food ads	38,841
Per cent devoted to retailers' private labels	37.1%
Cost to a manufacturer to duplicate this newspaper advertising nationally for one year	$36,700,000

A second point to consider in accounting for the lower retail price of private label food products *vis a vis* nationally advertised brands is the possibility that the lower cost of the private label may be the result of a lower value.

We recently tested two of our major products in white unbranded packages against their major private label competitors. Here is what we found:

Blind Product Test

Breakfast Food

Preferred Quaker Product X	55%
Preferred Leading Private Label ...	38
No Preference	7

Pet Food

Preferred Quaker Product Y	64%
Preferred Leading Private Label ...	27
No Preference	9

Our brands were clearly preferred to the private label, even when the consumer didn't know which was which. Which lends support to the possibility that the real correlation may not be higher advertising costs, but higher consumer value.

Established Products

1972 Adv. Budget (in millions)	Average Price Per Pound
$3.4	$ .31
2.7	.35
2.6	.63
2.5	.76
2.2	.70
1.6	.78
1.4	.73
1.3	.59

Looking to Quaker products again for an example of the relationship between advertising and pricing. this chart shows our eight advertising budgets of $1,-000,000 or more matched with the price per pound of the product these budgets supported. What this chart shows is that at Quaker there is a negative correlation between the higher priced products and the higher advertising budgets. In our case, at least, the higher advertising budgets seem to be linked with the lower priced products.

This should surprise no one, because the answer to the question, "what is the relationship between advertising and pricing?" is, at least in markets that are reasonably mature: None. The relationship is between advertising and *cost*. Because advertising is just one of a dozen cost factors to be considered in developing, producing and selling any product, all products, advertised or unadvertised, must meet the identical pricing criterion, and that criterion is to be priced low enough to prove attractive enough to the consumer to result in reasonably consistent purchases.

Once this viable price has been established, all other decisions relate to the manufacturer's cost. Obviously there are many ways for him to cheapen the product, after it has been established. Cutting back on consumer communication is only one way he can do this.

Which brings us to the third current complaint about large advertising budgets: The complaint that they stifle competition from smaller but perhaps more innovative companies which lack the resources to advertise.

This erroneous supposition has been very forcefully countered by numerous experts, and most reasonable people seem to agree that advertising is not a barrier to market entry but rather the *means* for market entry.

Advertising Doesn't Inflate Prices

And so to sum up, then: It seems to me the time has come to do away with this tired old concept of how advertising works in the marketplace.

It is simply not an accurate model of what really occurs. It is not true that business controls the market by employing large advertising budgets to manipulate the consumer into buying its products. It is not true that advertising inflates the prices of these products, or that advertising serves to reduce competition. Rather, consumer needs, as researched or guessed at by business, lure business into offering products or services whose purpose is to meet those needs at a profit. To the extent that the product represents value to the consumer it will achieve a certain sales level. This sales level, in turn, determines the level of advertising the manufacturer can afford to prolong the life of the market and to maintain his share of it.

But while this model seems to me to be clearly more accurate in describing what happens in the marketplace, I am not suggesting for an instant that it is therefore any less vulnerable to criticism than its predecessor.

Critics who question business' ability or willingness to tackle society's major problems will be able to go right on questioning. Those who complain that our society produces too many goods of dubious intrinsic value will be able to go right on complaining.

Critics who deplore the fact that advertisers don't spend more money on products that "ought" to sell well but don't, can go right on deploring, because according to this model, advertising budgets are the result of product sales, not vice versa.

But no longer can critics complain that advertising is a barrier to competition. Quite the contrary, experience has shown there seems to be no effective mechanism to limit the number of market segments which advertisers may successfully develop, and as a result, the proliferation of products and advertising campaigns in some categories often seems quite wasteful from both a social and economic point of view.

Unfortunately, this seems to be the price we have to pay for a free enterprise system that welcomes maximum competition in every product category.

Reprinted from "Advertising Age," June 12, 1972, pp. 41, 44

The positioning era cometh

BY JACK TROUT AND AL RIES
Ries Cappiello Colwell

Today it has become obvious that advertising is entering a new era. An era where creativity is no longer the key to success.

The fun and games of the '60s have given way to the harsh realities of the '70s. Today's marketplace is no longer responsive to the kind of advertising that worked in the past. There are just too many products, too many companies, too much marketing "noise."

To succeed in our over-communicated society, a company must create a "position" in the prospect's mind. A position that takes into consideration not only its own strength and weaknesses, but those of its competitors as well.

Advertising is entering an era where strategy is king.

A Tale of Two Ads

If you had to pick an official date to mark the end of the last advertising era and the start of the new one, your choice would have to be Wednesday, April 7, 1971. In the *New York Times* that day was a full-page ad that seemed to generate very little excitement in the advertising community.

But then, an abrupt change in the direction of an industry isn't always accompanied by the blowing of bugles. You sometimes need the vantage point of history to realize what has happened.

The ad that appeared that spring morning in 1971 was written by David Ogilvy. And it's no coincidence that the architect of one era called the tune for the next.

In the ad, the articulate Mr. Ogilvy outlined his 38 points for creating "advertising that sells."

In first place on his list was a point Mr. Ogilvy called "the most important decision." Then he went on to say, "The results of your campaign depend less on how we write your advertising than on how your product is positioned."

■ Blow the bugles, the positioning era has begun.

Five days later, in the *New York Times* and in AD-VERTISING AGE, another ad appeared that confirmed the fact that the advertising industry was indeed changing direction. Placed by Rosenfeld, Sirowitz & Lawson, the ad listed the agency's four guiding principles.

In first place was, you guessed it. According to Ron Rosenfeld, Len Sirowitz and Tom Lawson, "Accurate positioning is the most important step in effective selling."

Suddenly the word and the concept was in everybody's ads and on everybody's lips. Hardly an issue of ADVERTISING AGE passes without some reference to "positioning."

You Can't Beat 'em Head-On

In spite of Madison Ave.'s current love affair with positioning, the concept had a more humble beginning.

In 1969, one of us (Jack Trout) wrote an article entitled "Positioning is a game people play in today's me-too marketplace," which appeared in the June, 1969, issue of *Industrial Marketing*. The article made predictions and named names, all based on the "rules" of a game called positioning.

One prediction, in particular, turned out to be strikingly accurate. As far as RCA and computers were concerned, "a company has no hope to make progress head-on against the position that IBM has established."

The operative word, of course, is "head-on." And while it's possible to compete successfully with a market leader (the article suggested several approaches), the rules of positioning say it can't be done "head-on."

Three years ago this raised a few eyebrows. Who were we to say that powerful, multi-billion-dollar companies couldn't find happiness in the computer business if they so desired?

Desire, alas, was not enough. Not only RCA, but also General Electric bit the IBM dust.

With two major computer manufacturers folding one right after another, the urge to say, "I told you so," was irresistible.

Last November, a follow-up article, "Positioning revisited: Why didn't GE and RCA listen?" appeared in the same publication.

We're an Over-Communicated Society

As GE and RCA found out, advertising doesn't work anymore. At least, not like it used to. One reason may be the noise level in the communications jungle.

The per-capita consumption of advertising in the U.S. is approaching $100 a year. And while no one doubts the advertiser's financial ability to dish it out, there's some question about the consumer's mental ability to take it all in.

Each day, thousands of messages compete for a share of the prospect's mind. And, make no mistake about it, the mind of the battleground. Between six inches of grey matter is where the advertising war takes place. And the battle is rough, with no holds barred and no quarter given.

The new ball game can prove unsettling to companies that grew up in an era where any regular advertising was likely to bring success. This is why you see a mature, sophisticated company like Bristol-Myers run through millions of dollars trying to launch me-too products against strongly dug-in competition. (If you haven't noticed, Fact, Vote and Resolve are no longer with us.)

To understand why some companies have trouble playing in today's positioning game, it might be helpful to take a look at recent communications history.

'50s Were the Product Era

Back in the '50s, advertising was in the "product" era. In a lot of ways, these were the good old days when the "better mousetrap" and some money to promote it were all you needed.

It was a time when advertising people focused their attention on product features and customer benefits. They looked for, as Rosser Reeves called it, the "Unique Selling Proposition."

But in the late '50s, technology started to rear its ugly head. It became more and more difficult to establish the "USP."

The end of the product era came with an avalanche of "me-too" products that descended on the market. Your "better mousetrap" was quickly followed by two more just like it. Both claiming to be better than the first one.

The competition was fierce and not always totally honest. It got so bad that one product manager was overheard to say, "Wouldn't you know it. Last year we had nothing to say, so we put 'new and improved' on the package. This year the research people came up with a real improvement, and we don't know what to say."

In '60s, 'Image' was King

The next phase was the image era. In the '60s, successful companies found their reputation or "image" was more important in selling a product than any specific product feature.

The architect of the image era was David Ogilvy. As he said in his famous speech on the subject, "Every advertisement is a long-term investment in the image of a brand." And he proved the validity of his ideas with programs for Hathaway shirts, Rolls-Royce, Schweppes and others.

But just as the "me-too" products killed the product era, the "me-too" companies killed the image era. As every company tried to establish a reputation for itself, the noise level became so high that relatively few companies succeeded. And most of the ones that made it, did it primarily with spectacular technical achievements, not spectacular advertising.

But while it lasted, the exciting, go-go years of the middle '60s were like a marketing orgy.

At the party, it was "everyone into the pool." Little thought was given to failure. With the magic of money and enough bright people, a company felt that any marketing program would succeed.

The wreckage is still washing up on the beach. Du Pont's Corfam, Gablinger's beer, Handy Andy all-purpose cleaner, *Look* magazine.

The world will never be the same again and neither will the advertising business. For today we are entering an era that recognizes both the importance of the product and the importance of the company image, but more than anything else stresses the need to create a "position" in the prospect's mind.

Positioning Era Dawns

The great copywriters of yesterday, who have gone to that big agency in the sky, would die all over again if they saw some of the campaigns currently running (successful campaigns, we might add).

Take beer advertising. In the past, a beer copywriter looked closely at the product to find his copy platform. And he found "real-draft" Piels, and "cold-brewed" Ballantine. Back a little farther he discovered the "land of the sky blue waters" and "just a kiss of the hops."

In the positioning era, however, effective beer advertising is taking a different tack. "First class is Michelob" positioned the brand as the first American-made premium beer. "The one beer to have when you're having more than one" positioned Schaefer as the brand for the heavy beer drinker.

But there's an imported beer whose positioning strategy is so crystal clear that those old-time beer copywriters probably wouldn't even accept it as advertising.

"You've tasted the German beer that's the most popular in America. Now taste the German beer that's the most popular in Germany." This is how Beck's beer is effectively positioning itself against Lowenbrau.

Then there's Seven-Up's "Un-Cola" campaign.

And *Sports Illustrated's* "Third Newsweekly" program.

All of these positioning campaigns have a number of things in common. They don't emphasize product features, customer benefits or the company's image. Yet, they are all highly successful.

Old Word Gets New Meaning

Like any new concept, positioning isn't new. At least not in the literal sense. What is new is the broader meaning now being given to the word.

Yesterday, positioning was used in a narrow sense to mean what the advertiser did to his product. Today, positioning is used in a broader sense to mean what the advertising does for the product in the prospect's mind. In other words, a successful advertiser today uses advertising to position his product, not to communicate its advantages or features.

Positioning has its roots in the packaged goods field where the concept was called "product positioning." It literally meant the product's form, package size and price as compared to competition.

Procter & Gamble carried the idea one step forward by developing a master copy platform that related each of their competing brands. For example: Tide makes clothes "white." Cheer makes them "whiter than white." And Bold makes them "bright."

Although the advertising for each Procter & Gamble brand might vary from year to year, it never departed from its pre-assigned role or "position" in the master plan.

■ The big breakthrough came when people started thinking of positioning not as something the client does before the advertising is prepared, but as the very objective of the advertising itself. External, rather than internal positioning.

A classic example of looking through the wrong end of the telescope was Ford's introduction of the Edsel. In the ensuing laughter that followed, most people missed the point.

In essence, the Ford people got switched around. The Edsel was a beautiful case of internal positioning to fill a hole between Ford and Mercury on the one hand, and Lincoln on the other. Good strategy inside the building. Bad strategy outside where there was simply no position for this car in a category already cluttered with heavily-chromed, medium-priced cars.

If the Edsel had been tagged a "high performance" car and presented in a sleek two-door, bucket-seat form and given a name to match, no one would have laughed. It could have occupied a position that no one else owned and the ending of the story might have been different.

Remember the Mind Is a Memory Bank

To better understand what an advertiser is up against, it may be helpful to take a closer look at the objective of all advertising programs—the human mind.

Like a memory bank, the mind has a slot or "position" for each bit of information it has chosen to retain. In operation, the mind is a lot like a computer.

But there is one important difference. A computer has to accept what is put into it. The mind does not. In fact, it's quite the opposite.

The mind, as a defense mechanism against the volume of today's communications, screens and rejects much of the information offered it. In general, the mind accepts only that new information which matches its prior knowledge or experience. It filters out everything else.

For example, when a viewer sees a television commercial that says, "NCR means computers," he doesn't accept it. IBM means computers. NCR means National Cash Register.

The computer "position" in the minds of most people is filled by a company called the International Business Machines Corp. For a competitive computer manufacturer to obtain a favorable position in the prospect's mind, he must somehow relate his company to IBM's position.

Yet, too many companies embark on marketing and advertising programs as if the competitor's position did not exist. They advertise their products in a vacuum and are disappointed when their messages fail to get through.

Seven Brands Are Mind's Limit

The mind, as a container for ideas, is totally unsuited to the job at hand.

There are more than 500,000 trademarks registered with the U.S. Patent Office. In addition, untold thousands of unregistered trademarks are in use throughout the country.

During the course of a single year, the average mind is exposed to more than half a million advertising messages.

The target of all this communications ammunition has a reading vocabulary of no more than 25,000 to 50,000 words, and a speaking vocabulary of one-fifth as much.

■ Another limitation: The average human mind, according to Harvard psychologist George A. Miller, cannot deal with more than seven units at a time. (The eighth company in a given field is out of luck.)

Ask someone to name all the brands he or she remembers in a given product category. Rarely will anyone name more than seven. And that's for a high-interest category. For low-interest products, the average consumer can usually name no more than one or two brands.

Yet in category after category, the number of individual brands multiply like rabbits. In 1964, there were seven soft drinks advertised on network television. Today there are 22.

■ To cope with complexity, people have learned to reduce everything to its utmost simplicity.

When asked to describe an offspring's intellectual progress, a person doesn't usually quote vocabulary statistics, reading comprehension, mathematical ability, etc. "He's in seventh grade" is a typical reply.

This "ranking" of people, objects and brands is not only a convenient method of organizing things, but also an absolute necessity if a person is to keep from being overwhelmed by the complexities of life.

You see ranking concepts at work among movies, restaurants, business and military organizations. (Some day someone might even come up with a rating system for politicians.)

Mind Puts Products on Ladders

To cope with advertising's complexity, people have learned to rank products and brands in the mind. Perhaps this can best be visualized by imagining a series of ladders in the mind. On each step is a brand name. And each different ladder represents a different product category.

Some ladders have many steps. (Seven is many.) Others have few, if any.

For an advertiser to increase his brand preference, he must move up the ladder. This can be difficult if the brands above have a strong foothold and no leverage or positioning strategy is applied against them.

For an advertiser to introduce a new product category, he must carry in a new ladder. This, too, is difficult, especially if the new category is not positioned against an old one. The mind has no room for the new and different unless it's related to the old.

That's why if you have a truly new product, it's often better to tell the prospect what the product is not, rather than what it is.

■ The first automobile, for example, was called a "horseless" carriage, a name which allowed the public to position the concept against the existing mode of transportation.

Words like "offtrack" betting, "lead-free" gasoline and "tubeless" tire are all examples of how new concepts can best be positioned against the old.

Names that do not contain an element of positioning usually die out. The "Astrojet" name dreamed up by American Airlines is an example of a glamorous, but unsuccessful name, because it lacks a positioning idea.

Leading Brand Has Big Edge

The weather forecast for the old, traditional ways of advertising is gloomy at best. And nowhere was this more clearly demonstrated than in the recent Atlanta study conducted by Daniel Starch & Staff.

According to Starch, about 25% of those noting a television commercial attributed it to the competition. With virtually no exceptions, high scoring commercials were the brand leaders in their category.

The also-rans didn't fare nearly as well. A David Janssen Excedrin commercial was associated with Anacin twice as often as Excedrin. A Pristeen commercial helped F.D.S., the brand leader, more than it did Pristeen.

This shattering turn of events is certainly "positioning" at work in our over-communicated society. It appears that unless an advertisement is based on a unique idea or position, the message is often put in the mental slot reserved for the leader in the product category.

Clutter is surely part of the reason for the rise of "misidentification." But another, even more important factor is that times have changed. Today, you cannot advertise your product in splendid isolation. Unless your advertising positions your product in relationship to its competition, your advertising is doomed to failure.

Creativity No Longer Enough

In the positioning era, "strategy" is king. It made little difference how clever the ads of RCA, General Electric and Bristol-Myers were. Or how well the layout, copy and typography were executed. Their strategy of attacking the leaders head-on was wrong.

Even creativity in the form of a slogan no longer serves much of a purpose if it doesn't position the product.

"If you got it, flaunt it" and "We must be doing something right" achieved enormous popularity without doing much for Braniff and Rheingold. And we predict that "Try it, you'll like it" won't do much for Alka-Seltzer.

As far as advertising is concerned, the good old days are gone forever.

As the president of a large consumer products company said recently, "Count on your fingers the number of successful new national brands introduced in the last two years. You won't get to your pinky."

Not that a lot of companies haven't tried. Every supermarket is filled with shelf after shelf of "half successful" brands. The manufacturers of these me-too products cling to the hope that they can develop a brilliant advertising campaign which will lift their offspring into the winner's circle.

Meanwhile, they hang in there with coupons, deals, point of purchase displays. But profits are hard to come by and that "brilliant" advertising campaign, even if it comes, doesn't ever seem to turn the brand around.

No wonder management people turn skeptical when the subject of advertising comes up. And instead of looking for new ways to put the power of advertising to work, management invents schemes for reducing the cost of what they are currently doing. Witness the rise of the house agency, the media buying service, the barter deal.

Ads Don't Work Like They Used To

The chaos in the marketplace is a reflection of the fact that advertising just doesn't work like it used to. But old traditional ways of doing things die hard. "There's no reason that advertising can't do the job," say the defenders of the status quo, "as long as the product is good, the plan is sound and the commercials are creative."

But they overlook one big, loud reason. The marketplace itself. The noise level today is far too high. Not only the volume of advertising, but also the volume of products and brands.

To cope with this assault on his or her mind, the average consumer has run out of brain power and mental ability. And with a rising standard of living the av-

erage consumer is less and less interested in making the "best" choice. For many of today's more affluent customers, a "satisfactory" brand is good enough.

Advertising prepared in the old, traditional ways has no hope of being successful in today's chaotic marketplace.

■ In the past, advertising was prepared in isolation. That is, you studied the product and its features and then you prepared advertising which communicated to your customers and prospects the benefits of those features.

It didn't make much difference whether the competition offered those features or not. In the traditional approach, you ignored competition and made every claim seem like a preemptive claim. Mentioning a competitive product, for example, was considered not only bad taste, but poor strategy as well.

In the positioning era, however, the rules are reversed. To establish a position, you must often not only name competitive names, but also ignore most of the old advertising rules as well.

In category after category, the prospect already knows the benefits of using the product. To climb on his product ladder, you must relate your brand to the brands already there.

Avis Took 'Against' Position

In today's marketplace, the competitor's image is just as important as your own. Sometimes more important. An early success in the positioning era was the famous Avis campaign.

The Avis campaign will go down in marketing history as a classic example of establishing the "against" position. In the case of Avis, this was a position against the leader.

"Avis is only No. 2 in rent-a-cars, so why go with us? We try harder."

For 13 straight years, Avis lost money. Then they admitted they were No. 2 and have made money every year since. Avis was able to make substantial gains because they recognized the position of Hertz and didn't try to attack them head-on.

VW Made 'Ugly' Position Work

A company can sometimes be successful by accepting a position that no one else wants. For example, virtually all automobile manufacturers want the public to think they make cars that are good looking. As a result, Volkswagen was able to establish a unique position for themselves. By default.

The strength of this position, of course, is that it communicates the idea of reliability in a powerful way. "The 1970 VW will stay ugly longer" was a

powerful statement because it is psychologically sound. When an advertiser admits a negative, the reader is inclined to give them the positive.

A similar principle is involved in Smucker's jams and jellies. "With a name like Smucker's," says the advertising, "you know it's got to be good."

Battle of the Colas

The advantage of owning a position can be seen most clearly in the soft drink field. Three major cola brands compete in what is really not a contest. For every ten bottles of Coke, only four bottles of Pepsi and one bottle of Royal Crown are consumed.

While there may be room in the market for a No. 2 cola, the position of Royal Crown is weak. In 1970, for example, Coca-Cola's sales increase over the previous year (168,000,000 cases) was more than Royal Crown's entire volume (156,-000,000 cases).

Obviously, Coke has a strong grip on the cola position. And there's not much room left for the other brands. But, strange as it might seem, there might be a spot for a reverse kind of product. One of the most interesting positioning ideas is the one currently being used by Seven-Up. It's the "Un-Cola" and it seems silly until you take a closer look.

"Wet and Wild" was a good campaign in the image era. But the "Un-Cola" is a great program in the positioning era. Sales jumped something like 10% the first year the product was positioned against the cola field. And the increases have continued.

The brilliance of this idea can only be appreciated when you comprehend the intense share of mind enjoyed by the cola category. Two out of three soft drinks consumed in the U.S. are cola drinks.

By linking the product to what's already in the mind of the prospect, the Un-Cola position establishes Seven-Up as an alternative to a cola drink.

■ A somewhat similar positioning program is working in the media field. This is the "third newsweekly" concept being used by *Sports Illustrated* to get into the mind of the media buyer.

It obviously is an immensely successful program. But what may not be so obvious is why it works. The "third newsweekly" certainly doesn't describe *Sports Illustrated*. (As the Un-Cola doesn't describe Seven-Up.)

What it does do, however, is to relate the magazine to a media category that is uppermost in the prospect's mind (as the Un-Cola relates to the soft drink category that is uppermost in the mind).

Both the Seven-Up and the *Sports Illustrated* programs are dramatic reminders that positioning is not something you do with the product. Positioning is something you do with the mind. That is, you position the product in the mind of the prospect.

You Can Reposition Competitor

In order to position your own brand, it's sometimes necessary to reposition the competitor.

In the case of Beck's beer, the repositioning is done at the expense of Lowenbrau: "You've tasted the German beer that's the most popular in America. Now taste the German beer that's the most popular in Germany."

This strategy works because the prospect had assumed something about Lowenbrau that wasn't true.

The current program for Raphael aperitif wine also illustrates this point. The ads show a bottle of "made in France" Raphael and a bottle of "made in U.S.A." Dubonnet. "For $1.00 a bottle less," says the headline, "you can enjoy the imported one." The shock, of course, is to find that Dubonnet is a product of the U.S.

Plight of Airline X

In the positioning era, the name of a company or product is becoming more and more important. The name is the hook that allows the mind to hang the brand on its product ladder. Given a poor name, even the best brand in the world won't be able to hang on.

Take the airline industry. The big four domestic carriers are United, American, TWA and an airline we'll call Airline X.

Like all airlines, Airline X has had its ups and downs. Unfortunately, there have been more downs than ups. But unlike some of its more complacent competitors, Airline X has tried. A number of years ago, it brought in big league marketing people and pushed in the throttle.

Airline X was among the first to "paint the planes," "improve the food" and "dress up the stewardesses" in an effort to improve its reputation.

And Airline X hasn't been bashful when it comes to spending money. Year after year, it has one of the biggest advertising budgets in the industry. Even though it advertises itself as "the second largest passenger carrier of all the airlines in the free world," you may not have guessed that Airline X is Eastern. Right up there spending with the world-wide names.

For all that money, what do you think of Eastern? Where do you think they fly? Up and down the East Coast, to Boston, Washington, Miami, right? Well, Eastern also goes to St. Louis, New Orleans, Atlanta, San Francisco, Acapulco. But Eastern has a regional name and

their competitors have broader names which tell the prospect they fly everywhere.

■ Look at the problem from just one of Eastern's cities, Indianapolis. From Indianapolis, Eastern flies *north* to Chicago, Milwaukee and Minneapolis. And *south* to Birmingham and Mobile. They just don't happen to fly *east*.

And then there is the lush San Juan run which Eastern has been serving for more than 25 years. Eastern used to get the lion's share of this market. Then early last year American Airlines took over Trans Caribbean. So today, who is number one to the San Juan sun? Why American, of course.

No matter how hard you try, you can't hang "The Wings of Man" on a regional name. When the prospect is given a choice, he or she is going to prefer the national airline, not the regional one.

B. F. Goodrich Has Identity Crisis

What does a company do when its name (Goodrich) is similar to the name of a much larger company in the same field (Goodyear)?

Goodrich has problems. They could reinvent the wheel and Goodyear would get most of the credit.

If you watched the Super Bowl last January, you saw both Goodrich and Goodyear advertise their "American-made radial-ply tires." But which company do you think got their money's worth at $200,000 a pop?

We haven't seen the research, but our bet would be on Goodyear, the company that owns the tire position.

Beware of the No-Name Trap

But even bad names like Eastern and Goodrich are better than no name at all.

In *Fortune's* list of 500 largest industrials, there are now 16 corporate nonentities. That is, 16 major American companies have legally changed their names to meaningless initials.

How many of these companies can you recognize: ACF, AMF, AMP, ATO, CPC, ESB, FMC, GAF, NVF, NL, PPG, RCA, SCM, TRW, USM and VF?

These are not tiny companies either. The smallest of them, AMP, has more than 10,000 employes and sales of over $225,000,000 a year.

What companies like ACF, AMF, AMP and the others fail to realize is that their initials have to stand for something. A prospect must know your name first before he or she can remember your initials.

GE stands for General Electric. IBM stands for International Business Machines. And everyone knows it. But how many people knew that ACF stood for American Car & Foundry?

Furthermore, now that ACF has legally changed its name to initials, there's presumably no way to even expose the prospect to the original name.

An exception seems to be RCA. After all, everyone knows that RCA stands for, or rather used to stand for, Radio Corp. of America.

That may be true today. But what about tomorrow? What will people think 20 years from now when they see those strange initials. Roman Catholic Archdiocese?

And take Corn Products Co. Presumably it changed its name to CPC International because it makes products out of lots of things besides corn, but you can't remember "CPC" without bringing Corn Products Co. to mind. The tragedy is, CPC made the change to "escape" the past. Yet the exact opposite occurred.

Line Extension Can Be Trap, Too

Names are tricky. Consider the Protein 21/29 shampoo, hair spray, conditioner, concentrate mess.

Back in 1970, the Mennen Co. introduced a combination shampoo conditioner called "Protein 21." By moving rapidly with a $6,000,000 introductory campaign (followed by a $9,000,000 program the next year), Mennen rapidly carved out a 13% share of the $300,-000,000 shampoo market.

Then Mennen hit the line extension lure. In rapid succession, the company introduced Protein 21 hair spray, Protein 29 hair spray (for men), Protein 21 conditioner (in two formulas), Protein 21 concentrate. To add to the confusion, the original Protein 21 was available in three different formulas (for dry, oily and regular hair).

Can you imagine how confused the prospect must be trying to figure out what to put on his or her head? No wonder Protein 21's share of the shampoo market has fallen from 13% to 11%. And the decline is bound to continue.

Free Ride Can Be Costly

Another similar marketing pitfall recently befell, of all companies, Miles Laboratories.

You can see how it happens. A bunch of the boys are sitting around a conference table trying to name a new cold remedy.

"I have it," says Harry. "Let's call it Alka-Seltzer Plus. That way we can take advantage of the $20,000,000 we're already spending to promote the Alka-Seltzer name."

"Good thinking, Harry," and another money-saving idea is instantly accepted.

But lo and behold, instead of eating into the Dristan and Contac market, the new product turns around and eats into the Alka-Seltzer market.

And you know Miles must be worried. In every tv commercial, the "Alka-Seltzer" gets smaller and smaller and the "Plus" gets bigger and bigger.

Related to the free-ride trap, but not exactly the same, is another common error of judgment called the "well-known name" trap.

Both General Electric and RCA thought they could take their strong positions against IBM in computers. But just because a company is well-known in one field doesn't mean it can transfer that recognition to another.

In other words, your brand can be on top of one ladder and nowhere on another. And the further apart the products are conceptually, the greater the difficulty of making the jump.

In the past when there were fewer companies and fewer products, a well-known name was a much greater asset than it is today. Because of the noise level, a "well-known" company has tremendous difficulty trying to establish a position in a different field than the one in which it built its reputation.

You Can't Appeal to Everyone

A human emotion called "greed" often leads an advertiser into another error. American Motors' introduction of the Hornet is one of the best examples of the "everybody" trap.

You might remember the ads, "The little rich car. American Motors Hornet: $1,994 to $3,589."

A product that tries to appeal to everyone winds up appealing to no one. People who want to spend $3,500 for a car don't buy the Hornet because they don't want their friends to think they're driving a $1,900 car. People who want to spend $1,900 for a car don't buy the Hornet because they don't want a car with $1,600 worth of accessories taken off of it.

Avoid the F.W.M.T.S. Trap

If the current Avis advertising is any indication, the company has "forgotten what made them successful."

The original campaign not only related No. 2 Avis to No. 1 Hertz, but also exploited the love that people have for the underdog. The new campaign (Avis is going to be No. 1) not only is conventional "brag and boast" advertising, but also dares the prospect to make the prediction not come true.

Our prediction: Avis ain't going to be No. 1. Further prediction: Avis will lose ground to Hertz and National.

Another company that seems to have fallen into the forgotten what made them successful trap is Volkswagen.

"Think small" was perhaps the most famous advertisement of the '60s. Yet last year VW ran an ad that said, "Volkswagen introduces a new kind of Volkswagen. Big."

O.K., Volkswagen, should we think small or should we think big?

Confusion is the enemy of successful positioning. Prediction: Rapid erosion of the Beetle's position in the U.S. market.

The world seems to be turning faster.

Years ago, a successful product might live 50 years or more before fading away. Today, a product's life cycle is much shorter. Sometimes it can be measured in months instead of years.

New products, new services, new markets, even new media are constantly being born. They grow up into adulthood and then slide into oblivion. And a new cycle starts again.

Yesterday, beer and hard liquor were campus favorites. Today it's wine.

Yesterday, the well-groomed man had his hair cut every week. Today, it's every month or two.

Yesterday, the way to reach the masses was the mass magazines. Today, it's network tv. Tomorrow, it could be cable.

The only permanent thing in life today is change. And the successful companies of tomorrow will be those companies that have learned to cope with it.

The acceleration of "change" creates enormous pressures on companies to think in terms of tactics rather than strategy. As one respected advertising man commented, "The day seems to be past when long-range strategy can be a winning technique."

But is change the way to keep pace with change? The exact opposite appears to be true.

The landscape is littered with the debris of projects that companies rushed into in attempting to "keep pace." Singer trying to move into the boom in home appliances. RCA moving into the boom in computers. General Foods moving into the boom in fast-food outlets. Not to mention the hundreds of companies that threw away their corporate identities to chase the passing fad to initials.

While the programs of those who kept at what they did best and held their ground have been immensely successful. Maytag selling their reliable appliances. Walt Disney selling his world of fantasy and fun. Avon calling.

And take margarine. Thirty years ago the first successful margarine brands positioned themselves against butter. "Tastes like the high-priced spread," said a typical ad.

And what works today? Why the same strategy. "It isn't nice to fool Mother Nature," says the Chiffon commercial, and sales go up 25%. Chiffon is once again the best selling brand of soft margarine.

Long-Range Thinking Important

Change is a wave on the ocean of time. Short-term, the waves cause agitation and confusion, but long-term the underlying currents are much more significant.

To cope with change, it's important to take a long-range point of view. To determine your basic business. Positioning is a concept that is cumulative. Something that takes advantage of advertising's long-range nature.

In the '70s, a company must think even more strategically than it did before. Changing the direction of a large company is like trying to turn an aircraft carrier. It takes a mile before anything happens. And if it was a wrong turn, getting back on course takes even longer.

To play the game successfully, you must make decisions on what your company will be doing not next month or next year, but in five years, ten years. In other words, instead of turning the wheel to meet each fresh wave, a company must point itself in the right direction.

You must have vision. There's no sense building a position based on a technology that's too narrow. Or a product that's becoming obsolete. Remember the famous "Harvard Business Review" article entitled "Marketing Myopia"? It still applies.

If a company has positioned itself in the right direction, it will be able to ride the currents of change, ready to take advantage of those opportunities that are right for it. But when an opportunity arrives, a company must be ready to move quickly.

■ Because of the enormous advantages that accrue to being the leader, most companies are not interested in learning how to *compete* with the leader. They want to be the leader. They want to be Hertz rather than Avis. *Time* rather than *Newsweek*. General Electric rather than Westinghouse.

Historically, however, product leadership is usually the result of an accident, rather than a preconceived plan.

The xerography process, for example, was offered to 32 different companies (including IBM and Kodak) before it wound up at the old Haloid Co. Renamed Haloid Xerox and then finally Xerox, the company has since dominated the copier market. Xerox now owns the copier position.

Were IBM and Kodak stupid to turn down xerography? Of course not. These companies reject thousands of ideas every year.

Perhaps a better description of the situation at the time was that Haloid, a small manufacturer of photographic supplies, was desperate, and the others weren't. As a result, it took a chance that more prudent companies couldn't be expected to take.

When you trace the history of how leadership positions were established, from Hershey in chocolate to Hertz in rent-a-cars, the common thread is not marketing skill or even product innovation. The common thread is seizing the initiative before the competitor has a chance to get established. In someone's oldtime military terms, the marketing leader "got there firstest with the mostest." The leader usually poured in the marketing money while the situation was still fluid.

IBM, for example, didn't invent the computer. Sperry Rand did. But IBM owns the computer position because they built their computer fortress before competition arrived.

And the position that Hershey established in chocolate was so strong they didn't need to advertise at all, a luxury that competitors like Nestle couldn't afford.

You can see that establishing a leadership position depends not only on luck and timing, but also upon a willingness to "pour it on" when others stand back and wait.

■ Yet all too often, the product leader makes the fatal mistake of attributing its success to marketing skill. As a result, it thinks it can transfer that skill to other products and other marketing situations.

Witness, for example, the sorry record of Xerox in computers. In May of 1969, Xerox exchanged nearly 10,000,000 shares of stock (worth nearly a billion dollars) for Scientific Data Systems Inc. Since the acquisition, the company (renamed Xerox Data Systems) has *lost* millions of dollars, and without Xerox's support would have probably gone bankrupt.

And the mecca of marketing knowledge, International Business Machines Corp., hasn't done much better. So far, the IBM plain-paper copier hasn't made much of a dent in Xerox's business. Touché.

The rules of positioning hold for all types of products. In the packaged goods area, for example, Bristol-Myers tried to take on Crest toothpaste with Fact (killed after $5,000,000 was spent on promotion). Then they tried to go after Alka-Seltzer with Resolve (killed after $11,000,000 was spent). And according to a headline in the Feb. 7 issue of ADVERTISING AGE, "Bristol-Myers will test Dissolve aspirin in an attempt to unseat Bayer."

The suicidal bent of companies that go head-on against established competition is hard to understand. They know the score, yet they forge ahead anyway. In the marketing war, a "charge of the light brigade" happens every day. With the same predictable result.

One Strategy for Leader

Successful marketing strategy usually consists of keeping your eyes open to possibilities and then striking before the product ladder is firmly fixed.

As a matter of fact, the marketing leader is usually the one who moves the ladder into the mind with his or her brand nailed to the one and only rung. Once there, what can a company do to keep its top-dog position?

There are two basic strategies that should be used hand in hand. They seem contradictory, but aren't. One is to ignore competition, and the other is to cover all bets.

As long as a company owns the position, there's no point in running ads that scream, "We're No. 1." Much better is to enhance the product category in the prospect's mind. Notice the current IBM campaign that ignores competition and sells the value of computers. All computers, not just the company's types.

Although the leader's advertising should ignore the competition, the leader shouldn't. The second rule is to cover all bets.

This means a leader should swallow his or her pride and adopt every new product development as soon as it shows signs of promise. Too often, however, the leader pooh-poohs the development, and doesn't wake up until it's too late.

Another Strategy for Non-Leaders

Most companies are in the No. 2, 3, 4 or even worse category. What then?

Hope springs eternal in the human breast. Nine times out of ten, the also-ran sets out to attack the leader, a la RCA's assault on IBM. Result: Disaster.

Simply stated, the first rule of positioning is this: You can't compete head-on against a company that has a strong, established position. You can go around, under or over, but never head-to-head.

The leader owns the high ground. The No. 1 position in the prospect's mind. The top rung of the product ladder.

The classic example of No. 2 strategy is Avis. But many marketing people misread the Avis story. They assume the company was successful because it tried harder.

Not at all. Avis was successful because it related itself to the position of Hertz. Avis preempted the No. 2 position. (If trying harder were the secret of success, Harold Stassen would be president.)

Most marketplaces have room for a strong No. 2 company provided they position themselves clearly as an alternative to the leader. In the computer field, for example, Honeywell has used this strategy successfully.

"The other computer company vs. Mr. Big," says a typical Honeywell ad. Honeywell is doing what none of the other computer companies seems to be willing to do. Admit that IBM is, in fact, the leader in the computer business. Maybe that's why Honeywell and Mr. Big are the only large companies reported to be making money on computers.

Some 'Strong' Positions Aren't

Yet there are positions that can be taken. These are positions that look strong, but in reality are weak.

Take the position of Scott in paper products. Scott has about 40% of the $1.2 billion market for towels, napkins, toilet tissues and other consumer paper products. But Scott, like Mennen with Protein 21, fell into the line-extension trap.

ScotTowels, ScotTissue, Scotties, Scottkins, even BabyScott. All of these names undermined the Scott foundation. The more products hung on the Scott name, the less meaning the name had to the average consumer.

When Procter & Gamble attacked with Mr. Whipple and his tissue-squeezers, it was no contest. Charmin is now the No. 1 brand in the toilet-tissue market.

In Scott's case, a large "share of market" didn't mean they owned the position. More important is a large "share of mind." The housewife could write "Charmin, Kleenex, Bounty and Pampers" on her shopping list and know exactly what products she was going to get. "Scott" on a shopping list has no meaning. The actual brand names aren't much help either. Which brand, for example, is engineered for the nose, Scotties or ScotTissue?

In positioning terms, the name "Scott" exists in limbo. It isn't firmly ensconced on any product ladder.

Eliminate Egos From Decision Making

To repeat, the name is the hook that hangs the brand on the product ladder in the prospect's mind. In the positioning era, the brand name to give a product is probably a company's single, most important marketing decision.

To be successful in the positioning era, advertising and marketing people must be brutally frank. They must try to eliminate all ego from the decision making process. It only clouds the issue.

One of the most critical aspects of "positioning" is being able to evaluate objectively products and how they are viewed by customers and prospects.

As a rule, when it comes to building strong programs, trust no one, especially managers who are all wrapped up in their products. The closer people get to products, the more they defend old decisions or old promises.

Successful companies get their information from the marketplace. That's the place where the program has to succeed, not in the product manager's office.

■ A company that keeps its eye on Tom, Dick and Harry is going to miss Pierre, Hans and Yoshio.

Marketing is rapidly becoming a worldwide ball game. A company that owns a position in one country now finds that it can use that position to wedge its way into another.

IBM has 62% of the German computer market. Is this fact surprising? It shouldn't be. IBM earns more than 50% of its profits outside the U.S.

As companies start to operate on a worldwide basis, they often discover they have a name problem.

A typical example is U.S. Rubber, a worldwide company that marketed many products not made of rubber. Changing the name to Uniroyal created a new corporate identity that could be used worldwide.

Creativity Takes Back Seat

In the '70s, creativity will have to take a back seat to strategy.

ADVERTISING AGE itself reflects this fact. Today you find fewer stories about individual campaigns and more stories about what's happening in an entire industry. Creativity alone isn't a worthwhile objective in an era where a company can spend millions of dollars on great advertising and still fail miserably in the marketplace.

Consider what Harry McMahan calls the "Curse of Clio." In the past, the American Festival has made special awards to "Hall of Fame Classics." Of the 41 agencies that won these Clio awards, 31 have lost some or all of these particular accounts.

But the cult of creativity dies hard. One agency president said recently, "Oh, we do positioning all the time. But after we develop the position, we turn it over to the creative department." And too often, of course, the creativity does nothing but obscure the positioning.

In the positioning era, the key to success is to run the naked positioning statement, unadorned by so-called creativity.

Ask Yourself These Questions

If these examples have moved you to want to apply positioning thinking to your own company's situation, here are some questions to ask yourself:

1. What position, if any, do we already own in the prospect's mind?

Get the answer to this question from the marketplace, not the marketing manager. If this requires a few dollars for research, so be it. Spend the money. It's better to know exactly what you're up against now than to discover it later when nothing can be done about it.

2. What position do we want to own?

Here is where you bring out your crystal ball and try to figure out the best position to own from a long-term point of view.

3. What companies must be outgunned if we are to establish that position?

If your proposed position calls for a head-to-head approach against a mar-

keting leader, forget it. It's better to go around an obstacle rather than over it. Back up. Try to select a position that no one else has a firm grip on.

4. Do we have enough marketing money to occupy and hold the position?

A big obstacle to successful positioning is attempting to achieve the impossible. It takes money to build a share of mind. It takes money to establish a position. It takes money to hold a position once you've established it.

The noise level today is fierce. There are just too many "me-too" products and too many "me-too" companies vying for the mind of the prospect. Getting noticed is getting tougher.

5. Do we have the guts to stick with one consistent positioning concept?

With the noise level out there, a company has to be bold enough and consistent enough to cut through.

The first step in a positioning program normally entails running fewer programs, but stronger ones. This sounds simple, but actually runs counter to what usually happens as corporations get larger. They normally run more programs, but weaker ones. It's this fragmentation that can make many large advertising budgets just about invisible in today's media storm.

6. Does our creative approach match our positioning strategy?

Creative people often resist positioning thinking because they believe it restricts their creativity. And it does. But creativity isn't the objective in the '70s. Even "communications" itself isn't the objective.

The name of the marketing game in the '70s is "positioning." And only the better players will survive.

Reprinted from "Advertising Age," April 24, 1972, pp. 35, 38; May 1, 1972, pp. 51-52, 54; May 8, 1972, pp. 114, 116

No, this is not the era

of positioning

BY LEO GREENLAND
President, Smith/Greenland Co.
New York

We in advertising take one hell of a lot of abuse. We all know how people feel about advertising and the kind of continuing scathing criticism to which we are constantly subjected. Advertising people are regarded by some as being shallow, glib, superficial and hucksterish.

People don't believe us, and sometimes for good reason. All too often one amongst us will rise up and offer a panacea for all that ails products that aren't selling. All too often someone will come along and whittle the practice of advertising down to magic formulas and pseudo-scientific findings.

I admit that it is often a great temptation to embrace a new ghuru when our products aren't selling. It is tempting to look for new buzzwords, new terminology, new analytical techniques, new position papers—in short, anything that will move a product off a shelf.

ADVERTISING AGE has devoted a great deal of space to a series of articles that prophetically told us that the answer to advertising in the '70s is positioning (AA, April 24 to May 8). I was sufficiently intrigued by these articles to read them fully. If the biblical and divinely sounding title was enough to turn me on, the substance of the articles' point of view did the exact opposite.

■ I was amused when I read these articles. It became clear to me that we don't really live in an era of positioning at all. We live in an era of cultists, and each cult has the ultimate answer to the ultimate problem of advertising. In fairness to each cult, both old and new, I think we should begin identifying ourselves by wearing certain clearly recognizable arm bands on our grey flannel suits. One would say, "Positionist"; another would say, "Segmentationist"; a third, "psychographicist," and so on. In this way the advertiser will know which cult we belong to and can worship at the altar of the cult of his choice.

And when we go to the mountain and implore our two new ghuru theorists to tell us what to do, a bolt of typewriter ribbon will come down, and a voice will say, "Creativity is dead. Positioning in the '70s is the answer. Long live the king."

A Good Idea Still Helps

If I sound cynical, it's because I am. I am bored with prophetic new formulas for successful advertising. Not only bored, but downright embarrassed.

What today's ghuru twins fail to tell us after we have carefully analyzed why our products do not sell is, "Dumb-dumb, what you really need is one hell of a good idea!"

I can understand why our profession isn't taken seriously when someone comes along and blurts out in all seriousness that creativity is dead and on to the next solution. Creativity is not only alive and well, but is living here, not Argentina. And contrary to the limited insights of the authors of the positioning series, positioning of products isn't beginning in the '70s. It's been with us for many, many years.

Basically, where I take issue with the positionist cultists—or any cultist for that matter—is in the assessment of one ingredient always being more important to successful advertising than any other ingredient. The cultist becomes dogmatic and inflexible in his approach to advertising because he is saying that it is positioning and nothing else that matters.

Forgive me for saying something you're all probably sick of hearing by now, but sometimes basics need to be said. We all know the ingredients that take a product from inception to a consumer's home. And we all know that a brilliantly conceived message will tip the marketplace in favor of your product.

The magic in advertising is in making the message exciting, breathtaking, pro-vocative, memorable and motivating. Of course strategy is absolutely fundamental and vital—but that's not the only answer. The answer is shaping a creative strategy so that it comes alive.

And why, for heaven's sake, do the positionist cultists signal the end of the importance of product-message advertising as if product features and performance were suddenly of no interest to consumers in their supposed new positioning era? It's a good thing that Timex got in under the gun of the 1940s. If they'd invented the tough little watch during the 1970s, they'd have had to sell it as the timepiece that sits between the sun-dial and Accutron, and totally ignore its incredible performance story.

Positioning Is Only Part of It

The point is that positioning need not be viewed as a technique apart from product message. It isn't either/or. Who can argue that distinctive positioning *plus* a product differentiation message will inevitably be more persuasive than a positioning distinction alone?

For example, you are responsible for a 100mm cigaret. You now must tell the world about the wonders of this new cigaret. That, basically, is the strategy.

The creative strategies for Benson & Hedges and for Pall Mall had to be fairly similar. The execution of the campaign for one of these was brilliant and masterful. It had all of America laughing over, and remembering the name of, the long cigaret which was cut off by closing car windows and elevator doors. It was everything advertising should be: Newsy, memorable, attractive. The execution of the other campaign was competent—very competent—but competence lost out to creativity. And we're just not talking aesthetics either. Benson & Hedges took over the lion's share of the 100mm cigaret *because* of brilliant creative strategy.

I'm here today to explore with you how cultists oversimplify and run from basics in advertising. To do so, I'm afraid I must refute the logic of the positionist cult. By so doing, I hope I can symbolically discourage the advent of future cults. Then I'd like to explore the creative elements of some famous campaigns to analyze what made them great and why they sold products. And last, I'd like to do my own assessment of what the '70s really hold in store for us.

Positioning Through the Ages

Let's begin with positioning. Is it new? It's as new as Columbus. Here's a quote from an advertising trade publication on positioning: "The old omnibus advertising began to give way to the advertisement designed as a special tool to reach the special class of people automatically selected by the given publication in which it appeared."

Are we talking about 1972? No. This quote appeared in *Printers' Ink* in 1908.

Here is a description of product positioning in 1926 taken from the same magazine. "This was a device for fastening clothing designed to take the place of buttons, hooks and eyes and other fastening methods. In 1926 the Hookless Fastener Co. (now Talon Inc.) set out upon an advertising and merchandising program to establish the product definitely in the public mind and give it an identity apart from whatever product it might be used on."

And how about this *Printers' Ink* evaluation of a famous cigaret campaign of 1928: " 'Reach for a Lucky instead of a sweet' shows positioning of a product for a particular kind of consumer."

These are all examples of an early understanding of positioning. It wasn't new then, just as it isn't new now. It was just as basic to advertising as all the other elements. Even the historically competitive soap market was engaging in positioning advertising as early as 1901. Cuticura soap advertised itself to the athlete who was bothered by "golf rash, heat rash, or any irritation produced by athletics."

Upstart Plymouth Used It in 1932

Almost everybody in advertising will admit that the late J. Sterling Getchell's advertising for Plymouth in 1932 is one of the alltime greats. It is a classic example of creative positioning. For those of you who don't remember it, it's often referred to as the "Look at All Three" ad. It positioned Plymouth with the leaders in the low-price field. Plymouth was entering its third year, having been launched in 1929. It was naturally a very new and a very small contender in the low-price field then dominated entirely by Ford and Chevrolet.

At the time, Chevrolet was in a very good position, having out-styled and out-sold the old Model A Ford, and had obtained a very strong hold on the market while Ford had been out of production retooling. Hardly anyone knew or cared about Mr. Chrysler's new Plymouth—until the ad which broke tradition and referred to the competition. Under the banner headline of "Look at All Three" ran the line, "But don't buy any low-priced car until you've driven the new Plymouth with floating power." Under the subhead was a photograph of Walter P. Chrysler staring earnestly at you from the page, followed by a statement from him.

The day the ad was published in newspapers all over the country, the reaction was unmistakable. Plymouth, over night, had become a real contender in the low-price field, and has remained so ever since. By 1941, sales ran well over 600,000 cars a year.

I could go on and on with these kinds of examples to show that positioning has always been an important factor in advertising. Positioning is no different from any other traditional technique of merely distinguishing a product within its competitive marketplace. Positioning —whether through consumer segmentation, imagery or product distinction, put-up or price-point differentiation, you name it—are all part of the same phenomenon. And none of them can legitimately be described as new.

How No-Cal Positioning Flopped

I would now like to move on to the subject of positioning without creativity to demonstrate that one without the other equals failure.

No-Cal offers us a classic example. Here's a company (Kirsch Beverages Inc.) that did everything our positionist cultists tell us is their secret for marketing success. They had a beat on the soft drink industry because they were the first to come up with a calorie-free, diet soft drink when we were all becoming very weight conscious. Not only that, but the company did what the positionists tell us can't fail—they named their product after the marketing position they assumed—No-Cal. So there we have it. They were there first with a unique product, and had a great position going for it.

From the positionist point of view, one would think that No-Cal dominated its field the way IBM and Polaroid did theirs. As you know, the answer is no. No-Cal did not. Why? Because No-Cal went through one of the most bland advertising campaigns I've ever seen. Every other diet soft drink that came along kicked No-Cal's bubbles in with better advertising and execution—a classic example of a company being there first with a product and losing the subsequent market share because of ineffectual execution of the unique selling proposition.

I think you'll agree that the message is just as essential as the position. George Eastman seemed to be aware of that at the beginning of this century when his new product was merchandised to Americans with the promise, "You press the button—we do the rest." As early as 1903, Ford was the "Boss of the Road" and Packard was confidently advising people to "Ask the man who owns one." We started "Watching the Fords go by" in 1907, and the Cadillac of 1912 was already the "Standard of the World."

Remember These Slogans?

Throughout the history of advertising, literally thousands of catchy phrases made for instant recognition. I'll give you all a little quiz. I'll rattle off a handful of famous advertising phrases and see if you can identify the product:

"We'll take good care of you"; "And away go troubles down the drain"; "Babies are our business . . . our only business"; "The best aid is first aid"; "The beer that made Milwaukee famous"; "The biggest should do more. It's only right . . ."; "Born in 1820, still going strong"; "Breakfast of Champions"; "The brisk tea"; "The Champagne of bottle beer"; "The coffee-er coffee"; "Come alive"; "A cut above the commonplace"; "Does she . . . or doesn't she"; "The extra care airline"; "Filter, flavor, flip-top box"; "Helps build strong bodies 12 ways"; and "Look for this famous name in the oval."

Fun, isn't it? But now, I want to make a point about the role of creativity relative to positioning. And to show why it's so important, let's assume that you've developed a sound marketing strategy for a product, and all signals indicate that the product can't miss. It's a good product, it's positioned well, your consumer testing rates high, and so on . . . all the signs of strong product life. Now you're ready for the advertising message, the essential ingredient that hits the point home hard and effectively.

But what if you should miss the boat on the proper expression and execution of that all important message? Just as in my earlier example of Benson & Hedges and Pall Mall, the advertising message that is memorable will surely consummate a well-planned marketing strategy.

Seven-Up wisely decided to position itself as an alternative to the cola drinks which had the overwhelming share of the soft drink market. Excellent positioning. But what if its message had been less brilliant? Would the impact have been the same if the message read "7Up Is *Not* a Cola" rather than "7Up. The *Un*-Cola?" Would Heinz have been effective if the line read "Heinz's Ketchup Runs Slowly" rather than "The Slowest Ketchup in Town?"

Do These Slogans Grab You?

Let's play another little game. Let's see what happens if we alter one or two words in some advertising lines that we have come to accept as classics. Let's see if the impact remains the same. I'll give the "positioning-style" copy lines. See if you can remember the lines as some great writers shaped them. "Let us drive you in our bus instead of driving your own car." "Shop by turning the pages of our directory." "If you're going to drink a lot of beer, Schaefer is a good beer to drink." "We don't rent as many cars, so we have to do more for our customers." "The luxury standard of bottled beers." "You'll find a sympathetic ear at Chase-Manhattan."

Well, you get the idea.

Another premise developed by the positionist cultists is that when a well-known brand places more products using the same brand name on the market, the less meaning the name has to the average consumer. The cultists called this marketing strategy the "line-extension trap," and Scott was used as the victim, and Charmin as the victor. It is claimed that the housewife wasn't going to write the name "Scott" on her shopping list because the name has no meaning in and by itself.

We'll let Scott speak for itself, but the positionists had better start loosening their arm bands if they're going to use logic that can be refuted so easily.

Creative ideas, truly big ideas can do more to establish a position than the product itself, particularly if there is no basic difference in products in the same

brand category.

Take the case of Ajax cleanser. As told by Richard Bowman of Norman, Craig & Kummel, the last thing anyone needed in 1964 was another detergent. Colgate had an excellent product, but competitive advertising was spending in excess of $60,000,000. The competition was in many shapes and forms—high sudsers, low sudsers, liquids, powders and pills and packets.

■ The strategy for Ajax was relatively simple. Colgate wanted Ajax to stand for power, to be the strongest detergent the housewife could put in her laundry machine safely, plus take advantage of the Ajax name. Their research showed that it's no surprise that what a woman wants isn't really clean clothes. She *has* to get them clean because they're dirty. What the woman wants is no dirt at all. The problem is, she *hates* dirt. It was on that premise that the agency got the line "stronger than dirt."

Next was not how do we stay clean, but how do we get on the lady's side and help her win her fight against dirt which is really a fight for good versus evil. It was within that framework that the Ajax White Knight was unlocked as the mythical helper that turned a product into a hero. As a result of the "stronger than dirt" campaign with White Knight graphics, Colgate's House of Ajax line climbed to the 20% market share level by 1967.

Did VW Creativity Boom or Bust?

Everyone in this room is familiar with the Volkswagen success story and the brilliant advertising by Doyle Dane Bernbach which will always serve as a milestone for the advertising industry. I don't have to recall to you how Doyle Dane broke new ground by taking such unprecedented steps that I'm certain

even Volkswagen management was somewhat skeptical at the beginning. Imagine assuming a stance that made your product ugly, a bug, a lemon and all sorts of other epitaphs that must have made Detroit rub its hands in glee.

What happened is history, of course, but the real breakthrough in the VW campaign was Doyle Dane's deep psychological understanding of its consumer prospect.

■ Call it psychological positioning or call it brilliant conceptual creativity; it doesn't matter. The fact is that it was as bold and daring an advertising approach as it was for Volkswagen management to attempt to sell a car of such dimensions and style to an American market.

In 1949, VW sales in this country totaled two cars. A year later, 330 cars were sold. In 1969, U.S. sales topped 569,000. The numbers tell the story.

Ad 'Science' Will Fail

The '70s are *not* the era of positioning, nor will the '80s be the era of point of purchase supremacy, nor the '90s the era of psychogalvanomic attitudinal reflexibility—whatever the hell that means. I must warn the cultist that all attempts to treat basic marketing as a science can only result in consistent, dismal failure. For no art form has yet proved responsive to formularization without winding up with a paint-by-the-numbers result.

The '70s will find that creativity lives and that its influence will be felt by every single facet of marketing. Creativity will be needed at more levels of marketing than ever before. The positioning era pundits notwithstanding, the basics of advertising will remain the same. They'll simply have to be better than anything we've ever seen, and the ad agencies who can rise to the occasion will sell the products.

Reprinted from "Advertising Age," July 10, 1972, pp. 43-44, 46

Put people in positioning

BY JACK SPRINGER
The First Team Inc.
New York

The staging of a marketing theory is usually about as exciting as a cricket match. One normally appears—tentative as a crocus—via the "Harvard Business Review," or perhaps a scholarly paper handed down at a congress of marketers. But when ADVERTISING AGE threw its full influence behind the concept of positioning with a dramatic and powerful three-part series, the theory sprang to life seemingly full-grown—bold as Jack's beanstalk.

Yes, this is certainly radically different from the usual slow-evolution of theories. And it shows. Because like all theories, those on business need to be challenged; that is, modified, ramified and hammered into shape before they become good marketing tools.

What's happened is that the Trout/Ries essay was so full of useful information and so beautifully packaged that a lot of people now think they know all about positioning. Now this is causing me considerable aggravation since, (1) I make a large part of my living positioning and re-positioning products, (2) some of my best clients have actually mentioned the articles to me and (3) the essay, though lengthy, cannot be considered comprehensive.

All Purpose Message Won't Work

Astonishingly, despite all its thousands of words and charts and examples, the articles never once discussed positioning in terms of people's needs! This is so flagrant an omission that one can only conclude that the authors have decided all consumers are exactly alike.

Consumers (unfortunately) are people. And people (rather fortunately) are as unalike as—well, people. The needs and life style of a man of 40 are clearly different from the needs and life style of his 15-year-old daughter. To get your message into both their heads, you need, literally, to speak two different languages. I don't know why most advertising agents hate to admit this. But they do. They hang in there with the forlorn hope that they can create one, all-purpose message that says all things to all people.

Forget it.

Certainly, we can't prepare a special communication for every consumer-person. The best we can do is to find clusters of people with similar needs and similar life styles. And then prepare special communications (or even products) to suit them. I am speaking, of course, about market segmentation which, although some marketers seem determined to fight it to the death, is a fact of life. The point being that the concept of positioning is a poor marketing tool *unless it is accompanied by an understanding of market segmentation.*

The essayists Trout and Ries have not understood. In the first place, they discuss positioning as a way of capturing a share of *everybody's* mind, which is rarely necessary. But assuming that you did need to, the strategy of comparing your product to an existing product is doing it the hard way. This advice is based on the faulty assumption that people's minds are already brim full of information.

Indeed, Messrs. Trout and Ries are so bold as to assert: "The (modern) mind has no room for the new and different unless it is related to the old." This is not only nonsense, but also a critical error. Because if you buy it, you are left with only one course of action—teaching old dogs new tricks, which is the path of greatest resistance.

But you don't have to buy it. Because Trout and Ries are wrong. There *is* one part of the human brain that is wide open and anxious for new information. In fact, it's the largest part there is. It is the I part. The Me. The Ego. The Self-centered part.

It's the part that is constantly saying, "I live in a certain way that is partly good and partly not-so-good; I have certain needs that are not always satisfied; I have certain desires that are not always fulfilled; I am always on the lookout for more fulfillment and more satisfaction."

Find Your Segment

Now if you can identify a significant segment of people who have similar needs and desires and can explain your product in those terms, you are then following the path of least resistance. They will gladly remember what you have to say. You are doing positioning the smart way.

I guess the question is, "If a positioning fell in a forest and nobody was under it, would it make any noise?"

Obviously, it wouldn't. No matter how one defines it, positioning's only reason for being is to help advertising help products and services find their best place in a segmented market.

This is undeniable because no one marketer any longer owns any market category. And for as long as we are committed to free enterprise, no one ever will. All that you have is a piece of a category—and you'll only have that until someone offers your customers a better deal, which is inevitable. (The comforting thing is that that someone can be anyone, including you.)

Furthermore, the more profitable your piece of the action, the more action you'll stir up. If you're making money, never doubt that someone else is studying your best customers, probing their needs, examining the changes and expected changes in their way of life. In short, even as you read, someone is looking for an angle to change your customers' mind about you.

7Up Not Positioning Success

These days, this kind of competition almost always leads to value-added *new* products. Rarely anymore does it lead to the introduction of new parity products whose only virtue is a new positioning or advertising strategy, despite what Mr. Trout and Mr. Ries would like to believe. But naturally, since advertising has become such a hideously inefficient way to sell packaged goods, we must expect agency people to lead their best cards.

For example, it is probably true that the Uncola campaign is a smash success. But this is a success story for *ad-*

vertising (brilliant execution and the willingness to spend maybe $75,000,000); it is hardly a good example of deft positioning. A most sophisticated marketing man, Dr. Alfred Remson, tells me the secret is *not* that 7Up positioned itself as an alternative to Coke or Pepsi. He says that by mere association with the magic word "cola," 7Up convinced people their product is a soft drink rather than a mixer. That's clever, but still rather clumsy as positioning.

Compare it to the truly great example of positioning soft drinks. Charlie Brower's stunning concept for Pepsi—The Pepsi Generation. People who *think young*. On the surface, this simply said that if you drink Coke, you're a fossil. But it came out at a time when there were more people (a segment) under 20 than ever before in history! That's positioning.

Or compare it to today's Hamburger Helper campaign which says to women, "You can be a lazy cook—and still win praise for dinner." There are a lot of women out there who don't give a damn about fancy cooking. And a lot of those women feel guilty about it. Or used to. These relieved women are going to be buying nearly $60,000,000 worth of Hamburger Helper this year. Now *that's* positioning—brand manager style.

Tijuana Smalls Tell Who They're For

Let's look at another insightful example: The difference between the campaigns for Camel Filters and Tijuana Smalls.

The Camel advertising reads like the first half of a "Let's Go After The Individualist" strategy. The copy says, "We're not for everybody." But it never goes on to say just who Camel Filters *are* for. This is not very helpful to, say, a Marlboro man. He already knows he's not everybody—he's a maverick cowboy. But he gets no clues at all from Camel in finding out if maybe he's also their kind of smoker. In other words, Camel marketers know what positioning is, but they don't know how to make it work.

Tijuana Smalls do much better. Their strategy is basically the same. The advertising says, "We're not for everybody —are we for you? Maybe, you know who you are." But they then go on to show us explicitly who Tijuana Smalls *are* for: The individualist who sees himself as youthful (but not young), modern (but not far out), health-conscious (a jogger) and a very gregarious fellow. Pretty good positioning since there are probably ten million people (a segment) who fit that profile exactly—and another twenty million who wish they did (a segment).

One more example from the tobacco industry, which is particularly interesting to study since it is nearly static and

therefore predictive of what's going to happen in most categories: A constant number of suppliers competing for a constant number of customers. Philip Morris, by virtue of good timing and magnificent advertising, quickly captured a very profitable 1.5 share of the market with Virginia Slims. More significant for the long run though was the genius of their positioning. Rather than greedily position themselves as the cigaret for women (not a segment), they positioned themselves as the cigaret for *modern* women (a segment). This at a time when nearly every woman in America is wondering whether she's liberated or not. (How would you like to try to bring out a woman's cigaret today, knowing you'd already be classfied as un-modern?) Enviable work. Enviable position.

Positioning Isn't Just Comparing

All of which leads us to a definition: When you find a specific segment of people and tell them how your product satisfies their needs and fits into their life styles, that is positioning. Which is quite a different thing from comparing a product to another product. Or a company to another company. Or a new logo to an old logo.

But, let me hasten to admit that the word, positioning, can, with validity, mean different things to different people. It is perfectly reasonable for the officers of a business machines company to plan their products *vis-a-vis* a competitor's with an eye to producing better machines or cheaper machines or complementary machines. Indeed, if your competitor is IBM, you'd have to be pretty dumb not to. At any rate, you can call this sort of planning positioning, if you wish.

It is also reasonable for advertising strategists to distinguish a product or a service from a competitor's by making or implying a comparison. This, too, could be called positioning.

But the theory of positioning runs deeper than that. And it is by no means a new notion. It is part of an immutable progression in marketing which dawned first on packaged goods marketers, the best of whom have been practicing it for at least 40 years without benefit of an 11-letter name.

We can define these companies like this: Any manufacturer who actively, aggressively and continually promotes two or more functionally equivalent brands, is run by people who know how to position products.

Marketers Face Three-Way Crunch

These companies are the ones which first recognized the desirability of having multiple entries in a category rather than a single (vulnerable) one. This was

what necessitated the strategy of promoting similar products in different ways, which came to be called positioning.

It is scarcely surprising that a smart professional like David Ogilvy would recognize this trend and would (to quote Trout & Ries again) "on a spring morning in 1971" trumpet in the "Era of Positioning." What makes it so singularly unsurprising is that Mr. Ogilvy's agency enjoys the Maxwell House, Instant Maxwell House, Maxim and Max Pax business, a situation that a non-positionist would consider an egregious conflict. Mr. Ogilvy simply positioned himself as a man who understood positioning, thus opening the door to all kinds of multi-product entries in other categories.

And so, even though positioning for packaged goods has been and will be the prime application of the art, all American manufacturers need to understand the theory. It is important that they do because of a dynamic three-way crunch that is going on:

1. The extreme difficulty of further economic colonialism.

2. The war for shelf space due to the infeasibility of building retail outlets any bigger than they are now.

3. The imminent stabilization of a population whose ability to consume more is already questionable.

In other words, the battleground for consumer marketing will not be getting bigger. The outer boundaries are set, and only the fittest will survive. Or, as Joe Louis put it, "You can run, but you can't hide."

Considering this crunch in the long view, it is no longer unthinkable that it will eventually lead to an ever smaller number of large manufacturers who will ultimately eat each other up, thus ending "capitalism as we know it." Indeed, it is completely thinkable. One can clearly see that certain overpowering giants can, practically at will, exert unbearable pressure on their competitors. These companies, like P&G, GM and IBM, are approaching dominance precisely because they are multi-brand marketers. By encouraging inter-company, multi-product competition, and by mastering the art of positioning their various entries, they have actually created the phenomenon known as market segmentation. And, having created it, they know best how to control it.

In the meantime, there's still plenty of life in the jungle. Plenty of targets still to shoot at. Plenty of fabulous advertising campaigns still to be written. And the marketing professionals who understand positioning in terms of life styles and market segments will have little trouble picking off those who don't.

Reprinted from "Advertising Age," Sept. 4, 1972, pp. 31-32

Advertising of services, not products, will be the wave of the future

BY STEVE UNWIN
Assistant Professor of Advertising
University of Illinois, Urbana, Ill.

Advertising, as it is used today, has come under attack because it has not adjusted to the realities of the post-industrial society. Three anachronisms contribute to this effect:

First, most of current advertising continues to offer product satisfactions in a service economy. Second, in order to relate to new consumer wants, advertising endows products with unreal, non-product satisfactions. And third, advertising has been little used to channel new wants toward real, non-product satisfactions. Advertising finds itself perpetuating the old values, while plagiarizing the new.

Advertising is the tool of the mass persuader, versatile but compliant, expressing exactly the aims and wishes of those who use it. These anachronisms are not, therefore, the fault of advertising itself. The responsibility lies with those who use advertising too much, and those who use it too little; with the manufacturers, who continue to dominate the advertising media in a service economy; and with the service industries, which, undermarketed and underpromoted, still behave like quasi-charitable institutions in the midst of post-industrial plenty.

Material abundance has these results, each of which has profound significance for advertising: It provides the material foundation on which a prosperous service economy can be built. It permits the manufacture of an increasing number of new products. It brings affluence to the consumer, and with affluence, a changed hierarchy of consumer wants.

The literature is full of references, mostly somewhat colored, to consumer distaste for the fruits of affluence. M. W. Thring, in "Man, Machines and Tomorrow," believes that "at the beginning, new-found material wealth leads to actual happiness in its contrast with the straitened and narrow life many of us had led before, but after a while pleasure in possessions reaches a saturation point and there is disillusionment."

Toynbee, Others Look Askance at Us

One of advertising's fiercest, yet most esteemed critics, Arnold Toynbee, has written in AA (Nov. 21, '73), "I guess that a hungry and destitute Indian peasant is less unhappy than a western conveyor-belt worker who eats steak for dinner and has a refrigerator, a tv set, an air-conditioning apparatus and a car." Only the most ardent conservationist would go as far as Mr. Toynbee.

But it cannot be escaped that, even with present shortages, western man is considerably richer in manufactured artifacts than in non-material comforts. People are prone to want what they lack, rather than what they already have. Frank Knight's analysis of wants (in "The Ethics of Competition") is truer today than 50 years ago: "What the individual actually wants is not satisfaction for the wants which he has, but more and better wants."

And yet, the newly affluent, and somewhat surfeited, consumer is met at every turn by a stream of advertising for new products, most of which are not much different from those he already has. Last year, 52 new items went on supermarket shelves in a typical week. In 1971, one food company was responsible for the launch of 24 new products, AA reported. A. C. Nielsen Co. recorded 1,154 new product introductions in the grocery and health and beauty aids fields in the same year. Most of these failed to meet a demand. Of the 9,500 new supermarket brands introduced in 1968, only 20% met their sales goals.

It's Still 3:1 for Product Advertising

This new product casualty rate not only says something about the present state of demand for new products; it also does much to explain consumer annoyance and irritation with advertising. Similarly, the continued three-to-one ratio in favor of product advertising over non-product advertising can make little sense to post-industrial consumers, who, according to the U.S. Census Bureau, now spend more than half their income on services.

Americans, for example, now spend as many dollars ($350,000,000) with one of the smaller fast-food hamburger businesses as on all brands of toothpaste, and yet toothpaste advertisers outspend this fast-food business seven to one. In 1972, 85 of the 100 leading national advertisers were classified as manufacturers in 15 product categories. Ethical drug manufacturers spent $400,000,000 reaching the nation's doctors, whereas the 50 United States together combined to spend less than $100,000,000 advertising to all their citizens.

The Gallagher Report estimates that as much as 85% of today's ad expenditures are intended to move products. Affluent consumers still want to be informed about new products, and reminded about old products, but not to the exclusion of all else. The increased share of consumer expenditure in such non-product service areas as recreation, education, vacation, sport, hobbies, travel, health and handicraft has not been balanced by an equivalent increase in share of advertising expenditure. The product/service persuasion ratio is the inverse of the product/service spending ratio.

This is not to say that affluent consumers no longer need products. They do. They depend on them, but increas-

81

ingly as items of necessity. They are valued for their utility as much as their status. Alvin Toffler says in AA (Nov. 21, 1973): "We are witnessing a decline in possessiveness. The consumer is no longer as concerned with possession as he is with use." Hence the current consumer interest in product performance, reliability of product claims, and more informative product advertising.

Consumer Feels Cheated by Ad Themes

The advertising practitioner knows, however, that the mere repetition of product data does not give a brand much competitive edge in a market already crowded with many very similar products. He, therefore, seeks to differentiate his brand by giving it an added value. The values he selects reflect those wants which affluent consumers feel most strongly, and focus on non-material rewards instead of product benefits. Thus, beer is advertised as if it were a vacation trip or a passport to immortality. A motor oil is euphemized as an initiation to young adulthood. A car wax is transformed into an erotic experience. A tonic permits the carefree, country life of the gentleman farmer. And so on.

These ads sell. They sell because they motivate people to buy. Consumers identify and respond to these themes. But over a period of time they begin to feel cheated and deprived. The psychological rewards advertising has invested in the product seem flimsy counterfeit to the hardened product consumer of today. When needs are advertised as wants, consumers experience an expectation gap between promise and performance. They start to criticize when advertising masquerades their wants.

People are not inclined to resist or resent want-provoking appeals if they harmonize with their predispositions. As Theodore Levitt tells us, "Advertisements are the symbols of man's aspirations." People do not quarrel with embellishments which enhance the goals of their wants. Advertising helped to accomplish the technological revolution. It must now perform a similar role for the service revolution. This is advertising's new horizon. As people demand more and better services, it is advertising's job to seek out, identify, stimulate and guide these newly-felt wants toward their satisfactions by service industries.

Service Industry Is Cinderella

There are two major obstacles to this logical development—the economic entrenchment of the manufacturing establishment, and the lowly status and poor performance of the service industries. Society expects and receives many excellent products, but only a few excellent services. Some 123 out of the 154 ma-

jor U.S. corporations are manufacturers, a *News Front* study tells us. The manufacturer dominates the consumer market in size, organization and influence.

On the other hand, most service industries are regarded as inefficient and lacking in prestige. Although allowing for one or two notable exceptions, like the Bell Telephone System, Peter F. Drucker has noted the absence of defined goals and measurable results in the "public service institutions." John Kenneth Galbraith deplores the exclusion of many of the less organized service companies from what he terms the "planning system."

Often overstaffed and usually underpriced, the service industries stagger from one crisis to the next. Despite their overwhelming aggregate dollar volume (the health industry is now the second largest in the country) they still carry a Cinderella image.

Mr. Drucker has pointed to the paradox: People say they want more services, but are not prepared to pay for them, either out of pocket or out of taxes. Services are still somehow seen as the prerogative of the very rich or as charity for the very poor. The pre-industrial image of services lingers on in an era when material abundance has at last made professional services available to all. The affluent consumer earns twice as much as he did 20 years ago.

And yet, despite technical advances in both health care and automobiles, he is happier to pay the dealer $4,000 for a new car than the hospital $1,000 for a new family member. The need to run sweepstakes to subsidize Chicago mass transit tells a similar story in the public sector. The nation cannot long continue to allow 70% of its GNP to be treated as "good works" or "free handouts."

James Webb Young in AA cited advertising's ability to "overcome inertia— the great drag on all human progress, economic or non-economic, as represented by the sociological term, 'cultural lag'." Even Mr. Toynbee allowed that "advertising is the art of persuading, and persuasion can be used for preaching a new way of life." Creative advertising can articulate the abstract benefits of services, and help convince the affluent consumer that such intangible satisfactions as freedom, fulfilment, health, love and security are more faithfully and fully supplied by services than through the surrogacy of a product.

What Service Advertising Can Do

Further than that, advertising can particularize abstract benefits. The bank's "friendly image" can be spelled out in terms of receptiveness to inquiries for loans, a relaxed atmosphere in which to discuss matters of personal financial se-

curity and risk, and the avoidance of banking jargon.

Advertising can demonstrate that the personal involvement of time and effort required in the "consumption" of many services and activities, such as education and sport, can be more edifying than the more immediate, but usually more superficial, satisfactions of product consumption.

Advertising can raise the social and economic status of services, and persuade the affluent consumer that service values justify payment. Opportunities for advertising will increase with the growth of private and personal services in education, entertainment, health and other areas. As a result, the service industries will be encouraged to become goal and consumer oriented, and advertising will be doing the job it does best, and which only advertising can do, which is to stimulate wants, create demand and motivate action.

The competing claims of advertisers will act as a spur to services development. The persuasive art of advertising will again be in harmony with the economic system.

Advertising Can't Be Coy

Advertising will not realize its full potential in the post-industrial economy so long as there are service industries that do not recognize advertising as a viable medium for curing their awareness problems, preventing apathy and gaining public support.

Such coy and defensive attitudes to advertising are exemplified in the self-imposed restrictions on advertising of pharmacists and architects. The tenuous ethical arguments put forward to outlaw the advertising of prescription services and home designing seem incongruous in a society now accustomed to the advertising of churches, colleges and schools. Neither does it make much sense to condone the advertising of the medical product, but not its dispenser; the constructed home, but not its designer.

All suppliers of services will hopefully come to accept advertising as a highly flexible tool of communication, which can be adapted, like all modes of communication, to suit their special needs, and which can lead to higher consumer expectations and, thereby, to better qualities of services.

Advertising Isn't Morality Play

It is also to be hoped that the shift of advertising support from products to services will forestall further attempts to meddle with its synchronizing capability. Formal disclosure and other regulatory ploys, which threaten to turn advertising into a sort of latter-day morality play, or legal tort, miss the point of advertising's function. The purpose of advertising is to accelerate consumption, expedite changes in attitudes, and to achieve goals in a shorter period of time. Advertising is the persuasive use of mass communication to help men keep pace with all the other fast-moving elements in a technological society.

Advertising helps to synchronize modern social and economic processes. To restrict its use to the provision of information and to muffle its persuasive power would impede its synchronizing function. It would also be a misuse of the medium. Because of the vast number of competing messages, advertising has to communicate its meaning fast. It makes at best a fleeting impression. Because it is fast, it has to be short. One advertisement should not attempt to convey more than one or two basic points. Otherwise, it will never be noticed, let alone remembered.

Because it is fast and short, and because it has to maintain momentum behind a product, service or idea, advertising is essentially a medium of repetition. A fast, short and repetitive medium is neither a suitable nor efficient vehicle for the dissemination of detailed information. Packages, leaflets, catalogs and consumer reports, available immediately prior to and following purchase, are far more appropriate media for this purpose. Mail order, some industrial and some new consumer products require informative advertising, but not established, fast-moving, consumer brands.

Advertising that was forever informing people about things they did not want to know would make media exposure an almost unbearable experience, especially for those not in the target audience. Also, the advertising business should not be misled into thinking the more informative advertising will pacify the critics and satisfy the regulators. In fact, the opposite is more likely, with more demands for substantiation of product information and further threats of affirmative disclosure.

Regulation Slows Flow of Goods

Attempts to change advertising into a purely informative medium are as mistaken as those which seek to curb corporate power by transforming the manufacturer into an agent for social welfare. There are few obvious parallels between the profitable manufacture and distribution of products and the professional planning and administration of social services. Manufacturers do not have the training, experience or expertise to perform effectively in the social area. For similar lack of qualification the military have traditionally made bad policemen, artists poor administrators, and faculty indifferent accountants.

Just as corporate deficiencies in the social area do not deter the corporate critic, so the ultimate purpose of advertising regulation is not to make an "honest" medium of it, but to slow down the flow of goods and services. Advertising people should take note of the ominous link between consumerism and the concept of a "no-growth" economy. Consumerists have shown little interest in using advertising to boost the service sector. Regulation is not designed to improve advertising performance for products or for services. An advertising business castrated by controls has serious implications for the future health of the nascent service economy.

Advertising's Role in New Society

Thriving service institutions, "the real growth sector of a modern society," as Mr. Drucker says, are vital to the further development of western civilization. There are many visions of the future society to which we are headed. Mr. Thring envisions a "creative society" where men find fulfilment through mental and manual creative activity; Mr. Toffler describes the imminence of an "experiential economy," where goods and services are valued according to their psychological reward; and there are other versions ranging from the cultural to the spiritual.

But it is certain that none of these will transpire, unless they can take place within a prosperous and well-ordered service environment. There is a natural progression from the agricultural economy to the industrial economy to the service economy and, soon, to the cultural economy. Each depends on the former for its existence. Each builds on the achievements of its predecessor. Each adds to, but does not subtract from, the wealth of the previous economy. Advertising, which helps to synchronize change and ease transition, has a role to play at every stage.

As the carrier of messages for the industrial economy, advertising has had its wings clipped; its feathers ruffled. It should now take its head out of the sand, and learn to fly in new directions.

Reprinted from "Advertising Age," May 27, 1974, pp. 39-40

PART 4 **Society and Advertising**

How government

regulates advertising

Name a national problem and someone will almost certainly find a way to blame it on advertising.

Whether it is the energy crisis, crime in the streets, or meals lacking nutritional balance, there inevitably are those who will believe advertising made it happen. So the era of modern consumerism sparks endless debates over proposals to restrict advertising to children; to require specific types of information in ads for gasoline, cars, food and drugs; or to curtail forms of advertising, such as billboards, and specific uses of advertising, such as messages for cigarets or liquor.

While the problems are often easy to recognize, answers are often elusive. For a restriction on the advertiser's right to be heard may also represent a restriction on the consumer's ability to be informed. And even the best motivated restraints on the freedom of advertisers can have unanticipated consequences in a competitive marketplace where product innovation and consumer welfare may be closely intertwined.

■ Restrict ads to children? Who will foot the bill for the entertainment and information programs?

Make ads more informative? How much information can consumers absorb from a 30-second tv spot?

Blame advertising for tantalizing the under-employed with visions of luxurious living beyond their reach? Are our conversations to be in hushed tones lest we be overheard by some 'for whom the American dream is not yet a reality?

The controversies surrounding advertising are real, and literally inescapable, for advertising is involved in so much of what goes on in American society. As a communications technique suited to the needs of a complex society,

advertising takes a multitude of forms and serves an infinite variety of purposes. Consumers see advertising as a source of information; but the vendors of goods and services who are doing the advertising may be pursuing more limited strategies which they judge to be in their own best interests. Every American is exposed to hundreds of advertising messages daily—many intrusive and unwanted—and each of these individuals perceives these messages not only in terms of truth or falsity, but also from the standpoint of such subjective standards as taste and moral values.

There is, of course, considerable screening of advertising by various agencies of self regulation. But in the free American marketplace, access to advertising in one form or another is readily available to virtually anyone who wishes to advertise. Taste and values, however, do not readily lend themselves to censorship even by well-motivated citizens; so the degree of restraint, as well as the quality of information in the message, reflect the integrity of the advertiser as much as the requirements of law.

The federal government's efforts to cope with advertising abuses date back 100 years to the earliest postal fraud laws. But the number of regulators and the forms of regulation have proliferated to keep pace with the sophisticated selling techniques of an increasingly impersonal marketplace.

The earliest issues tended to be clear cut: Fraud and deception. Now, prodded by consumerists, regulators are becoming increasingly demanding. Given the complex nature of many modern consumer products, is it unfair to fail to disclose technical information which will enable consumers to make value comparisons? Is there such a thing as "puffery?" Or is puffery a device for imply-

ing claims which the advertisers could not possibly substantiate? In the race to be first to advertise new products, do advertisers rush into the marketplace without properly testing their drugs or appliances? Do they design products for eye and promotional appeal rather than quality or safety? Do they encourage large numbers of people to live beyond their means?

Advertising people, who long ago regarded themselves as members of one of the nation's most regulated professions, were baffled by the demands for change when modern consumerism began to emerge about a decade ago. They angrily resisted demands for laws which would prescribe the kinds of information required on packages; for laws regulating the promotion of instalment credit; for the elimination of cigaret advertising from radio and television.

'Fairness' Emerges

Once the federal responsibility was no longer limited to fraud and deception, regulators were able to escalate rapidly to a new plateau. "Fairness" emerged as the new and more hospitable legal standard for the regulators, and the demands on advertisers multiplied: When must an ad disclose shortcomings or hazards, as well as advantages? When products are essentially alike, is it fair to stress their merits without disclosing that competing products do exactly the same thing? Should products that children don't use be advertised to children in the hope that the child will become a "surrogate salesman," recommending them to his parents?

With an influx of imaginative young staff people, and with aggressive leadership, the Federal Trade Commission discovered unsuspected powers, including cease-and-desist orders which require corrective ads to offset previous misstatements. The Food & Drug

Administration, with more than ten times the budget it had less than a decade ago, began to pinpoint the kinds of ingredients and the types of nutritional information that should appear on package labels for foods, cosmetics and over-the-counter drugs. An entirely new Consumer Product Safety agency was created to assure that safety design and pre-market testing were not overlooked in the rush to move innovative household products into the marketplace.

■ The consumer specialist emerged as a new profession. Most government departments and major agencies included a consumer specialist at the highest staff levels; and, in the White House, beginning in the Kennedy Administration, the consumer advisor to the President participated in the preparation of administration policy on all matters involving the consumer's welfare. Even these changes, however, failed to satisfy those who contended that the advertiser had too many advantages, whether in the marketplace, or in the formulation of government regulation. And consumerism continues to consider as its highest priority legislative goal the creation of a special agency which will speak for the consumer in the courts and regulatory agencies. Meanwhile, business watches nervously—fearful that such an agency would become the spawning ground for more and more regulation.

This process of turbulent change has exacted a heavy price. Practices which seemed reasonable to advertisers at the time they used them no longer were acceptable under the emerging standards of permissible behavior. Those who resisted change paid the price in damaging publicity. For reformers and regulators were able to dominate the news media, sometimes overstating their cases and inflicting lasting damage on advertisers who got caught in the crossfire.

These experiences were remindful of a lesson which responsible business men had learned long ago: That the business man who is accused of unfair or illegal practices can't possibly come out ahead. In purely pragmatic terms, he alienates the public and sacrifices good will. Nowadays he also invites retribution from regulatory officials at all levels of government, and from the new "public interest" groups which function as volunteer overseers over the workings of the marketplace.

■ An inquiry from Ralph Nader, or from any of the dozens of individuals and organizations that have followed in his footsteps, is no small matter for a business man. For it may be the advance warning of painful, adverse publicity in the offing, or the beginning of a dispute which will result in damaging regulatory and costly legal proposals.

Nor is the visit of a federal investigator a minor event. He may be collecting background information which will eventually surface as a regulation or law changing or curtailing advertising and promotional tactics which are productive for the business man. If he is from a regulatory agency, his report could have lasting impact. The mere citation for false advertising means bad publicity. If the charges are sustained, the advertiser will find himself under a cease-and-desist order which hangs permanently as a threat over his head in the event of future violations. Even if the charges are eventually dismissed—as they have been in a number of highly publicized cases in recent years—the government's retraction does not overcome the original injury.

History of Regulation

How did it happen that the growth of advertising was matched by the expansion of federal regulatory activity aimed at spotlighting and rooting out deceptive advertisers?

Post Office fraud laws effective as early as 1872 provided criminal and civil remedies against the use of the mail to defraud. But it was not until 42 years later, in 1914, that Congress passed the Federal Trade Commission Act to provide a broad legal weapon for federal action in the advertising field. This act was approved at a time when the public was demanding a number of reforms to protect consumers. In the 59 years since, the FTC's authority has been greatly enlarged, and at least half a dozen other federal agencies have been given important responsibilities in the policing of advertising.

Early demands for reform were generated by outrages committed by charlatans who populated the food and drug industry at the turn of the century. In 1906, Congress passed the Pure Food & Drug Act, the first major federal law for the protection of consumers. But there was still no mechanism for curbing the fraudulent advertising that flooded the mails and filled the advertising columns of many publications.

■ Five years later—in 1911—as a first move against swindle-by-advertising, the ancient postal fraud laws were overhauled. Where the original laws tried to curb a schemer from swindling a pre-selected victim, the revised law was intended to deal with the wholesale distribution of fraudulent advertising offers by mail.

The advertising industry—during this same period—was providing militant support for the adoption of model state laws against deceptive advertising. It was in this atmosphere that Congress worked for the adoption of the Federal Trade Commission Act.

The FTC, as conceived in 1914, constituted a radically new idea. The newly accepted federal responsibility to battle monopoly and guard against unfair methods of competition involved an area of law where few guideposts existed. The FTC's sponsors hoped the new agency would identify unfair business practices and help the business world recognize them and avoid them.

The commission's efforts to protect consumers from deceptive advertising eventually ran into legal snares in a period when the Supreme Court was refusing to stretch the literal meaning of the laws already on the books. In 1931, the court dismissed an FTC complaint against a company on the ground that deception of consumers was not an adequate basis for action under the FTC Act as it had been enacted in 1914. The commission appealed to Congress for new authority, and in 1938 it received a solid legal basis for action in the advertising field—including authority to seek court injunctions against potentially dangerous advertisements for foods, drugs and cosmetics.

■ Then, during the New Deal years of President Roosevelt, several other federal agencies received specific assignments involving the regulation of advertising. Fraud laws administered by the Post Office Department were strengthened. Special laws providing for stringent actions against deceptive ads for securities, banks and savings institutions were administered by the Securities & Exchange Commission, the Federal Deposit Insurance Corp., and the Federal Home Loan Bank. Labeling laws administered by the Food & Drug Administration were tightened; the Federal Alcohol Administration Act vested sweeping controls over liquor advertising and labeling in the Treasury Department; responsibility for dealing with unfair and deceptive advertising by airlines was given to the Civil Aeronautics Board.

What Is the Truth?

The ever-present question hanging over the enforcement of laws in the advertising field is: What is the truth?

Outright deceptions are easily recognized, but even well-meaning advertisers sometimes find themselves embroiled with regulatory officials on claims that— from the advertiser and agency standpoint at least—seem no more than "puffery."

The courts have traditionally taken the view that an advertisement must be written so that it will not deceive "the trusting as well as the suspicious, the casual as well as the vigilant, the naive as well as the sophisticated." While the commission has long stopped short of putting a literal interpretation on statements that represent nothing more than bragging, it has cautioned advertisers that "puffery" will not be an acceptable explanation for any statement which could be regarded by the public as a performance claim.

In former years, most of the cases handled by the FTC were based on letters from indignant citizens, or from tips secretly supplied by competitors. More recently, however, the commission has put increasing reliance on its own monitoring of the marketplace, as well as on information it gets through consultation with public interest groups, government officials, and business groups.

■ The commission's authority over advertising rests largely on a passage in the FTC Act which outlaws "unfair methods of competition in commerce and unfair or deceptive acts or practices in commerce." The FTC also enforces several specialized laws related to textile labeling, as well as portions of the Truth in Packaging, Truth in Lending, and the Fair Credit Reporting Act.

Enforcement is vested in five commissioners appointed by the President and confirmed by the Senate for seven-year terms. No more than three of the five may be of the same political party. One commissioner, designated as chairman by the President, exercises special initiatives in selecting top staff personnel and handling the agenda and assignments of commission matters and cases. The actual investigative work and preparation of cases in the advertising field is under the Bureau of Consumer Protection, which has about 250 lawyers and

135 "consumer specialists" on its staff.

The FTC is more concerned with preventing future offenses than in punishing past errors in a criminal sense, but there has been a major change in its viewpoint in recent years. Formerly it issued cease-and-desist orders which did little more than define past deceptions and forbid their use in the future.

More recently the FTC has recognized a need to serve the public and the respondent's competitors by restoring conditions as they were before the deception took place. Some recent cease-and-desist orders contain sections requiring the respondent to use advertising which "corrects" his earlier misstatements. Others require remedial payments to persons who were misled. Still others seek to avert future deception through such requirements as "cooling off" periods for door-to-door sales transactions involving large amounts of money.

■ When the FTC believes a deception has occurred, its staff drafts a proposed complaint. If this is accepted by the commission, it may be publicly announced, often naming the advertising agency involved, in addition to the advertiser. Negotiations toward settlement are offered at this point, and many succeed. If no settlement is indicated, a formal complaint is issued, and hearings are conducted before an administrative judge who issues a decision. His decision can be appealed to the full commission, and is subsequently reviewable in a court of law.

Business men, indignant over what they consider unfair adverse publicity, contend they should have an opportunity to settle cases before the initial complaint is publicly announced. While this was the procedure for many years, the FTC's leadership decided that it was unfair to the public because the public was not aware that any dispute existed during the months—even years— that negotiations continued. Meanwhile, the controversial ads ran, uninterrupted, throughout that period.

Where an ad for a food, drug, cosmetic or a device represents a serious threat to the public, the commission may apply to the federal courts for a temporary restraining order. There has been substantial support for legislation which would enable the FTC to seek court restraints in any unfair or deceptive situation involving serious risk to the public.

In the early 1970s, the commis-

sion focused on national advertising, particularly in the food field. Late in 1971, it held a landmark hearing which explored in depth the various aspects of modern advertising practice which could lead to unfair or deceptive selling methods.

■ Individual litigation is traditionally the cutting edge of FTC activity, singling out a particular ad to test its legality, and to send a "signal" to other advertisers. In recent years the FTC has tended to give lower priority to the kinds of issues which dominated its calendar in the past—bait-and-switch, fictitious price ads, misuse of words like "guarantee," and failure to disclose foreign origin. Its emphasis has been on much broader matters, such as the kinds of proof an advertiser should have before making a claim.

Prove Your Claims

Under its "advertising substantiation" program, it has required most industry members in more than a dozen industries—including makers of cars, toothpaste, cough remedies, air conditioners and others—to submit the proof behind claims in their current ads. While only a handful of cases have resulted, many of these companies were exposed to public embarrassment when the FTC released the results of these investigations for scrutiny.

For many years, the commission has tried to move toward non-punitive industry-wide techniques, and away from time-consuming, case by case litigation. In some situations, such as deceptive pricing, guarantee offers, and recently, endorsements in ads, its staff has released "guides" which are advisory, rather than legally binding.

Recent court decisions have apparently cleared the way for the use of "rules" which are, in effect, "mini laws," issued by the FTC and legally enforcible. "Rules" have been issued on such subjects as textile labeling, gasoline octane rating posting, retail food special ads, and the use of giveaway games as retail store promotions. There are indications that in the mid-1970s rule-making will be used extensively by the FTC to define the kinds of information required in point of sale materials and ads.

Role of FDA

Paralleling the work of the FTC, to some extent, are the policing efforts of the Food & Drug Administration with respect to the "labeling" of foods, drugs and cosmetics.

A congressional decision in 1938 divided the regulation of foods, drugs and cosmetics between the two agencies, with the FTC retaining responsibility for "advertising" in promotional media, and the FDA assuming power over any claims that appear on the label or the package.

In the prescription drug field, legislation passed by Congress in 1962 gives FDA almost unlimited authority to require disclosure of side effects and other possible complications in advertising as well as in labeling materials. For other products, the FDA is confined only to issues involving statements made on the label.

For many years a rivalry persisted between the two agencies which resulted in overlaps, but the old antagonisms have given way to close collaboration. The FDA with its extensive scientific resources and its close contacts with the scientific community, determines acceptable labeling claims. The FTC, with limited scientific resources, relies on the FDA's findings in reviewing the ads.

While the FDA is confined to the "label," its role is broader than the word implies. If it finds that a claim in an ad is not supported by the information on the label, the FDA can proceed with a "misbranding" action. So its interest in ads is more direct than may appear.

■ The FDA, because it handles matters related to health and safety, has a choice of criminal or civil remedies, and it uses procedures which are much faster than the FTC's. When it believes a product is "misbranded," it gets a court order, and seizes the product. The issues are argued before a judge after the product is off the market. In its regulation of prescription drug advertising, the FDA pioneered in introducing the "corrective" ad penalty.

It took nearly a decade for the FDA to complete its scientific reviews covering claims for all prescription drugs that were on the market when the 1962 law passed. Then, beginning in 1972, it began using a network of scientific advisory groups to review permissible claims for various categories of over-the-counter drugs, beginning with analgesics and antacids. Literally tens of thousands of products are involved, but they have been divided into about 25 groups. As the panels complete a review for each group, all products are ordered to adjust their labels accordingly, with the FTC, in the background, to assure that the ads are changed, too.

For many years, when it operated under stringent budgets, the FDA concentrated its resources on drugs, in an effort to cope with the explosion in drug therapy. More recently, under more generous budgets, it has played an active role in food and cosmetic marketing.

Through the use of standards of identity, it has traditionally served as the expert on "nomenclature" important to truthful advertising of food products. Under the Truth in Packaging law it defines the kinds of information that must be displayed on food, drug and cosmetic packages, including the use of promotional offers, such as cents-off sales.

■ The FDA has cooperated with the food industry in the development of standardized nutritional labeling systems for foods, and is currently working with the cosmetic industry toward new arrangements which are expected to provide ingredient information on cosmetics. Through its review of chemical additives, such as saccharin, the FDA controls the destiny of entire product categories. As the agency responsible for cosmetic safety, the FDA is able to ban or require warnings on products. After the FDA ruled they have no therapeutic value, feminine hygiene deodorant sprays became feminine deodorant sprays.

Postal Service

Closely allied to the FTC and the FDA in much of the regulatory activity is the fraud staff of the Postal Service. Armed with both criminal and civil power to proceed against mail fraud, it has found that many of its most persistent problems are in the food and drug field.

The postal fraud staff gets its information from the public and its own inspection force. Because fraud, from a legal standpoint, involves "intent to deceive," the Postal Service cases ordinarily involve misrepresentations that go beyond the routine "false advertising" handled by the FTC.

The more serious postal fraud cases are turned over to the Department of Justice for presentation to a grand jury. A majority of the fraud cases are handled administratively in a civil procedure through hearings similar to those of the FTC.

■ Cases referred for criminal prosecution generally involve intent to obtain large sums on a broad scale. Under the criminal fraud law the use of the mail at any stage of the enterprise is sufficient to represent "fraud by mail," even though the actual remittance may be arranged outside the mail. Conviction for criminal mail fraud can involve fines of $1,000 and imprisonment up to five years.

The Postal Service also has authority to handle cases involving either fraud or misrepresentation through administrative procedures which can result in an order cutting off all mail addressed to the person accused of fraud, and returning it to the senders. Fraud cases must involve the actual transmission of money. Misrepresentation cases are akin to false advertising situations. In both instances, civil "prosecution" before an administrative judge is conducted by the Consumer Protection Office of the Postal Service's general counsel office.

Similar administrative procedures are used by the Postal Service to stop any promotion by mail involving a lottery.

Also in the lineup of the federal agencies ready to move against deceptive advertising is the Federal Communications Commission. Since the commission regulates the broadcaster rather than the advertiser, it is not concerned with the advertisement itself. Its rules bar lotteries, fraud and obscenity on the air; they also require clear identification of all sponsored materials, including the disclosure of "payola." But the commission normally becomes concerned about individual advertisements only if it is convinced that the broadcaster knowingly carries false and deceptive commercials.

Through liaison arrangements with FTC and FDA, the commission keeps informed of questionable ads detected on the air. It has put the entire broadcasting industry on notice that failure to drop an ad that has been banned by the FTC or by other regulatory agencies will be regarded as an indication of irresponsible management, to be considered at license renewal time.

Consumerists have attempted to use the FCC's "fairness" doctrine as an indirect restraint on advertising appeals they consider objectionable. Courts have upheld their contention that stations which carry ads concerned directly with issues of public controversy are obliged to make time available for the other side of the question. The FCC, however, has rejected efforts to extend this to include product ads which may "implicitly" touch on issues of public importance. For example, the "fairness" doctrine was applied to an oil company ad which argued for the Alaskan pipeline, but in another case FCC refused to find that environmentalists are entitled to time because ads for large autos fail to disclose the potential environmental damage that might result from operating this kind of vehicle.

■ Access to the air for "counter advertising" was a major issue in 1972, with the FTC supporting public interest lawyers who contended that advertisers give the public only part of the story. An FTC petition to the FCC contended that specific amounts of time ought to be set aside for public interest groups and others wishing to comment on the implications of commercials which while not misleading in the legal sense, or unfair under the FCC's doctrines, are "incomplete." But the FTC move received a frigid reception from both the FCC and the broadcast industry. The FCC, with Supreme Court approval, has also upheld the right of broadcasters to refuse to sell time for ads dealing with public issues.

In addition to the FTC, FDA, Postal Service and the FCC, there are many other federal agencies with specialized roles touching on the regulation of advertising. Under the Packers and Stockyards Act, the Agriculture Department plays an FTC-like role in controlling promotional practices of the meat industry. The department also has a role similar to that of the FDA in passing on labels of meat products. The Environmental Protection Agency does for pesticide labels what the FDA does for food additives. The EPA has also published fuel performance information by brand for foreign and domestic autos as a forerunner of some regulatory activity, perhaps in conjunction with the FTC, which could involve the disclosure of fuel consumption on new car stickers, or in advertisements. The Consumer Product Safety Agency is calling on the ad industry to avoid any themes which may encourage unsafe use of products.

Many of the special federal laws adopted in the 1930s were designed to protect investors and savers. Under the Securities & Exchange Act, the SEC has issued strict regulations to control the

advance publicity for new stock issues and to require disclosure of truthful information about securities, brokers, dealers and advisers. To keep "puffery" out of the securities business, the SEC has a regulation calling for so-called "tombstone" advertising for new securities, a form of advertising which confines the ad to bare statistical information about the forthcoming issue, precluding any discussion of merits.

Other SEC regulations require the use of promotional materials which give both the favorable and the unfavorable facts with respect to investment opportunities. A regulation covering the advertising of investment advisers requires that any statement which discusses the successful suggestions offered by the adviser must be sufficiently comprehensive to include all the other suggestions the adviser made during a full year.

■ The Federal Deposit Insurance Corp. and the Federal Home Loan Bank Board both exercise close supervision over the advertising practices of banks and savings and loan associations. On several occasions, they have proposed regulations to restrict the use of earnings claims in advertising and to put a limit on the premiums offered by financial institutions.

Under the Truth in Lending Law, the Federal Reserve Board regulates instalment credit ads by banks. The department of housing and urban renewal enforces SEC-like rules requiring disclosure of facts in promotion materials for interstate land sale ads. Among the other government agencies regulating advertising and labeling are the Treasury's bureau of alcohol, tobacco and firearms and the Civil Aeronautics Board. As the agency responsible for enforcing the Federal Alcohol Beverage Act, the Treasury enforces a comprehensive advertising code which prevents vendors of alcoholic beverages from using many of the techniques available for other commodities.

Its regulations specifically ban any theme which implies therapeutic benefits from using alcoholic beverages, and they stringently regulate the use of flags or insignia implying official endorsement, or brand names which may misrepresent the

country of origin. A high percentage of alcoholic beverage advertising is submitted for screening by federal officials under a voluntary arrangement.

■ The Civil Aeronautics Board concerns itself with many forms of aviation industry advertising activity. Airlines and travel agents are subject to CAB action for misrepresenting fares and facilities, and there have been several instances where airlines have been called to account for using advertising which misrepresents their fares, or the kind of aircraft that are regularly used on their routes. In most cases, these complaints originate with a competing airline that feels it has been injured by the advertising.

Like other federal agencies, the CAB has been under close consumerist scrutiny, and has updated its attitudes. In one recent case involving misrepresentation of package tour rates, the CAB required a major airline to run corrective ads. Another required refunds to tourists who were misled about accommodations included in a package tour offer.

But the regulation of content is only one aspect of the government's developing relationships with advertising.

■ Under the Highway Beautification program, for example, government is removing commercial signs from non-industrial portions of interstate and primary highways. Esthetic values and safety are offered as justifications. But the absence of ads is proving a handicap to the traveling public, which needs information about food, lodging and services, and there are strong demands for modification of the program.

"Regulation by jawbone" is another favorite government tactic, particularly for Virginia Knauer, the President's adviser on consumer affairs. Working with industry leaders, she has tried to rally business support for grading standards which would help consumers shop for commodities like fruit drinks and auto tires. In industry after industry—carpets, opticians, auto repairs and appliances, for example—she has encouraged the creation of voluntary consumer complaint-handling mechanisms.

Reprinted from Advertising Age," Nov 21, 1973, pp. 144, 147, 149, 154-155

Ads push thousands

of public causes

Although advertising is almost instinctively thought of as a tool of business, and frequently as the special darling of "big business," a very considerable amount of advertising is used on behalf of non-commercial causes and enterprises, not excluding many which are highly critical of advertising.

No separate figures are available, but a very substantial portion of the estimated $23.1 billion of U.S. advertising is made up of appeals for contributions by religious, educational, charitable and civic organizations, groups and societies, many of which are engaged in promoting points of view inimical to advertising. (We are eliminating here the advertising, estimated well up in the billions of dollars, which has been and is being contributed by the volunteer non-profit Advertising Council, whose activities on behalf of public causes are detailed elsewhere in this issue.)

Thousands of non-commercial organizations and enterprises use advertising routinely, in exactly the same way in which commercial organizations do, and for the same reasons—to "sell" memberships or gain support, to develop favorable consideration for a cause or a concept, and in general to encourage action which the sponsoring organization deems worth while

Thousands of churches buy advertising in newspapers to promote attendance at their services, and revivals, retreats, and other special religious events are often intensively advertised. Religious programs on radio and television, sponsored and paid for exactly like other commercial programs, are quite common, along with the public service religious programs aired without cost by the networks and numerous individual stations. Special purpose religious advertising campaigns, such as the long-running Knights of Columbus effort to disseminate information about Catholic doctrine, are also well established.

■ Hundreds of colleges and universities, as well as preparatory schools, camps and others, regularly use advertising in newspapers and magazines to promote enrolment, to feature special schools and courses, and sometimes to solicit gifts and endowments.

Government has always been an important user of advertising, and in the past year or so has become a substantially larger user. As ADVERTISING AGE pointed out in its issue of Aug. 27, 1973, "the surprising upsurge in advertising by the various branches of the U.S. government in 1972" catapulted it into the position of the 22nd largest advertiser in the country, with expenditures of $65,828,000 "on ad messages ranging from Army and Navy recruitment spots to public service messages on nutrition in print and tv for the Food & Drug Administration." And ADVERTISING AGE commented: "The fact that the government has turned to advertising as a persuasive tool is a strong argument for the power and value of advertising."

All state, county, municipal and other governmental bodies make use of the advertising mechanism routinely to the extent of publishing required legal notices. But numerous governmental bodies also use advertising more aggressively—to promote publicly-owned utilities, including transportation companies, water, light and power companies, etc. Toll roads, port authorities, and numerous other public and quasi-public institutions with services to sell—states and cities interested in attracting tourists and/or industry to their areas—state boards, commissions and agricultural marketing organizations—all find advertising useful in carrying out their tasks.

■ Labor unions use advertising—to promote the union label, or help move the products of an employing industry, or to state their positions in labor disputes or on public issues. Political parties and individual office seekers use advertising extensively to help sell their doctrines, their candidates and themselves to the public—a use which is currently causing intense public debate and numerous efforts to clean up and limit some of the practices in this area which have been carried to undesirable extremes.

Advertising is a selling tool and it is much used by business to sell goods and services at a (hoped for) profit. But it is equally adaptable to the selling of any commodity, service, idea or concept—including the concept that advertising is evil *per se* and should be prohibited! An interesting example is the direct mail advertising renewal notice to *Moneysworth* subscribers, which boasts of its success in attracting 700,000 subscribers through various forms of advertising and at the same time attributes much of its success to the fact that "*Moneysworth* has made a specialty of debunking advertising."

A great deal of non-commercial advertising consists of direct mail efforts by charitable, religious and similar non-profit organizations, and strange as it may seem, some of the aspects of direct mail which are most vehemently criticized are cited by observers as special favorites of non-profit groups. Sending unasked-for merchandise, souvenirs, etc., one of the most severely criticized of direct mail tactics, seems currently to be involved almost exclusively in charitable mailings which seem to delight in sending out sheets of perforated stamps, name labels, key rings, small religious symbols, envelopes filled with "holy" dirt, etc., in apparently fruitful efforts to induce more and larger contributions.

■ In a discussion of direct mail and its critics earlier this year, *Advertising & Sales Promotion* asserted that in 1972 some $3 billion went into the production and distribution of some 25 billion pieces of direct mail. "In addition to the $50 billion in sales produced by direct mail," said *A&SP*, "another $8 billion in contributions is generated through mail appeals." The publication also said, "At least 1,000,000 jobs are linked to direct mail."

While direct mail advertising is a favorite of charitable, religious and other groups seeking contributions and members, the entire gamut of advertising media is used for this and other "non-commercial" advertising. Newspapers, magazines, outdoor advertising, broadcasting and other advertising and promotional media are frequently used, and some have special rates for non-commercial groups as well as contributing a considerable amount of free time and space for worthy causes.

The *Washington Post* is an example of a newspaper which carries a considerable amount of non-commercial advertising, which it lists under an inclusive category called "editorial advertising." Some 100,000 lines of such advertising appeared in the paper during the first six months of 1973, the majority sponsored by individuals, coalitions and *ad hoc* groups attempting to influence Congress or the executive branch of the government, with environmentalists accounting for about one-third of the total this year.

Such advertising, the *Post* reports, sells at the appropriate local or general rate, except for a special charity rate available only to local charitable organizations which meet specific requirements of the newspaper.

■ Among magazines, *The New Yorker* carries a substantial volume of non-commercial and charitable advertising; in 1972 it ran about 27½ pages of free advertising (including 13 pages contributed to Advertising Council projects) and almost 45 pages of charity advertising at half its regular rates. *The New Yorker* defines a charity, for rate purposes, "as a tax-exempt organization from which needy individuals receive direct financial benefits." But even if the organization meets this requirement, it cannot get the charity rate if it "charges an admission or sells a product such as Christmas cards or magazine subscriptions, or is advertising for any commercial purpose other than the direct solicitation of funds."

In an effort to make some determination of the extent to which trade associations, churches, organized charities, schools and varied organizations and institutions use advertising, ADVERTISING AGE queried some 50 such charities and organizations, more or less at random.

As was to be expected, answers ranged all the way from that of Erma Angevine, who has since resigned as executive director of Consumer Federation of America, who said the CFA has used direct mail advertising for only one short sample project, hiring a public relations company to handle the entire project, to details of the extensive advertising effort of Christian Children's Fund, whose income of some $30,000,000 involves a major advertising effort.

■ Jerald E. Huntsinger, director of public relations for the Christian Children's Fund Inc., headquartered in Richmond, Va., reports that the fund depends "100% upon magazine advertising and direct mail to raise funds" for its worldwide child care program.

"As far as I can determine," he says, "Christian Children's Fund is the only major non-profit organization that has been able to utilize national magazine advertising over a long period of years, but the experience might be less positive if full commercial rates had to be paid across the board." The charity negotiates rates on an individual basis, but runs advertising in some magazines that give no discount, and in others that provide as much as a 50% discount. It also makes considerable use of "remnant space," which is space available at a discount because a particular magazine may have sold perhaps eight of ten of its geographic editions for a particular advertiser, and has this space unsold in the remaining two geographic areas.

■ Mr. Huntsinger reports that "fund raising costs are limited by policy of the board of directors to 10% of gross income, and says that "to my knowledge, this fund raising cost is among the lowest of the major non-profit organizations in America. Income for this fiscal year will be approximately $30,000,000. . .

"CCF does not use the traditional methods of fund raising, such as celebrity names, bazaars, benefit appearances, free merchandise, etc. Rather, the marketing program consists of public service spots on radio, television, magazine advertising and direct mail.

"While the ultimate goal is fund raising," Mr. Huntsinger asserts, "the marketing techniques are the same as you would find in most contemporary marketing organizations equipped with sophisticated computer analysis.

"In brief, it has been my experience that traditional fund raising techniques result in excessive fund raising costs, while contemporary marketing techniques result in an acceptable fund raising percentage."

■ An example of the use of advertising on a fairly modest scale by a university is provided by Elston Hillman, director of motion picture services, University of Pennsylvania, Philadelphia. The university used advertising to secure applications for admissions to some schools; for example, the Wharton Evening School budgets $7,600 annually for advertising in the three Philadelphia dailies, and the College of General Studies and Summer School budgets $6,000 for advertising in these newspapers and in six or seven college publications. The Graduate School of Education and the School of Social Work have modest budgets for advertising in professional journals, and various other budgets add up to a total of $18,100.

In addition, the university publishes a quarterly magazine which accepts advertising and "The Almanac," circulated to faculty and staff, which does not.

"Aside from advertising and promotion," comments Donald T. Sheehan, university director of public relations, "the U. of P. public relations program consists basically of the dissemination of public information and activities to both print and broadcast media, a motion picture unit, and internally, the publishing of a weekly newspaper for faculty and staff."

The National Urban League reports that it does "a great deal of mail solicitation" through its national headquarters, and the Freedoms Foundation at Valley Forge reports that it uses a periodic newsletter, sent to some 53,000 individuals at a cost of about $5,000 per mailing, as a fund solicitation vehicle.

■ Among other organizations which supplied ADVERTISING AGE with information about their advertising and promotional activities were Consumers' Research Inc. and Consumers Union. F. J. Schlink of Consumers' Research says his organization does direct mail advertising to solicit subscriptions to its magazine, but does not use an advertising agency. Paul Goldberg, promotion director of the considerably larger Consumers Union, reports that "we use large quantities of direct mail, straight space, radio and television" to solicit subscriptions for *Consumer Reports,* whose circulation is now over 2,000,000. March Advertising, New York, handles the Consumers Union account, and Michael R. Fabian, exec vp of that advertising agency, provided the following detail:

"Direct mail speaks for itself. Space efforts include the use of general media, full-page insert units in magazines, and free-standing stuffers in newspapers. Broadcast effort includes spot radio and tv in markets throughout the country. All advertising is placed on a measurable basis—coupons in print, call-ins and write-ins in the broadcast field.

"Since Consumers Union is a non-profit organization whose revenue depends in a large part on income derived from subscribers, a great deal of effort is expended to make their circulation efforts self-supporting, which, means translated into other words, means that we must maintain a relatively high degree of advertising effectiveness."

Edgar C. Bundy, executive secretary of the Church League of America, Wheaton, Ill., reports that his organization does not budget particular amounts for advertising; "we simply advertise as money becomes available." Direct mail is their principal medium, with Potomoc Arts Ltd., McLean, Va., handling creative and production.

"The AFL-CIO makes only very limited use of advertising techniques because our function is largely legislative," Albert J. Zack, director of the department of public relations, tells ADVERTISING AGE. "Several international unions, however, make more frequent use of advertising. For example, the Retail Clerks International Assn. is a sponsor of the baseball All-Star game on radio, as well as on NBC's Monitor program, and the Communications Workers of America has used newspaper advertising in several ways."

Maurer, Fleisher, Zon & Associates, Washington advertising agency, handles a number of unions and the infrequent advertising needs of AFL-CIO. AFL-CIO publications do not accept advertising, but some unions do, and a considerable amount is handled through the International Labor Press Assn. in Washington.

Henry Fleischer of the agency says the union advertising they handle "falls into three general categories: (1) General advertis-

ing in support of legislative issues or policy positions of the union, or for general community public relations work; (2) in support of specific collective bargaining objectives or policies; and (3) in support of strikes—or in support of the union's position in disputes that are not necessarily at strike level.

"We have placed this kind of advertising for a number of unions including AFL-CIO, Communications Workers of America, the Amalgamated Meat Cutters and Butcher Workmen, the Sheet Metal Workers International Assn., the Oil, Chemical & Atomic Workers, and the Textile Workers Union of America.

"The bulk of this advertising is placed in newspapers; occasionally, as in the case of the recent Oil Workers strike against Shell, we use radio spots in a few selected cities."

■ Political advertising in the U.S. dates back to the 1930s, but it has been only since perhaps 1964 that selling candidates to the electorate has become more or less scientific—and probably more ubiquitous, obtrusive and expensive.

An estimated $200,000,000 was spent at all levels on advertising in the 1964 elections. That outlay was exceeded in 1968, when all elections took about $300,000,000, and was exceeded again in 1972, when the cost rose to some $400,-000,000. It has been estimated that the campaign to reelect President Nixon last year consumed $50,000,000, while another $28,-000,000 was paid out in the vain effort to elect Senator McGovern. The broadcast industry alone is said to have sold $59,600,000 worth of air time to politicians last year.

"Although the $4.5 billion spent annually for national advertising for consumer products has compiled a pretty competent record of irritating growing segments of the public," commented E. B. Weiss, ADVERTISING AGE columnist, "the $400,000,000 spent for political campaigns probably outdid the $4.5 billion as a public irritant. The unprecedented use of direct mail and the telephone demolished the right of privacy, and, of course, the intelligence level of the messages broke through the bottom of the intelligence scale."

■ Some advertising agencies will not handle political campaigns, others believe that "as long as politicians are running for office and using media, advertising people ought to take their chances with the ones they trust." Those opposed say that politicians insist on making unsubstantial claims; that they are slow-pay clients;

and that the time consumed on political campaigns could better be used on behalf of product advertisers.

Others propose that advertising media space and time be donated without cost, otherwise the mounting costs of elections inevitably lead to corruption (donations to political parties for advertising by organizations expecting privileged treatment in return).

Whatever the solution, E. B. Weiss has expressed the belief that "major changes" will be made in political advertising in coming years, perhaps by 1980.

An interesting exposition of the promotional activities of the Salvation Army is provided by Maj. Ernest A. Miller, public relations secretary in territorial headquarters in Chicago, who points out the Salvation Army operates in more than 1,000 cities in the U.S. and in 79 countries, and that each center is essentially self-supporting, so that diverse patterns are the rule rather than the exception.

"There are, however, various patterns which are reasonably uniform throughout the U.S.," says Major Miller. "Some of these patterns and related principles may include the following:

"1. Paid advertising is held to a minimum. Essentially the only purpose for which it is used is to advertise for annuities in those few journals and newspapers which may be most useful for this highly specialized type of advertising.

"2. Mass advertising is used, but on a basis of donated space. J. Walter Thompson Co. and other agencies prepare ads without fee.

"3. Direct mail is used extensively in hundreds, if not thousands, of cities and communities. Each local community has its own budget, its own goals, and often its own materials for this. There is a trend, however, toward uniformity and the use of computerized lists and mailing facilities.

"4. The Salvation Army publishes several journals including: *The War Cry, The Young Soldier, The Musician, Home League Programaids,* and many others. No advertising is solicited or accepted for any of them.

"The circulation of the Christmas issue of *The War Cry* is in excess of 4,000,000 copies. Weekly issues circulate approximately 200,000 copies in the U.S.

"5. Broadcast media are used on a free time basis only. No time is purchased. Promotion projects include television spot announcements, radio spot announcements, the 30-minute radio drama 'Heartbeat Theatre' (540 stations), and other features."

92

Reprinted from "Advertising Age," Nov. 21, 1973, pp. 144, 147, 149, 154-155

How U.S. uses advertising

Some say it's not advertising at all. Some say it's advertising of the strongest kind, with Big Brotherish potential. Others, probably a majority, merely get an impression: Officialdom promoting ideas and actions that usually sound sensible.

Whatever you call it—and by dictionary definition advertising is as good a name as any—the federal government is deeply into it.

The government's expenditure to send out all kinds of advertising messages to the public in all kinds of media will be in the neighborhood of $110,000,000 this fiscal year if the appropriations requested are approved and spent. So far only a few, amounting to about $20,000,000, are considered possible targets for congressional questioning. The big military recruiting chunk of about $80,000,000—up $24,000,000 from last year —might even be hiked further by Congress because of pressures brought on by discontinuation of the draft.

The total expenditure, led by the military but also boosted considerably by increased spending elsewhere, has gone up sharply in the past few years. In 1971 the government put an estimated $43,000,000 into the preparation of ads and informational messages, plus payments for time (an Army test of paid tv) and space.

■ Last year the promotional figure was close to $66,000,000, a total offered by official sources which did not view as government advertising a payment of $10,000,000 to Cotton Inc., the cotton industry's advertising and research arm. Cotton Inc. puts about a third of that money into advertising. Another $3,000,000-to-$5,000,000 could be added to cover the salaries of government employes who work on, or have an important connection with, inhouse activities on ads and promotional materials. (This last figure may be conservative in view of a General Accounting Office report describing Pentagon figures on public affairs spending as misleading for omitting $24,000,000 in projects and jobs, some overlapping into advertising and promotion.)

Considering these costs, plus a possible $2,000,000-to-$3,000,000 additional military boost since Congress is worried about recruiting, it is conceivable that the government could put more than $120,000,000 into advertising and closely related activities in the current fiscal year.

■ This possible total does not include the costs of informational materials handed out to the press and the public at federal facilities throughout the country, though some of this borders on advertising in a broad sense—i.e., when the government advises you to file your income tax early. In the context of a tax guide booklet, it's not quite advertising, but the promotional message is there. You're not required by law to file your tax return early.

Nor would this $120,000,000 total include U.S. Information Agency programs, or military tv film handouts of the kind that might be characterized as program-length commercials by the Federal Communications Commission if the subject were real estate or chinchilla ranches. And none of the total takes into account the value of donated public service time and space, which came to $224,000,000 for eight campaigns last year handled through the Advertising Council. Add military public service ads, which are not placed through the Council, and the value reaches the neighborhood of $1 billion.

As for the $110,000,000 that is actually scheduled or proposed to be spent by the government on advertising and promotion this fiscal year, the question is: Where does it all go?

■ The answer would have been easy 20 years ago: U.S. savings bonds, Smokey the Bear, a few social service drives. The military services were spending only $10,000,000 on recruiting ads in 1960.

Smokey and savings bonds are still very much in evidence in annual campaigns by the U.S. Forest Service and the Treasury Department, but there's also Dana Andrews' plea for sober driving, Julie Nixon Eisenhower promoting the use of special educational facilities for handicapped children; a sale of long-forgotten silver dollars, "the coins Jesse James never got." Thousands of workers are being told that "exports create jobs." An even bigger campaign by the National Commission on Productivity will promote "better productivity." There are civil rights, job rights and housing rights campaigns and drives for safety, health, social security and veterans' benefits. Mass transportation will soon be promoted. There are tourism ads abroad and expanding environmental campaigns at home.

Military. By far the biggest government advertising effort is for military recruiting. The total armed services recruiting ad budget now before Congress is $80,000,000. An additional $8,000,000 is being requested by the Department of Defense for a one-year tryout of "umbrella" corporate-type advertising for all the services.

With the draft ended, the Army is relying heavily on paid print ads as well as public service broadcasting, and it proposes to spend a total of $34,000,000 this fiscal year. Just under a third of this is expected to go into paid magazine and newspaper advertising via the N. W. Ayer & Son advertising agency, reappointed by the Army a year ago. The decision to continue with Ayer and the ad theme, "Today's Army Wants to Join You," produced a major controversy over selection procedures that some competing agencies felt were stacked in favor of the incumbent. Added to this was internal dissatisfaction with the ad theme, which a group of career officers said was weak and failed to draw "dedicated" men. This year the "Army Wants to Join You" theme has been dropped down to a signature on recruiting ads that have a variety of new headline themes.

The Navy and Air Force, no longer alternatives to the draft and foot-soldiering, are also pushing harder for recruits. They're increasing expenditures by about $5,000,000 each to totals of $25,000,000 and $17,000,000, respectively. Grey Advertising held onto the Navy account in competition last spring that was joined in by only three other agencies out of 40 invited to participate. The Air Force held no competition this year and continues with D'Arcy-MacManus & Masius; and the Marine Corps, whose spending is up by $1,000,000 to a total of $7,400,000 for fiscal 1974, is into its 27th year with the J. Walter Thompson Co.

■ The Army is the government's biggest user of paid advertising, putting between $5,000,000 and $6,000,000 into magazine and newspaper space in fiscal '73. The Navy and Air Force combined put just over $2,000,000 into space purchases, mostly in magazines. The trend is toward more payment for ad space, but there is some opposition to this in Congress on the grounds it makes it more difficult for the services to get free time and space as a public service. The argument of the services is that they can't get their public service ads into print at the times and in the positions they want. The same argument is made even more vigorously regarding television and radio, and there is pressure, most notably from Sen. Richard S. Schweiker (R., Pa.), to permit the services to buy broadcast time regularly to reach the widest possible audience of potential recruits.

The possibility that armed forces recruitment advertising will reach the $100,000,000 mark in the next few years is not remote. Top Army men are worried not only about the failure to reach required manpower quotas but also that the new all-volunteer service is drawing minority recruits at a rate disproportionate with their numbers in the total population. They feel more

"recruiting balance" is needed to maintain support for the military from all sectors of the public. Part of the thinking behind plans for the $8,000,000 umbrella ad and promotion drive starting late this year or early next is that a general, dramatic sell on service to the country could be the attention-getter the individual branches need to get young men and women with diverse educational and economic backgrounds.

U.S. Postal Service. USPS sources say at least $5,000,000 will be spent to advertise old and new postal services this year. The figure might be somewhat suspect, since USPS was understood to have budgeted close to that amount last year. Now officials say they put closer to $3,000,000 into about half a dozen test campaigns for express mail service for business, postal money orders, security mail service, overnight letters, even old fashioned air mail. The express mail test was in regional issues of national magazines and the postal money order tryout used mainly spot tv.

USPS is coming out this fall with national campaigns for its services, possibly including drives for pre-stamped stationery, post office boxes and facsimile letters with ads stressing same-day delivery between cities. The service will continue to use public service time and space for its mail-early Christmas and Zip code messages. Needham, Harper & Steers is the agency.

Amtrak. The two-year-old government-sponsored intercity passenger train system started advertising in earnest last fall and early this year. Its initial six-month campaign through the spring of 1973 was a $3,000,000 effort and plans for 1974 indicate an annual expenditure in the neighborhood of $5,000,000. So far, Amtrak has stressed "comfort, convenience, safety" in newspaper and radio ads in 171 cities along the six main rail corridors in the country. Headlines like "Take the tension out of your trip" also make it clear that the system is after airline business and automobile drivers who might be happier in an Amtrak seat.

Whether Amtrak will become an even more important government advertiser is hard to say. It's been having trouble getting the funds it says are necessary to make the system attractive and efficient without pricing it too

close to the airlines, and it may never expand into the big market many officials would like to give it—commuter rail service. If it did, Ted Bates & Co., Amtrak's agency, would hardly be expected to object.

· **U.S. Travel Service.** "The Great American Adventure" in England and other English-speaking countries and similar campaigns in Europe cost about $2,000,000 this year. USTS is another government unit that hasn't been getting quite what it wants in the way of backing. The White House cut back on its plans for a $3,000,000-plus program to lure tourists to the U.S., but a boost will reportedly be sought again even though the flow of visitors is said to be increasing as a result of the dollar devaluation. Young & Rubicam is the USTS agency.

■ Most of these expenditures by the government are fairly easy to pin down, and, with the exception of military recruiting ads run on a public service basis, the time and space is paid. The area where the extent of government advertising activities gets hazy is in the creation and production of public service print and broadcast campaigns and drives that departments and offices start up on their own and put before the public in various ways—spot and regional public service ads directed at special groups, poster campaigns in plants and public places, transit drives, direct mail, classified, etc. In the view of some, including a few government officials, this is where government should be curbed or at least made to evaluate its aims and the effects of its deluge of messages on the public and the economy as well as on the federal treasury.

Curb Smokey the Bear? There have been complaints that the forest fire prevention campaign is irrelevant in urban areas and shouldn't take up tv time there. But the forest service says urban people go to the forests. Also, the drive fits in with environmental and preservation movements, as does a companion public service campaign against littering national parks and forests. It features a character called Woodsie Owl. Together, the campaigns cost about $300,000 a year to create and produce via Foote, Cone & Belding and Carson/Roberts.

■ Other public service drives with expenditures and aims that are fairly simple include the

Treasury Department's "Buy U.S. Bonds" campaign (cost about $360,000); the ACTION campaign to get volunteers for the Peace Corps ($250,000); the Interior Department's Johnny Horizon bicentennial cleanup campaign (also about $250,000); the office of education's drive to inform people of government programs for the handicapped ($50,000 to $100,000), and the highway safety ad program, which costs in the neighborhood of $300,000 to produce.

But for each of these there are two or three drives that no one in particular has a grip on as to cost, and that few officials can discuss in terms of aim or effect. Civil Defense spends something like $250,000 on public service messages on what to do in emergencies. The Immigration and Naturalization Service, at an expense that has not been revealed, notifies aliens of registration requirements in the person of a public service cartoon character who looks like he's just been prepared for the electric chair. There are Commerce Department campaigns to inform workers that "exports create jobs" (What is the worker supposed to do about that? Start exporting on his own?) and that good workmanship and more productivity are good for everyone. Transit and poster ads advise of job rights where no jobs are available, warn against housing discrimination where the audience is made up largely of people who can barely afford rent, and urge those who are most victimized by crime—inner-city blacks, many of them elderly—to do something about it. Perhaps buy guns?

■ There are also nutrition campaigns and anti-drug campaigns and alcoholism campaigns and mental health campaigns that may or may not have an effect in reducing the problems involved. Nobody really knows, but critics are beginning to see a target that's growing bigger all the time. Arguments have already been raised about a glut of government advertising and informational programs, one running into another until the messages are lost. There are charges that many of the efforts are either misdirected or examples of random government growth for the sake of government.

Some government officials feel the time and money involved could be put to better use at the core of the problems involved. Others point out that with some government social programs cut to the bone and funding for others at a minimum, the public should at least be made aware of problems that exist and solutions that can be brought about by self-help combined with government assistance.

They note that the cost is minimal compared to the bill for greatly expanded programs. Thus, while people who do little personally to cause pollution might feel helpless and irritated when told by Woodsie Owl to "stop pollution," they might also think twice before tossing a cigaret butt. It's the philosophy of most government message-makers that some good will comes of their efforts.

■ But despite contentions that the cost of government advertising campaigns is piddling compared with, say, military equipment expenditures, and ought to be left to grow as long as there are causes to be promoted, there's something of a new interest in the way taxpayers' dollars are spent to communicate with the public. It is evident in a study conducted by the White House Office of Telecommunications Policy that attempts to show the extent of in-house production of tv and radio spots and educational and training films throughout government.

■ The study shows that in-house production in departments like Agriculture and Health, Education & Welfare is on the decline and total costs for the programs are increasing. There are doubters in the tv spot and film production industry who say that work being contracted to them and to advertising agencies has been reduced by increased in-house production over the past several years.

Whether the OTP study will arouse more interest in the growth of government advertising or simply perpetuate a logistics debate is hard to say so soon after its completion. But it is the first time any aspect of government advertising as a whole has been given a thorough evaluation.

Serious thought about the effectiveness of advertising by government is also beginning to show up. At a recent conference of the American Marketing Assn., for instance, Lee Richardson, director of education and finance for the Office of Consumer Affairs, questioned "whether you can just turn on consumer education advertising and expect behavior to change. It doesn't seem to change things when you tell people to eat spinach . . . Maybe you just have to ban things and set minimum standards."

Reprinted from "Advertising Age," Nov. 21, 1973, pp. 160, 162

How agriculture

uses advertising

Ten years ago, a Department of Agriculture survey disclosed that 1,200 farm producer organizations operated promotion programs, spending $100,000,000 annually to promote their goods. The study is still in the process of being updated, but a department spokesman estimates that while the number of groups using promotion is still about 1,200, total budget figures have risen to $120,000,000 to $130,000,000.

While far from all the agricultural groups actively advertise their wares at the consumer level, the use of media advertising is becoming a growing factor in the industry.

There are three different types of farm organizations active in commodity marketing:

1. Voluntary producer groups. These are purely promotional and research groups such as American Dairy Assn. and Oregon-Washington-California Pear Bureau.

2. Farmer cooperatives. Individual farmers or growers join together to form this type of organization, which handles all marketing activities from packing and shipping to selling, and may or may not include advertising efforts for the industry. Sunkist Growers is an example of a co-op which relies heavily on advertising.

3. State boards, commissions and councils. These quasi-governmental organizations such as Florida Citrus Commission, California Milk Producers Advisory Board and Cling Peach Advisory Board, operate under marketing orders. The orders, established after a public hearing and vote of a certain number of the industry members, cover such areas as quality control, selling regulations and advertising.

Members of co-ops and state board-type groups are assessed a certain per cent of sales to cover costs of services rendered, including ad budgets for promotional efforts. Referendums are held when it is felt necessary to increase assessments.

Vernon Shahbazian, marketing bureau chief of the California department of food and agriculture, attested to the increase in promotional activities in recent years. In his state, which has a large number of agricultural groups, "promotions have more than doubled" in many cases, he said.

Thomas Randolph, senior vp at Foote, Cone & Belding, San Francisco, whose clients include several agricultural accounts such as Sunkist Growers, also noted that many groups have increased ad spending following selected weighted-market tests that convinced them of the benefits of solid advertising programs in moving their goods.

■ The promotion of peaches, avocados or milk, however, is a different matter from persuading the consumer to switch her loyalties from X brand to Y brand. Most agricultural items are not branded; many also have short growing seasons to contend with.

Advertising becomes a kind of constant repositioning of the product to make it relevant, given changing tastes and life styles. Efforts deal in benefits such as economy and nutrition rather than direct product comparisons. In some instances, the promotional thrust is concerned with building a new image for the product to expand its usage.

Last year, the per capita milk consumption in California increased 3.7% from the low point it hit in the late 1960s. Credited with the turnaround in milk drinking habits is a multi-media celebrity campaign created for the California Milk Producers Advisory Board in 1971 by Cunningham & Walsh, San Francisco.

In 1970, the American Dairy Assn. of California became the Milk Board through a state-created marketing order, and C&W was named as agency for the group. The problem at that time was the low rate of per capita consumption in the state, which had been declining since the mid-'60s. Initially, the agency began running radio spots with cow jokes and outdoor boards featuring bikini-clad girls and the line, "Every body needs milk," a theme purchased from Campbell-Mithun, which handles the Milk Foundation of the Twin Cities.

■ By mid-'71 declining consumption had been curbed. At that point, the board increased its ad budget by doubling the assessment on members to 1% of milk sales and the celebrity push was launched—beginning with Pat Boone in tv and radio. A variety of celebrities including Ray Bolger, Vida Blue and Mark Spitz have been used to date, and the effort has been expanded to include outdoor and print.

Success of the promotion for California has led to its expansion into Oregon and Washington, and the possibility of the approach being used in other markets.

■ This is just one example of the importance of advertising to the marketing of commodity products and illustrates the growing sophistication of ad efforts by agricultural organizations.

Sunkist Growers is another good example of advertising as an effective selling tool for agricultural products. When it was organized in 1893 as Southern California Fruit Exchange, oranges were a luxury product, consumed by very few persons with any regularity. The use of "Sunkist" as a trademark started in 1908 and has since been promoted to the tune of well over $100,000,000. Its success can be measured by the fact that today the group accounts for about 40% of all the fresh fruit sold nationally. The budget comes from an assessment of 16¢ per carton of oranges sold for the grower.

■ Sunkist deals mainly in eating oranges and lemons while another big spender, Florida Citrus Commission, puts most of its multi-million dollar budget behind orange juice and grapefruit.

A dramatic example of the effect promotion has had on this group's marketing occurred in 1959, when stocks of Florida frozen orange juice concentrate reached record levels. The commission lined up 22 producers of frozen orange juice to mount a special three-month $4,000,000 ad push. Examination of sales results for the period against patterns of previous years indicated that the campaign generated $18,000,000 in additional retail sales.

■ American Dairy has consistently held one of the largest promotional budgets, spending in tv, radio, magazines and newspapers for all kinds of dairy products. In addition to product promotion, the group has used advertising as a broad propaganda force in the health arena. Recently the group's ads have been hit by charges of making misleading claims regarding nutrition and the benefits of milk.

An animated spot themed "There's a new you coming every day," and featuring a stewardess getting instant energy from a glass of milk, and radio spots noting the low-fat content of whole milk (only 4% butterfat) were cited by government agencies as making misleading claims. This fall, the group is using live

action tv spots that tout a "fresh start the grade A way."

ADA's annual fall cheese promotion for '73, again themed "Cheese, It gives you ideas," offers a "Cheese Quickies" recipe booklet, and uses tv, radio, national magazine and newspaper backing. In-store materials are used not only in cheese sections but with related items such as fruits, nuts, ground beef, pizza mix and hot dogs.

■ Although most agricultural products are unbranded, those groups that use trademarks, such as Sunkist, Diamond Walnut Growers, Sun-Maid growers (raisins) and Sunsweet (prunes), have found them to be an effective selling tool. Earlier in 1973, Sunland Marketing was formed to

Ad spending by leading food associations: 1972

Group	Spot Television	Network Television	Magazines	Newspapers*	Spot radio	Net radio	Outdoor	Total
American Dairy Assn.	$ 5,489,400	$1,458,500	$ 640,700	$ 287,691	$ 642,200	$208,800	$141,200	$ 8,868,491
Florida Citrus Commission	269,100	5,232,100	1,109,300	280,946	—	—	—	6,962,946
Ocean Spray Cranberries	1,402,300	2,144,000	136,100	74,207	44,300	—	—	3,799,907
California Milk Producers Advisory Board	2,347,900	54,100	174,100	86,822	238,200	—	805,600	3,706,722
Sunkist Growers	1,221,800	338,900	1,463,500	190,415	133,100	—	—	3,357,725
California & Hawaii Sugar Assn.	834,700	—	300,400	79,705	1,300	—	—	1,216,105
American Sheep Producers Council	—	—	163,900	450,542	83,300	—	4,300	702,042
Cling Peach Advisory Board	661,100	—	—	7,000	—	—	—	668,100
California Prune Advisory Board	—	—	5,400	76,545	516,300	48,000	—	646,245
California Almond Growers	73,200	—	497,500	12,313	—	—	—	602,013
Diamond Walnut Growers	85,500	—	149,200	221,580	—	—	—	456,280
California Avocado Advisory Board	—	—	377,400	—	57,200	—	—	434,600
Dairymen's League Co-op Assn.	302,100	—	—	103,342	—	—	—	405,442
Idaho Potato Commission	—	—	—	—	392,600	—	—	392,600
California Canners & Growers	—	—	73,300	288,117	3,600	—	—	365,017
Cotton Producers Assn.	—	—	—	248,767	3,700	—	46,600	299,067
Texas Valley Citrus Commission	95,900	—	28,700	65,405	2,000	—	—	253 505
Sun-Maid Growers	—	—	221,400	—	—	—	—	221,400
Sunsweet Growers	—	—	199,900	—	—	—	—	199,900
Rice Council	—	—	180,800	—	—	—	—	180,800
Totals	$12,783,000	$9,227,600	$5,721,600	$2,473,397	$2,117,800	$256,800	$997,700	$33,577,897

*Newspaper includes supplements.

pool the marketing of Sun-Maid raisins, Sunsweet pitted prunes and Blue Ribbon figs, and forestall deeper penetration by private labels (almost 90% of current dried fruit sales are by national brands).

Commodities are very fragile products at times. If a crop is ruined by bad weather, a group can cut back on advertising and hope for fairer weather; when supplies are bountiful, ad-promotion efforts can be hypoed. Or in difficult times, a grower organization might follow the recent example of the California Avocado Advisory Board. When a small

crop in the 1971-72 growing season forced prices of the fruit upwards, the group used advertising to reposition the product out of the food category altogether.

■ Ads in *Cosmopolitan, Glamour, Harper's Bazaar* and *Vogue,* new territory for the item, extolled the cosmetic value of avocados.

Headlines such as "The Fresh Avocado Facial," and "Fresh Avocado Hair Care," were designed to arrest the reader's attention and then give her some beauty advice. A 44-page booklet of beauty aid recipes was offered for $1, featuring avocados with such other prod-

ucts as tomatoes, carrots, cranberries and cucumbers.

In 1960-'61, before the board was operating and promotions were spotty, value of the California crop was $9,998,152. In 1969-'70, with an ad investment of $826,144, crop value rose to $21,509,243. Ad investment for 1970-'71 rose to $1,200,000 with crop value growing to $24,500,000.

Ad investments are tied to crop value, rather than size, with assessment for promotion set at 4½% of dollar value to the grower. This arrangement enables consistent advertising, according to the group.

Reprinted from "Advertising Age," Nov. 21, 1973, pp. 162, 164

How labor uses advertising

Labor union advertising is aimed primarily at influencing political leaders on certain pieces of legislation and telling the public the union's side of a dispute during a strike.

Some unions, notably the International Ladies' Garment Workers Union (ILGWU), New York, still carry on "institutional" campaigns, urging consumers to buy union made goods, but for the most part have gotten away from ongoing campaigns and now use advertising on a rather *ad hoc* basis.

The AFL-CIO, Washington, for example, used to sponsor a radio show featuring Edward P. Morgan, five nights a week. The buy cost the AFL-CIO about $400,000 a year. After Mr. Morgan left ABC, the AFL-CIO dropped its sponsorship and began using its ad funds (received by charging a 10¢ per member per month tax) for irregularly scheduled campaigns.

About three and a half years ago, the AFL-CIO used the money for an extensive campaign to explain the union's side during a General Electric strike. Nothing of that magnitude has been mounted recently by the AFL-CIO. The most recent effort by the group was a newspaper ad in the *Washington Post* Sept. 16 urging legislators to override President Richard M. Nixon's veto of a bill to raise the minimum wage. The override attempt failed.

■ Another union that had used advertising extensively on a continuing basis but has since stopped such efforts is the United Auto Workers, Detroit.

The UAW had been spending about $1,000,000 a year in advertising up to 1970 when the General Motors strike almost bankrupted the union and all advertising had to be curtailed.

Prior to that time, the union had been recording a 30-minute radio program, "Eye Opener,"

using its own radio and tv production facilities. The show was a combination interview, news, commentary and music program that was placed in 20 markets.

The UAW also produced "Telescope," which was a tv interview show. The show was aired only in Detroit and was promoted heavily on radio-tv pages in Detroit newspapers. Both shows are now off the air and the union only does occasional radio advertising that addresses itself to current issues. It also has a Community Action Program, a one-column ad that runs in about six Michigan newspapers and deals with political topics.

The Communications Workers of America, Washington, uses advertising on a somewhat more regular basis than many other unions. CWA always runs an ad in local media when it has its national convention. The ad tells the public a little about the union and urges people to stop by and investigate it further. It also does strike advertising, which is usually funded out of a pr budget or a strike defense fund.

■ But by far, the union that has the most continuous and consistent advertising is the ILGWU which has been doing institutional and "buy American" type advertising for more than ten years. ILGWU funds its advertising by means of a 25¢ a member a month tax. The union had been using Solow/Wexton, New York, as its agency but is currently without one since Solow went out of business earlier this year. Until the close of Solow, the ILGWU had been running a consistent print ad campaign. The drive not only stressed buy American, but also urged consumers to look for the union label in garments.

One ad the union ran in the *New York Times Magazine* last year showed a garment finisher and carried the headline: "Once she's finished—you may be

through." Body copy stressed that many garment companies were sending products to other countries where the job of finishing paid about 16¢ an hour and that if the American finisher lost her job to a counterpart overseas, she could no longer purchase goods and services, thus harming the U.S. economy.

■ Another kind of job-retention plea came up in 1965 when the Brotherhood of Locomotive Firemen & Engineers ran a $100,000 advertising campaign to emphasize the need for the presence of firemen in locomotives. One ad showed a locomotive engineer who said that without a fireman "on the left side of my cab, my 'blind' side," railroading was "more difficult and dangerous."

The campaign was started about six months before the date set for renewing a rule allowing railroads to eliminate firemen from freight train locomotives. When renewal time came, different agreements were reached with different railroads. Some roads reinstated firemen on certain freight runs; other roads agreed to retain their firemen until they retired; still others agreed to continue the post, but as a training ground for future engineers.

Another safety campaign was one started in 1967—but this time involving the Uniformed Firemens Assn. of Greater New York, AFL-CIO. It resulted from many cases of open hostility exhibited toward the fire-fighters at a time of large-scale rioting in many American cities. The ads proclaimed, in English and Spanish, that "The fireman is your friend," and explained that he was doing his job "only to do good for you and your family," adding, "Let him do his job of rescue as quickly and efficiently as possible."

■ A notable campaign of the 1960s, one that ran for three

years, was sponsored by Local 1, Amalgamated Lithographers of America. Its advertising welcomed automation to the lithographic industry and spurred business for union shops with copy that pointed out that customers of ALA plants would not have to pay for "featherbedding or obsolete processes."

Another was a $500,000 effort by the Retail Clerks International Assn., Washington, to gain recognition for stores employing union members and to raise the standards of retail service. A third campaign involved Local 9 of the Brewery Workers Union and was designed to halt a decline in beer sales. One of the most celebrated union ads appeared over the signature of Local 746, International Union of Electrical, Radio & Machine Workers. The ad showed the latest of Westinghouse appliances, and proclaimed, "We're proud of them. They are America's finest . . . we know, because we build them."

Although good will campaigns like these appear from time to time, the unions apparently reserve their biggest advertising drives for contract-renewal periods. At such times, ads can vary from a this-is-what-we-want-and-why approach to a tough, hard-driving effort centering on complaints against company policies. Probably the biggest contract-renewal campaign in history ran in 1959 when the United Steel Workers began wage negotiations. The union sponsored full-page ads in 40 newspapers every week for four months. Copy explained how a $1 billion wage-increase for 1,250,000 steel workers would be beneficial to the American economy.

Steel industry managements countered with an advertising campaign of their own, using space in some 400 newspapers. The United Steel Workers spent an estimated $1,400,000 and the Iron & Steel Institute placed over $2,400,000 in advertising.

■ More recently, the Oil, Chemical & Atomic Workers Union, Denver, sponsored a newspaper and outdoor campaign against the Shell Oil Co. The advertising urged consumers to boycott Shell products. Outdoor boards showed the head of a man wearing a hard hat. Copy stated: "4,000 oil workers say SHELL? NO! Please DON'T BUY SHELL." The drive, which the union said marked the first use of national outdoor by a labor organization, was budgeted at $250,000, including newspaper ads.

Many local unions advertise regionally, with campaigns ranging, again, from good will types to hard sell efforts. Several locals of the International Brotherhood of Teamsters, for example, are currently running campaigns that urge safe driving. The Teamsters international headquarters does no advertising, however.

■ The Amalgamated Meat Cutters Union, Washington, ran a newspaper campaign in 35 markets last May that was a combination hard sell/union good will effort. The ad ran as meat prices began to climb higher and higher. They said, "Lady, please don't blame your butcher (for the rising prices)" and called for the resignation of Agriculture Secretary Earl Butz. The $40,000 one-week drive also asked consumers with complaints to get in touch with their congressmen. Maurer, Fleisher, Zon & Associates handled the campaign.

Media vs. Labor

Despite the fact many unions feel that they have a story to tell the consumer and that advertising is the best way to get the message across, the media may not always agree. A case in point is a legal battle that developed between the Amalgamated Clothing Workers of America and Chicago's four dailies—the *Daily News*, *Sun-Times*, *Today* and *Tribune*—in 1969 when all the papers refused a full-page union ad explaining why the union was picketing Marshall Field & Co., a Chicago based retail department store and a heavy newspaper advertiser. The store is also a part of Field Enterprises, publisher of the *Sun-Times* and *Daily News*.

The union was against Field's selling imported men's and boys' clothing, which the union said was taking jobs away from American workers. All four newspapers rejected the ad and offered no explanation. The union filed suit, charging infringement of free speech, since there were no other major dailies in the area. The union lost its case.

All in all, unions seem to have curtailed their advertising budgets in recent years. It appears not to stem from a lack of faith in advertising, however, but rather from a lack of funds.

Reprinted from "Advertising Age," Nov. 21, 1973, pp. 162, 164

The Advertising Council:

An American phenomenon

Now in its 32nd year of operation, the Advertising Council is still a private, non-profit corporation supported entirely by American business, including the advertising and communications industries. Since its inception early in 1942, when it was called the War Advertising Council, the organization has placed more than $7 billion worth of advertising for the public good.

For three decades, council campaigns conducted for private organizations and federal agencies have demonstrated that lives can be saved, natural resources conserved, diseases mitigated or eliminated, other pressing national problems alleviated, and vast sums generated for charitable organizations.

During its lifetime the Advertising Council has helped sell such ideas as "Register and Vote," "Prevent Forest Fires," "Buy U.S. Savings Bonds." More recently, in attempts to update and broaden its coverage of contemporary problems, the council has concerned itself with such thorny issues as drug abuse, pollution and crime prevention.

Although the council was originally founded during World War II to marshal the forces of advertising so they would be of maximum help to the national interest, the organization has continued to play a vital role in bringing to the American people peacetime programs for public service.

■ Today the council is a leading advertiser, sponsoring some 20-odd public service campaigns annually, and something of a national phenomenon. The nature of its work is to sell ideas that will promote the public weal. "In the area of public service," according to C. W. Cook, chairman of General Foods, "the Advertising Council is America's showcase to the world. Here is an amazing mix of managerial expertise; of technical facilities; of the economic, political

and behavioral sciences; of volunteer time and talent, of brains, work and money. Never before have business, labor communications, government, religion, education, medicine, the professions, and other material and spiritual resources been so effectively programed for public profit."

Back in November of 1941, while World War II was ravaging a good part of the globe, the leading figures in U.S. advertising and business were called to Hot Springs, Va., by the late Paul West, then president of the prestigious Assn. of National Advertisers, for a special "survival meeting."

■ Present at this first joint meeting in the history of the industry were representatives of the American Assn. of Advertising Agencies and various media groups. The subject of the meeting was how to upgrade the reputation of advertising in the public eye. Several speakers advocated a national consumer campaign explaining the purposes and mechanisms involved in the advertising process.

But the key speech was given by the late James W. Young, then a senior consultant to the J. Walter Thompson Co. and a former professor at the University of Chicago, who suggested that advertising skills and facilities be used to persuade and inform in non-commercial ventures.

Calling advertising "the most modern, streamlined, high-speed means of communication, plus persuasion yet invented by man," Mr. Young advocated its use "by governments . . . political parties . . . labor unions . . . farm organizations . . . churches . . . universities . . . It ought to be used to create understanding and reduce friction."

■ Most advertising men and other business men, then as now, felt their primary concern was "to run a company and make money." But they were challenged at the pre-Pearl Harbor meeting at Hot

Springs to "forget about advertising and start thinking about the war." And William L. Batt, then president of SKF Industries, added. "This profession has an obligation to find out what its clients ought to be doing for defense."

■ Thus was the idea of a War Advertising Council implanted. While some admen balked at the idea of such a voluntary group two months later, in January, 1942, a committee was formed that would place advertising at the service of the government. Agreement on such a group was reached by Mr. West of the ANA Frederick R. Gamble, then managing director of the Four A's, and Chester LaRoche, then president of Young & Rubicam who later started C. J. LaRoche & Co. The late Dr. Miller McClintock of Yale University was named executive director; Mr. LaRoche became board chairman; Harold Thomas of the Centaur Co. was elected vice-chairman. Mr. West served as secretary and Mr. Gamble as treasurer. The Four A's contributed the council's first funds, $25,000.

These men then planned, in conjunction with the Office of War Information, the council's initial assignments. The first task, it developed, was a campaign to promote converting the country from peacetime to wartime industrial production. Along with this job, the council tackled the problem of getting more Americans to purchase war bonds. This assignment was planned like a normal advertising agency operation as admen worked out campaigns and media schedules.

■ By the end of the war, more than 100 different home-front campaigns had been conducted. They included "Careless talk costs lives," venereal disease prevention, forest fire prevention and the promotion of victory gardens. By the end of 1945, American business had contributed more than $1 billion worth of time and space to these campaigns. President Truman hailed the dissemination of wartime information through advertising as a "vital" factor in telling Americans "the story of what had to be done to speed victory."

With the advent of peace, the War Advertising Council began making plans to disband. But this was not to be. Mr. West, Mr. LaRoche, and the director of the council, Theodore Repplier, kept it going. The group then became the Advertising Council and started working on the problems of reconversion to peacetime. The Red Cross and fire prevention programs obviously required continuation, and they were indeed continued.

■ The Advertising Council's policy today is basically the same as it was at its inception during the war. Its platform: "Accept no subsidy from government and remain independent of it. Conduct campaigns of service to the nation at large, avoiding regional, sectarian or special-interest drives of all kinds. Remain non-partisan and non-political. Conduct the council on a voluntary basis. Accept no project that does not lend itself to the advertising method. Accept no campaign with a commercial interest unless the public interest is obviously overriding."

The council currently consists of three major groups:

1. The board of directors— composed of 85 members who represent all branches of advertising, communications, business, and the constituent and sponsoring member organizations of the council. These are the Four A's, American Business Press, Assn. of National Advertisers, Newspaper Bureau of Advertising, Magazine Publishers Assn., National Assn. of Broadcasters, and the Outdoor Advertising Assn. of America. The board is broken down into a 24-member executive committee, plus 13 additional standing c o m m i t t e e s which deal, for example, with such subjects as campaigns review, finance, public relations and promotion, and with the various media.

2. The public policy committee—a select group of 28 representatives of public opinion drawn from such areas as labor, business, agriculture, medicine, religion, social work, journalism and education. This group's function is to review and make recommendations to the board of directors regarding all proposed campaigns,

except those originating with federal government departments.

3. The industries advisory committee—composed of 45 business leaders who assist in raising funds for the council and for campaigns which the council may itself sponsor. The committee also gives advice on campaigns of special interest to business and industry.

Then there are 28 volunteer advertising agencies and 24 volunteer coordinators, whose joint marketing, advertising and communications know-how is directed toward the creation of all council campaigns.

The Ad Council must determine which of thousands of possible public service efforts that are proposed truly lend themselves to the advertising methods geared for a mass audience. It must also prepare and distribute completed campaigns.

■ A request for Advertising Council sponsorship can be made by either private or governmental agencies; or it can be initiated by the council itself. However, all requests must first meet the council's "reasonable standards of integrity, public acceptance and general appropriateness for national media." The criteria are:

1. That, if the organization is a fund raising one, the Advertising Council will take into consideration whether or not it currently meets the standards of the National Information Bureau.

2. That the project be non-commercial, nonpartisan politically, and not designed to influence legislation.

3. That the project be national in scope, or sufficiently national so that the bulk of national media audience has an actual or potential interest in it.

4. That the appeal for support shall be one properly made to Americans generally. The project will not be rejected because it is in the interest of one group if it has such wide appeal—but it will be rejected if the appeal for participation is limited to special groups.

5. That the project be of sufficient seriousness and public importance to justify treatment before the national media audience.

Once the criteria have been met, the Ad Council board may accept or reject the proposed campaign. "If the campaign requested is covered by an Act of Congress which sets a policy, no further approval is needed to

make it a council project. However, if the board thinks the request may contain elements of controversy, it may be referred to the public policy committee, as are all projects requested by private organizations."

■ After this, the proposal is referred to the campaign review committee which studies it in detail, and recommends appropriate action to the council's board. Once the proposal has been accepted by the board, the Assn. of National Advertisers is called on to recommend a suitable coordinator, usually a top level advertising or marketing executive employed by a major advertiser. His principal function is to serve as liaison between the sponsoring organization for which the campaign is undertaken and the volunteer advertising agency, which is nominated by the Four A's to handle the project. Then the council appoints one of its staff members to serve as campaign manager to ensure cooperation among those involved in the creation of the campaign.

While everything is on a volunteer basis, some expenses are involved. The client organization is asked to pay for the materials which are later supplied free to the various media which are asked to help in the campaign. This money goes for such things as artwork, engravings, printing, paper, tv film and slides. Out-of-pocket expenses for a typical campaign now run from $75,000 to $150,000 annually. For each dollar spent on campaign materials, the recipient organization can expect to receive hundreds of dollars in advertising time and space to help further its program.

With the campaign fully prepared and produced by the volunteer agency, the council turns to the task of disseminating that message to the media, which contribute time and space to bring the public service advertising to the attention of the general public.

■ During 1972, the council received 244 requests for advertising support. Of these, 125 were eliminated for failure to meet its criteria, and of the 119 surviving requests then considered by the council's board, only 28 evolved as major campaigns distributed to some 20,000 media outlets. Media support for council campaigns last year totaled $525,-000,000 worth of space and time.

■ Robert Keim, who is now president of the Advertising Council, reported recently on some campaign results. He said:

"The Red Cross advised us that last year it received over $15,000,000 in contributions from our emergency Flood Relief campaign to help the victims of the June floods. The jobless rate for veterans has been cut in half, from 11% to 5.5%. The National Alliance of Businessmen has found employment for 1,019,062 disadvantaged persons. The United Negro College Fund raised $11,200,000 in 1972, a 20% increase in dollars over 1971 and a 15% increase in the number of gifts. In 1972, sales of Savings Bonds totaled $6.2 billion—the highest on record. The United Way campaigns achieved $910,000,000, a new record."

In addition, the National Safety Council has credited the Ad Council campaign for traffic safety with helping save 750,000 lives on the nation's highways in the last 25 years. The U.S. Forest Service has attested that the Smokey the Bear campaign has helped save $17 billion in natural resources since 1942.

■ As noted above, of the 119 surviving proposals made last year for council support, 28 wound up as major campaigns (either new ones or renewed efforts). But another 69 were published in the council's bi-monthly "Public Service Advertising Bulletin." These bulletins are mailed to 11,000 media outlets. The bulletin service is intended to win donations of space and time "over and above that devoted to the council's sustaining major campaigns." Some of them this year involve "Discover America," "Project Hope," "National Hospital Week," "National Safe Boating Week" and "Vocational Training."

Because the media also support these bulletin campaigns, there has been some fall-off recently in the council's "share-of-market" for its major projects. Mr. Keim recently pointed out that since media are pressured to support more and more "local" causes, the media "tend to forget that although our campaigns are distributed nationally, the action message has to apply locally or the council would not conduct the campaign in the first place."

This national-versus-local situation was a base from which an attack was made on the council in 1972 by David McCall, head of McCaffrey & McCall, who charged that the media time and space used by the council "is a crying waste" because the campaigns deal only with national problems, whereas the problems in this country "are overwhelm-

ingly local." Mr. McCall suggested that "it would seem like a good idea for the Advertising Council to disband," and some young activists, ecologists and nutritionists, seemed to agree with him. Mr. Keim retorted that the national campaigns of the council call for "local actions." He said, "It is in the local community that veterans are hired, seat belts fastened, Savings Bonds purchased, pollution stopped, babies conceived, or drugs avoided."

■ Advertising Council campaigns normally get support from radio and television, newspapers, magazines, business publications, outdoor advertising, transit advertising, direct mail and employe publications. The major broadcast networks are asked to put council messages on the air every three, four or five weeks (depending on length and frequency of the shows they program).

The International Newspaper Advertising Executives asks members to support four major council projects annually—one each quarter. Many consumer magazines carry council campaigns on a year-round basis. The business press runs thousands of campaign ads each year aimed at the business community. Outdoor advertising companies

in cities of 50,000 population and over contribute at least one 25-showing to council campaigns in four months of the year.

■ Companies in transit advertising contribute some 90,000 spaces to council car cards in public vehicles like buses and subways. The Direct Mail/Marketing Assn. makes council ads available as stuffers for inclusion in mass mailings by its members. About 3,400 company publications regularly receive public service ads for use in their pages and on company bulletin boards. It is a claim of the Advertising Council that each dollar contributed to it "results in $642 of advertising to help build a better America."

■ The Advertising Council, headquartered in New York, has a staff of 16 executives and 17 secretarial and clerical people. (It used to have offices in two cities and 42 people on staff.) Its operating expenses last year amounted to $709,000. Its projected income for the current fiscal year is $710,000. As a result, it will seek additional money from "major corporations which are now contributing less than comparable companies." Its total operating budget, incidentally, comes from the seven constituent and sponsoring organiza-

U.S. Savings Bonds campaign prepared by the Advertising Council includes talent donated by agencies and space donated by media.

tions, and from voluntary contributions made by many business companies, both large and small.

Whatever its financial problems, it would seem that the work of the Advertising Council will go on—if only because there is much unfinished business ahead of it. As broadcasting executive Donald McGannon has said, "If we didn't have the Advertising Council, we'd have to invent one to help communicate to the American people the things that need doing."

1972 media contributions to Ad Council

Business press	7,058 ads run
Consumer magazines	8,479 ads run
Newspapers	47,598,736 lines run
Newspaper cooperation plan	266,280 lines run
INAE newspaper plan	2,715,500 lines run
Car cards	1,233,678 cards displayed
Outdoor*	32,636 posters displayed
Three-sheets	6,297 posters displayed
Radio	70,840,091,000 listener impressions
Television	47,316,018,000 home impressions

*Painted bulletins — Four painted bulletins were displayed for each quarter of '72 in 21 major outdoor markets.

Reprinted from "Advertising Age," Nov. 21, 1973, pp. 172, 174, 177

Where advertising will fit in the future society

BY STEPHEN J. F. UNWIN
Assistant Professor of Advertising
University of Illinois, Urbana, Ill.

How can advertising help develop a more harmonious economic system? How can the advertising of services accelerate progress toward a more enlightened society? What other functions should advertising perform, and what forms should advertising take in the post-industrial economy?

To find the answers to these questions, we must first take a close look at the general trend and pattern of economic activities in which we are presently engaged. We know that since 1957 more Americans have been employed in the service industries than in manufacturing. We also know that the dollar volume of the service industries is not only larger than that of manufacturing, but it is growing at a faster pace.

What is not so well understood is that many service enterprises are in fact the "cutting edge" of entirely new industries, and which, as demand increases, first develop into mechanized systems and eventually into whole new ranges of manufactured products. Many of our modern industries would not exist without prior development as service operations. The private aircraft and the electronic communications businesses have both, for example, recently emerged from the service field. The innovating and expanding thrust of the new service industries is an important reason why they should receive strong advertising support.

Economists have traditionally pictured man's economic development as a straight line progression from the agricultural economy through the manufacturing economy to the service economy, with services as it were at the end of the line.

But services are not a dead end. They are a beginning—the initial formative stage of new industries catering to the needs of completely new markets.

For example, until the advent of Disney World 20 years ago, no one had heard of "theme parks." There are now dozens of these scattered across the na-

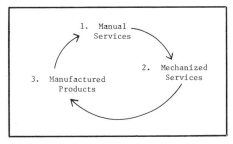

Diagram A

tion and it is estimated that by 1976 they will be visited by fully one-third of all Americans each year. Leisure and recreation constitute the second largest business in the nation. Affluence has sparked off an explosion of new personalized services. Diners-out like live music with their meals; working mothers demand live nursery staff to tend their offspring; and everybody who needs one expects a live psychiatrist.

Now We Dial Direct, Learn by Tape

Most services employ a lot of people at the start, when they are still exclusive and largely untried. As they become more experienced and established, their operations are organized into set routines. As demand increases, systems are introduced which lend themselves to mechanization. Eventually, the human element can be removed, and products are manufactured to perform the whole service.

Thus, the first telephone subscribers had all their calls connected manually; now they dial direct. Grocery items were first totaled by hand, then by check-out, and will soon be calculated by automatic systems. Professors used to repeat every lecture to every new class; now students learn from videotaped recordings on tv monitors. Once upon a time the housewife, or her maid, used to wash clothes, sweep floors and do the dishes. Now ... the list goes on and on. Each new service is a potential new industry.

We do not live in a *post*-industrial society, but a *new* industrial society. It is

only post-industrial in the sense that, as machines become more efficient, fewer people are required to operate them. People are freed from the manufacture of old products to provide an ever widening variety of new services.

Our Cycle Lacks Purpose

What should these new services be? Hopefully they will be less menial and more creative than those that have gone before. But the apparent cycle of "manual service" to "mechanized service" to "manufactured product" and then back to another new manual service seems to lack purpose and direction (*see Diagram A*).

It threatens to be a mindless, wasteful and rigid cycle of unending consumption. Herein lies the malaise that plagues the post-industrial society. It is a society spinning round in too small a circle; a circle which leaves no room for the input of ideals, for the option of leisure or for the husbanding of resources.

On closer inspection we find that it is only half a circle. It needs three more stages to transform it into the larger circle of an enlightened society, a society which could be more balanced, progressive and fulfilling than any other in the past.

The first stage to be added is "Human Concepts." These are the expression of man's desires and aspirations. These start the cycle and are not an afterthought to trim the excesses of a nine-to-five automaton. The post-industrial society, freed from the pressures of subsistence, can exercise choice. Choice now precedes action and sets its course.

■ The second stage to be added is "Leisure Activities." These encompass all those physically, psychically and spiritually rewarding activities in the arts, sports and education which are open to members of the post-industrial society. Thus, the enlarged six-stage model already allows for the impact of the next revolution, to follow the industrial and service revolutions, which is the cultural revolution, when employment in leisure activities will surpass that in services.

Thirdly, the model brings back agriculture under the wider definition of "Natural Resources," which also includes land, air, water, minerals and energy. Until the advent of the post-industrial economy the only major constraint was food, all other resources seeming infinite. Increased options for human activity are now matched by reduced options in natural resources.

Weight Reducing to Backyard Pools

The completed six-stage circle looks like Diagram B.

Each new human activity goes through the cycle stage by stage with each succeeding stage coming into effect in response to the demand set up by the previous stage. To show how the model works in practice we can apply it to a currently popular human concept, like weight reduction, and see how this concept is being developed through the leisure, service and manufacturing stages. The new concept initially prompts such leisure activities as walking, swimming and jogging. As more people become interested in losing weight, various forms of weight-reducing services are introduced. People go to PE classes at the Y, or join their local swim club.

As demand intensifies, the weight reduction business gets into its stride with computerized diets, programed meals, and all the apparatus of the modern health farm. Eventually, manufacturers will provide many of these items for private use at home. Backyard pools, for instance, are manufactured and marketed. These pools require extra supplies of water. Too much pressure on water reserves lends support to the concept of recycling water, thus creating a new concept, which starts a new cycle of activity.

Art Stays Non-Profit

Not every human activity needs, or should go through, the full cycle. For example, much artistic activity will remain a non-profit leisure pursuit for personal fulfilment and recreation. Much of medical diagnosis should be left literally in the hands of the physician. Many activities are best accomplished by human hand; hence the decision to send men as well as robots to the moon. No activity should move from one stage to the next unless people want it to. Performance capability, human satisfaction and, above all, value, fixed by price, will normally determine this.

If, in our example, shortage forced the price of water too high, weight reducers might prefer to settle for a sauna rather than a pool; just as some motorists have opted for smaller cars in the present gas shortage. It was the short supply and

high price of timber in 18th century England that first made coal a profitable substitute fuel, and led the way to the first industrial revolution.

The model is not an exact replica of every socio-economic activity correct to the last detail. It is a reference model to show how economic development and social advance can take place in a logical and orderly sequence. Technology becomes the instrument of progress, not its driving force. The model discourages the automatic recourse to technical solutions for all human problems. These are too often short-cuts which throw the system out of sync.

■ The wholesale manufacture of thousands of buses by General Motors is not necessarily the best way to gain acceptance for the concept of communal transportation on the ground. And so long as most Americans have not yet taken to the air there is little advantage in contemplating mass transit at supersonic speeds. Technology is not brought into play until the concept is accepted.

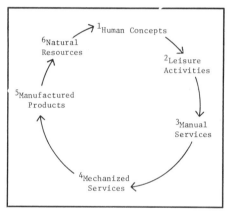

Diagram B

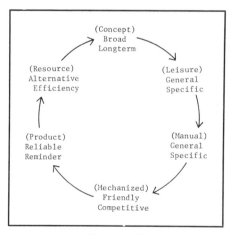

Diagram C

To take another example, consumers need to be sold on nutrition *per se* before they will respond to nutritional claims for specific brands of food. Lastly, by attracting employment to new services the model discourages the deterioration of older services into overstaffed, self-serving bureaucracies. The model shows how we live in a unified society; a society of human resources as well as natural resources, of ideas and culture as well as services and products.

It is not a model for a meritocracy, where intellect is power, but an all-embracing society for all human beings, be they good, dumb or beautiful. It is a model for the planning of social and economic activity; for marketing and advertising.

Now that we have a model for the enlightened society, we have a framework within which to discuss the future role of advertising. What can advertising do to help bring about such a society?

Advertising assists the development of an economy by accelerating demand. It speeds up awareness and adoption of new concepts. It helps man keep pace with the rapid changes in his environment. It promotes economic equilibrium. Advertising makes the economy move, like waves pushing the tide.

When Advertising Works Best

Advertising will expedite the enlightened society when more of its weight is placed at the beginning of the six-stage cycle. Advertising works best when it is promoting something new. Most advertising is now concentrated behind the older manufacturing industries, and not enough behind new concepts and services. This tends to perpetuate old life styles to the detriment of new leisure and service enterprises. Since it is people who receive the wages and not machines, it makes economic sense to promote their output more than that of machines.

The post-industrial economy is similar in one respect to an undeveloped economy. Men are not yet attuned to all its possibilities. Advertising can stimulate demand for new concepts and services by motivating people toward new forms of satisfaction. Whereas in an undeveloped economy it may be appropriate to motivate people to brush their hair, clean their teeth and wash their hands through the promise of enhanced status, such appeals have a somewhat stunting effect on the growth of a post-industrial economy.

Couples today in search of nature can enjoy this experience first-hand, and do not need it euphemized in a packet of cigarets. The writer's own research showed foreign students coming from affluent countries having significantly less response to advertisements for general consumer products than students from some of the poor countries. Also, people are unlikely to resent advertising's entreaties and praises if these mesh with the current longings and hopes.

Advertising should never try to create a want. It cannot do so. The want, however undeveloped, must already exist. Advertising can be no more successful in selling a bad concept than a bad product.

Changing Roles for Advertising

Advertising has a different role to perform at each stage of the economic cycle. At the concept stage advertising needs to articulate a basic human ideal or objective. The concept should be broad enough to permit varied development. The concept of clean water, for example, leads to less industrial pollution, better management of fishing reserves, infection-free lakes for swimming, better-quality drinking water, and so on. Because concepts are new and abstract, concept advertising takes longer to have an effect than the more immediate and tangible appeals of product advertising.

There is little point, therefore, in demanding instant action, or even suggesting courses of action. New ideas require fresh thinking, and this takes time to develop. Above all, concept advertising wants to be positive and offer real social benefits. Too much of today's social issue advertising chides and rebukes its readers for their past sins and shortcomings. This censorious tone may satisfy the advertiser, but it turns off the audience.

The headline, "If America dies, where will we bury it?" is unlikely to do America much good, and America's doctors, who sponsored the ad, even less good. "Love. It Comes in All Colors" evokes a more positive response for the Urban Coalition. If negative headlines do not work for products, there is no reason to think they should work for concepts.

Identify Venture, Spell Out Benefits

Because the human element is predominant, new leisure and service activities offer a wide variety of intangible satisfactions. Advertising, therefore, needs to combine the general with the particular both to give each new venture a clear identity and to spell out its many benefits. Thus, the People's National Bank offers its customers "13 delicious services for only $3.50 a month—a Banker's Dozen." The same "Banker's Dozen principle" is evident in "The Traveling Businessman's 10 Most Wanted List," available at Holiday Inns—"the Most Accommodating People in the World." The ad enumerates the separate benefits of the service and then caps them with an overriding theme.

This same principle is evident in myriads of service ads, ranging from "What a few good college men should know about the Marine Corps" to Henry Block's oft-repeated "17 Reasons Why." The trick is always to combine the general with the specific. The State of Oregon does it well with its "Come to Oregon and We'll Give You the World," followed by 28 separate vistas of that state, covering everything from the restaurants of Canton to Siberian sea lions.

When the growing new industry becomes mechanized, two things happen to change the advertising format. The industry gets more competitive, and the service gets less personal. Advertising now has to stress only a few competitive features and to convey a warm and friendly image. Public relations starts to substitute for people contacts. Companies like Chase Manhattan and Hewlett Packard come across in their advertising as organizations still composed of warm-blooded human beings. This impression is vital in automated enterprises that continue to deal directly with their customers.

Security Blanket Is Smart Move

At the manufacturing stage, once the new product has been successfully established, advertising should be cut back to a reminder role, since by this time in the evolution of a new industry, consumers are convinced of its benefits and accustomed to its use. Advertised features will now be narrowed to one or two at most. The company image is still important, with the emphasis now being placed on product quality and reliability. The service aspect of the manufacturing stage is also crucial. After-sales service and warranty plans are sometimes as important to feature as the products themselves, as evidenced by the AMC Buyer Protection Plan and the VW Security Blanket.

With the coming of more widespread affluence throughout the world, and the ensuing demands on shrinking reserves of natural resources, suppliers of raw materials should refrain from encouraging the profligate consumption of conventional resources. They should instead focus their advertising on promoting greater efficiencies in resource usage and diverting consumption to alternative sources of food, energy and minerals.

These then are the forms that advertising should take at each of the six stages of the cycle.

Who the Concept Sponsors Are

Who shall fund advertising in the enlightened society? To pay for their increased share of total advertising, service companies will need to raise their advertising/sales ratios nearer to that of manufacturers. Manufacturers, on the other hand, can reduce their product advertising budgets, and put more emphasis on service, distribution and price. The transfer of advertising dollars from products to services would be a simple bookkeeping matter for the diversified corporation.

Concept advertising should continue to be funded by all its present sponsors—by the Advertising Council, business and professional associations, voluntary groups, foundations and so on—but the list should be extended to include the full spectrum of social and economic institutions. The labor unions, the major universities and especially the corporations should allocate a larger percentage of their budgets to concept advertising. The corporations are searching for a social role. They may lack the talent for social work, but they are past masters in the art and science of mass communication. Let them put these skills to work in a new marketplace of ideas. Corporations can compete with each other and with other institutions in a new dimension—the dimension of ideas.

Corporations and other institutions should espouse a concept, such as literacy, modern health facilities, the performing arts, student study abroad, fuel efficiency and so on, and make this the cause they advertise and the concept with which they are identified. The concept should be in an area with which the corporation is not presently involved, thus earning public belief, trust and good will. The Atlantic Richfield Co. is already showing how this can be done for a series of concepts from cultural understanding to the free flow of information.

Keep Government Out of It

To avoid criticism of bias, the concept should be selected within the corporation by a process of consensus and have the support of the majority of everyone employed by the company, as well, perhaps, as its leading suppliers and customers. Concept advertising would not only be good for external pr, but would work as a strong unifying factor inside the company. It would not do harm to the corporate image, as some controversial corporate campaigns have in the past.

There is a real incentive for corporations to make this investment in future human endeavor, since they, after all, are among the ultimate beneficiaries of new industrial development. But to be successful, new concepts, just like new products or services, have to meet with public favor.

The only institution that should be excluded from concept sponsorship is the government. This would smack too much of big brother, and in any case the government is already a major advertiser of services, and will become larger still.

Samuel Eliot Morison, in his "Oxford History of the American People," states, "Advertising more than any factor has made the luxuries of yesterday the necessities of today." This is true, and advertising has done well in the industrial society. The headline for Metropolitan Life is also true: "The future always arrives a little before you're ready to give up the present." It is now up to advertising so to whet the appetite for the enlightened society that people go forward to greet it—and grasp it.

Reprinted from "Advertising Age," July 8, 1974, pp. 29-30, 34

PART 5 International Advertising

International advertising grows

If there is one development which stands out among all others in the past decade of hectic activity in international advertising, it is the forging of giant multi-national agency conglomerates.

Most assuredly, the global scene is also indelibly marked by government curbs and warnings, self-regulation, taxation, inflation, devaluation, consumerism and nationalism. And the impact of these developments is expected to continue for some time.

But the multi-national agency link-ups of the late 1960s were unique. They were fashioned despite government curbs on advertising, despite inflation, devaluation and nationalism.

In mid-1969, the Chicago-based Leo Burnett Co. startled the advertising world with its acquisition of the major agency parts of the London Press Exchange, at that time the second-largest London-based agency. SSC&B soon stirred things up anew with the announcement that it was acquiring a substantial interest in Lintas, then the No. 1 London-headquartered international shop and owned by the giant detergent company, Unilever.

■ For Burnett—an agency ensconced among the "silos of Michigan Ave.," in the facetious words of the late Leo Burnett—the acquisition of LPE gave it an instant overseas network of 23 offices in 19 countries. Thus Burnett became the fifth largest agency in the world and joined stride with J. Walter Thompson Co. and McCann-Erickson, which had been methodically piecing their empires together since the '20s and '30s.

SSC&B's acquisition became operative at the beginning of 1970, when it acquired a 49% interest in Lintas. Today the combined operation bills $409,700,000, compared with Burnett's current $471,200,000.

Another pact which caused much interest was the 1970 creation of Benson Needham Univas, marking the world's first three-way linkup of major advertising forces. The principals were Needham, Harper & Steers of the U.S., S. H. Benson Ltd. of England, and Havas Conseil, France's largest agency, whose holding company, Agence Havas, is 56% owned by the French government. The "U" in the new BNU network stood for Univas, the subsidiary company set up by Havas Conseil in 1968 to handle its international operations. BNU represented a combined billings force of $300,000,000 through 21 agencies in 13 countries.

■ But Benson later went public, and the Rothschild Investment Fund paid $11,040,000 to acquire all the properties of the Benson group. Rothschild, in turn, sold the Benson agencies to Ogilvy & Mather for $1,174,000 in cash and $984,000 in convertible stock. The sale ended Benson's participation in the Benson Needham Univas network and sent NH&S and Havas scurrying for another partner, which turned out to be KMPH Ltd., one of the most successful and aggressive young agencies in the U.K. The acquisitive-minded KMPH had earlier bought a number of other British agencies, including Clifford Bloxham Marketing Organization and Gerald Green Associates, and later the giant Pemberton Group.

■ Another momentous but short-lived international union was formed late in 1970 when D'Arcy Advertising and MacManus, John & Adams, both of the U.S., joined forces with Intermarco, the large Amsterdam-headquartered European network. This created D'-Arcy-MacManus-Intermarco with combined billings of more than $250,000,000. D'Arcy, which five years previously had been one of

four founders of Multi-National Partners, a European agency network, now dissolved its agreement with MNP.

D'Arcy-MacManus' affiliation with Intermarco broke up early in 1972. Later that year, D'Arcy-MacManus joined hands with Masius, Wynne-Williams, the huge London-based agency with an extensive European network. The agencies agreed to exchange a substantial minority interest. This brought together an agency power with combined billings exceeding $350,000,000.

Masius, Wynne-Williams had actually invaded the U.S. market in 1968 when it acquired Street & Finney. (It dropped the Street & Finney name in 1971.) Masius had wanted to go it alone in the U.S., but as A. J. (Tony) Abrahams, managing director of Masius, said at the time of the D'Arcy-MacManus pact, Masius "could not have been a major factor in the U.S. for 10 or 15 years, if at all. And the same was true in Europe for D'Arcy-MacManus. Both of us felt we needed to be in the top 12 among global agencies.

■ Following the break-up of D'-Arcy-MacManus-Intermarco, the latter was acquired by Publicis S.A., which is also the holding company for Publicis Conseil, the second-largest agency in France. This year, Publicis gained 100% control of the Swiss-based Dr. Rudolf Farner Advertising Agency Group. The Farner network has its major strength in Switzerland, Germany and Austria, while Intermarco has important operations in France, Benelux, Scandinavia and Spain. The Publicis-Intermarco-Farner combine represents billings of some $220,-000, making it the largest European-owned agency operation on the continent today, according to Claude Neuschwander, international director of Publicis and president of Intermarco.

■ Another late-comer on the international scene was Dancer-Fitzgerald-Sample, which early in 1970 entered into an agreement with Dorland Advertising Holdings Ltd. of London, and Dorland Werbeagentur of Munich through a nominal exchange of stock. Because of the broad holdings of the two Dorland agencies, the move gave D-F-S access to a global network. DDI (D-F-S Dorland International) then represented combined billings of $237,000,000.

The great surge in giant multinational mergers led a number of observers to predict that international agencies would continue to absorb smaller shops, until there would be only 10 or 15 remaining that could be regarded as truly international. This view has been expressed by such leaders as S. R. (Tim) Green, chief executive officer of SSC&B-Lintas International; Paul C. Harper Jr., chairman and chief executive officer of Needham, Harper & Steers, and Armand de Malherbe, chairman and managing director of Ted Bates S.A., Paris.

■ A strongly opposing point of view has been presented by Albert Stridsberg, international vp of The Solutions Group, a marketing consultancy, and a former international marketing specialist at J. Walter Thompson Co., who said the middle-size agency is "alive and well and living in Europe." He said that the middle-size agency, in addition to being free of bureaucracy, spares the European client "the Harvard razzle-dazzle, lets him talk his own language (the prevalence of English in giant agency management continues to offend), and puts him in touch with people doing business in the manner that is conventional to his country."

■ While the huge multi-national networks were being forged, other American agencies continued to piece together their own international operations link by link. These included Young & Rubicam; McCann-Erickson; Benton & Bowles; Doyle Dane Bernbach; BBDO; Ogilvy & Mather; Compton; Norman, Craig & Kummel; Foote, Cone & Belding; Ted Bates & Co., and Grey.

Nationalism Is on the Rise

One of the most significant developments in international advertising of late has been the upsurge of nationalism in many countries, particularly in Canada, Mexico, Australia and New Zea-

Ad volume in 74 nations: 1970

Country	Ad outlay in millions	GNP in billions	% of GNP	Country	Ad outlay in millions	GNP in billions	% of GNP
Argentina	$ 268.6	$ 21.0	1.28%	Malaysia, Singapore &			
Aruba	1.1	0.1	1.10	Brunei	70.2	5.7	1.23
Australia	456.5	31.6	1.44	Mauritius	1.1	0.2	0.55
Austria	198.4	15.3	1.30	Mexico	214.7	31.5	0.68
Belgium	207.9	25.8	0.81	Morocco	13.5	3.3	0.41
Bolivia	7.9	0.9	0.88	Nepal	0.7	0.8	0.09
Brazil	350.0	38.0	0.92	Netherlands	410.5	29.8	1.38
Canada	1,037.2	82.8	1.25	New Zealand	87.2	5.3	1.65
Ceylon	5.1	1.6	0.32	Nicaragua	1.6	0.8	0.20
Chile	38.8	6.3	0.62	Nigeria	13.3	5.2	0.26
Colombia	45.5	6.6	0.69	Norway	112.0	10.1	1.11
Costa Rica	9.2	0.9	1.02	Pakistan	14.5	17.2	0.08
Denmark	238.9	14.6	1.64	Panama	6.7	1.0	0.67
Ecuador	12.4	1.8	0.69	Peru	41.3	5.4	0.76
El Salvador	2.4	1.0	0.24	Philippines	35.1	8.5	0.41
Finland	119.4	10.2	1.17	Portugal	40.0	6.1	0.66
France	996.6	138.0	0.72	Puerto Rico	54.5	4.6	1.18
Ghana	3.2	2.3	0.14	Saudi Arabia	5.2	3.1	0.17
Greece	66.5	9.0	0.74	South Africa	99.1	16.8	0.59
Guatemala	3.8	1.7	0.22	South Korea	40.1	7.0	0.57
Honduras	1.9	0.7	0.27	Spain	275.5	30.1	0.92
Hong Kong	37.0	3.6	1.03	Sudan	3.3	1.6	0.21
Iceland	3.8	0.4	0.95	Sweden	386.8	29.4	1.32
India	73.4	50.0	0.15	Switzerland	428.0	19.6	2.18
Indonesia	1.5	12.8	0.01	Syria	1.8	2.1	0.09
Iran	20.0	9.9	0.20	Taiwan	39.8	5.2	0.77
Iraq	1.6	2.9	0.06	Thailand	14.8	6.8	0.22
Ireland	78.0	3.5	2.23	Trinidad & Tobago	4.9	0.9	0.54
Israel	27.9	5.1	0.55	Turkey	81.9	9.2	0.89
Italy	489.0	87.3	0.56	United Arab Republic	32.7	6.3	0.52
Jamaica	11.3	1.2	0.94	United Kingdom	1,264.8	111.8	1.13
Japan	2,115.3	185.6	1.14	United States	19,600.0	927.6	2.11
Jordan	2.8	0.6	0.47	Uruguay	6.3	2.0	0.32
Kuwait	2.7	2.9	0.09	Venezuela	55.4	10.1	0.55
Lebanon	15.0	1.3	1.15	West Germany	2,693.9	172.7	1.56
Liberia	0.6	0.3	0.20	Zambia	7.5	1.7	0.44
Luxembourg	6.9	0.9	0.77				

Source: "1970 World Advertising Expenditures," by International Research Associates and International Advertising Assn.

land. In Australia, it took the form of a breaking away from the Australian Assn. of Advertising Agencies by a splinter group made up entirely of locally-owned agencies. The militant new group is known as Australian-owned Advertising Agencies (AUSTAC).

Canada has had a groundswell of nationalism during the past few years, most prominently displayed in efforts to limit foreign ownership. The most recent tussle has been to reduce the amount of foreign-produced commercials on Canadian television and radio.

Some observers feel that a growing nationalism will be counter-productive to the growth of Europe's Common Market. Others feel that the sheer force of the European Economic Community, which last January was expanded to include England, Ireland and Denmark, will work to crush nationalism. The latter point to an increased flow of goods since the new members joined Germany, France, Italy, Belgium, Netherlands and Luxembourg in the EEC.

■ The first priority of the EEC Committee on Unfair Competition was to study the possibility of harmonizing legislation on misleading advertising. This raised a cry from several member nations, particularly England and Ireland, who contended that such legislation would be unfair and debilitating since the needs of each market vary widely.

With the enlargement of the Common Market, there is an increasing benefit for a manufacturer to have the same brand name, the same package available in all countries, and at least a similar look to his advertising across borders. One reason for this is the growing phenomenon of the migrant consumer. There is a continually growing number of Turks, Greeks, Italians, North Africans and Spaniards who move to Germany, France and other countries of Northern Europe where jobs are more plentiful.

Most of these migrants eventually return to their homelands, but they stay many years in their "second" countries, attracted by more jobs and better pay. When they do return to their native countries, they bring back with them new habits of consumption, and wise advertisers make it possible for such natives to recognize their newly favored brands on retail shelves. In addition to migrant workers, there is a growing number of tourists who

WORLD ADVERTISING: 1972	
1. U.S. and Canada	$20,637,000,000
2. Europe	8,016,000,000
3. Asia	2,447,000,000
4. Latin America	1,141,000,000
5. Australia & New Zealand	543,700,000
6. Middle East & Africa	333,200,000
Total (75 countries)	$33,119,600,000

Source: "1970 World Advertising Expenditures," by International Research Associates and International Advertising Assn.

make the necessity for brand name and packaging homogeneity all the greater.

■ One common denominator in the Common Market is youth. Young people in Europe, and the world over for that matter, tend to dress alike, eat similar foods and seek similar diversions. Youth is undoubtedly the key market segment spurring the rapid development of fast food outlets in Europe. Major factors in this move have been McDonald's and Kentucky Fried Chicken. Both have quickly expanded in Japan as well, where McDonald's alone already has more than 65 outlets.

The cross-fertilization that already exists among managements of multi-national companies will probably accelerate with the enlarged EEC. Already it's common to find a German marketing executive in Shell's office in The Hague, a Dutchman in Mennen's European headquarters in Brussels, and a Canadian with Cadbury Schweppes in London. And the national mix is so great at Swiss-based Nestle that Max Gloor, a director, has said, "We cannot be considered either as pure Swiss or as purely multinational. We are something in between, a breed of our own. In one word, we have a particular 'Nestle' citizenship."

Woes: Money, Consumerism

The devaluation of the U.S. dollar (8% in December, 1971, and 10% in February, 1973), with concurrent realignments of other currencies, has had an effect on the world marketing scene. But it has had no significant effect on U.S. multi-national conglomerates since they tend to be in local production, and thus operate much the same as a national company.

But the devaluation of the U.S. dollar has made some European companies more dependent than ever on European markets. Ger-

man and Japanese companies have been among the hardest hit by the dollar devaluation because their currencies were simultaneously revalued upward. This has sent the Japanese scouring Europe for new economic opportunities. At the same time, since most imports are cheaper in Japan, some foreign foods, namely cosmetics, liquor and chocolate, have begun to compete with domestic brands.

The consumer movement in Europe, as in the U.S. and Canada, has been gaining momentum. But this is not the case in Latin America where people in developing countries are more preoccupied with earning a living than with challenging advertising claims. Also, affluent consumers in Latin America frequently have maids who do the family shopping, thereby keeping well-heeled consumers removed from the marketplace.

Along with consumer moves, there have been strong government attacks on advertising in all corners of the globe. Legislation to regulate and control advertising has been proposed or is nearing passage in Australia, Canada, Finland, Germany, Japan, Norway, the United Kingdom and the U.S. Alfred L. Hollender, chairman of the International Advertising Assn., has noted that there is already a tax on advertising in all media in Sweden, and that advertising taxes have been proposed in many other countries.

According to Mr. Hollender, some Latin American countries are considering sharply curtailing foreign ownership of ad agencies, and the World Health Organization of the United Nations has issued directives covering the distribution and marketing of pharmaceuticals in the belief that advertising has contributed to over-consumption. The committee of ministers of the Council of Europe has adopted a resolution looking to the protection of consumers against misleading advertising.

■ Concern for marketing freedom has led the International Advertising Assn. to publish a white paper, "The Global Challenge to Advertising." According to Mr. Hollender, it is the "first step in a campaign to mobilize and strengthen the association's capability on dealing with the problems confronting advertising." The IAA will attempt to involve representatives of government and consumer groups for an exchange of views, a resolution of conflicts, and to foster systems of self regulation.

Canada is one of the world leaders in self-regulation. In fact, Canada's "Truth in Advertising" guidelines have set the pace for other countries to follow.

Governments vs. Advertising

Governments' primary concern appears to be cigaret advertising, which has been banned or will be soon in more than 25 countries. Australia and Austria are phasing out cigaret commercials from radio and television, while Mexico is limiting radio and tv commercials for both cigarets and alcohol.

The National Clearing House on Smoking & Health has reported that cigaret advertising is banned from all or some media in Canada, England, Ireland, France, Italy, Denmark, Norway, Sweden, Finland, Iceland, Switzerland, Russia, Czechoslovakia, Romania and Argentina.

Another category to receive governments' attention is advertising to children on television. Both Canada and Australia have set guidelines on advertising to kids.

One of the most controversial moves by a government on advertising came in 1966 when the Monopolies Commission in Britain charged Unilever and Procter & Gamble Ltd. with excessive spending in the advertising and promotion of their household detergents, resulting in alleged over-pricing of these products. Both companies were required to cut back their marketing expenses by at least 40% to produce an average reduction of 20% in wholesale prices.

On the other hand, governments do not disdain the use of advertising for their own purposes. The Swedish government directed a massive advertising and publicity program to promote a safe transition from left to right side of the road driving. The campaign cost more than

$5,000,000—a total that would be doubled if donated advertising and free time on the government-operated broadcasting system were included.

France, a longtime holdout against commercial television, finally allowed commercials for brands in October, 1968. Prior to that, only commercials for categories, such as the milk industry, were permitted on French tv.

Television commercials for specific brands began with a scant two minutes per day, but has increased each year. The European tv commercial average is still only 30 minutes per day.

The only west European countries still without commercial tv and radio are Belgium, Sweden, Norway and Denmark. (Britain, which has been without advertising on radio, except for

Ten world leaders in advertising volume

	1970	1961
1. United States	$19,600,000,000	$12,000,000,000
2. West Germany	2,700,000,000	1,100,000,000
3. Japan	2,100,000,000	600,000,000
4. United Kingdom	1,300,000,000	1,300,000,000
5. Canada	1,000,000,000	600,000,000
6. France	996,600,000	450,000,000
7. Italy	489,000,000	150,000,000
8. Australia	456,500,000	300,000,000
9. Switzerland	428,000,000	*
10. Netherlands	410,500,000	*

*Not in Top Ten in 1961
Source: "1970 World Advertising Expenditures," by International Research Associates and International Advertising Assn.

TOP TEN U.S. AGENCIES IN FOREIGN BILLINGS: 1972

1. McCann-Erickson		$417,300,000
2. J. Walter Thompson Co.		374,000,000
3. Young & Rubicam		205,800,000
4. Ted Bates & Co.		205,000,000
5. Ogilvy & Mather		199,200,000
6. Leo Burnett Co.		157,800,000
7. SSC&B		134,700,000
8. Norman, Craig & Kummel		101,200,000
9. Compton Advertising		75,000,000
10. Foote, Cone & Belding		72,200,000

Ten Biggest Foreign Agencies: 1972

1. Dentsu Advertising		$684,500,000
2. Hakuhodo		213,300,000
3. Havas Conseil Group		213,100,000
4. Daiko Advertising		128,200,000
5. Publicis Conseil		82,200,000
6. Intermarco		68,000,000
6. Euro-Advertising International		68,000,000
8. IMAA/Man-Nen-Sha		67,700,000
9. WPT Group		65,000,000
10. Tokyu Advertising Agency		63,100,000

(Chart does not include foreign agencies with U.S. affiliations; for example, SSC&B-Lintas International, which billed $409,700,000 in 1972. SSC&B Inc., New York, owns 49% of SSC&B-Lintas International).

the hey-day of off-shore pirate stations in the '60s, is getting commercial radio this year.) Canada followed the U.S. and Japan into color television in 1965, with Europe moving to color later.

Foreign Pay Scales Attract

There is a new breed of marketing executive emerging in Europe who is "multi-national in attitude and multi-lingual and young," according to Richard C. Christian, president of Marsteller Inc.

Eugene H. Kummel, president of McCann-Erickson International, noted five years ago that the refinement of international advertising had begun to attract young creative people in ever-increasing numbers—not just Americans, but every nationality. Despite this increasing interest, experienced creative people continue to be in short supply in many countries, including Germany, Italy, France, Mexico and Brazil.

In Italy, for example, agencies must sometimes pay creative people more than managing directors. In Brazil, a creative director in one of the ten largest agencies can ask for and get $50,000, and a top copywriter can command a salary between $30,000 and $35,000.

Copy isn't the only lucrative area in Brazil. A marketing director can get $50,000; a top art director perhaps $33,000, and an account supervisor about $26,000. In fact, everything is big in Brazil, which has been able to keep a previous runaway inflation in workable bounds, while achieving an 11.3% increase in its 1971 gross national product, the highest in the world.

■ The tremendous economic strides made by Brazil have opened the door to an eager market of 100,000,000 consumers. International companies and agencies are knocking at the door.

Inflation has not only been a condition in Brazil; it has plagued Western Europe, Japan and most developed countries. In conjunction, ad rates have been soaring. In 1968, it was estimated that ad rates increase 15% to 20% every three years. Now the increase is even steeper.

Nine Errors of U.S. Abroad

Arthur C. Nielsen Jr., president of A.C. Nielsen Co., has listed some of the basic errors made by U.S. companies in marketing abroad. Although the list is six years old, it still has relevance today:

1. Failure to adapt the product to the market.

2. Failure to gauge the underlying impact of custom, tradition and racial and religious differences.

3. Failure to exploit markets in the proper sequence.

4. Failure to enter potentially profitable markets due to a personal repugnance toward political institutions.

5. Failure to build a strong management of nationals.

6. Failure to appreciate differences in the connotation of words, regardless of whether the same language or a translation is involved.

7. Failure to understand differences in advertising. Media importance varies sharply with such factors as literacy levels, restrictive taxation and other forms of governmental interference with media playing a vital role.

8. Failure to achieve a domestic personality in the foreign country.

9. Failure to understand and weigh correctly the relative importance of the various types of retailers in the distribution of the product.

Big Innovators Overseas

The U.S. has no monopoly on product development. Ralph Z. Sorenson, professor of marketing at the Harvard Business School, said last year that the gap between Europe and the U.S. in product innovations is "closing rapidly." He noted that in the area of consumer goods, Europeans have led with such products as stainless steel blades, enzyme detergents, stainless steel flatware, cordless rotary head electric shavers (by Philips of Holland), yogurt with fresh fruit, instant and freeze-dried coffee, soft margarine, dried soups, Bic throw-away ballpoint pens and throw-away lighters. He added that in the automobile category, with the exception of automatic transmissions, power brakes and steering, almost every recent important product innovation has come from Europe.

While Mr. Sorenson was speaking of the European challenge, it is no less in the case of Japan. And in the future, we can expect greater marketing developments in the rest of the Pacific, as well as Latin America and eastern Europe.

The challenge is there, and the market is ever increasing. The world advertising total is expected to increase 150% from an estimated $93 billion at the beginning of the '70s to an estimated $93 billion at the beginning of the '80s, Edward M. Thiele, vice-chairman of Leo Burnett Co., has predicted. He estimated that two-thirds of the $93 billion will be outside the U.S.

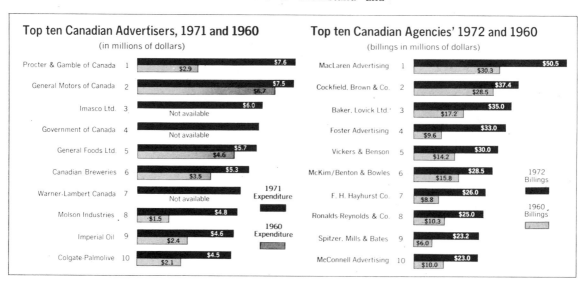

Reprinted from "Advertising Age," Nov. 21, 1973, pp. 184, 186, 188, 190

PART 6

The Case for Advertising:

Some Pros and Cons

Arnold Toynbee speaks

about advertising

BY ARNOLD TOYNBEE
The Royal Institute for International Affairs, London

A free press is a key part of the mechanism of the American Constitution. This truth has been rightly recalled, apropos of Watergate. Freedom of the press means freedom of the press itself to search and destroy, and freedom for members of the public to communicate their opinions in newsprint.

If the press were to muzzle the public, or if the administration were to muzzle the press, the freedom of the press would have been circumvented. The publication of this article in ADVERTISING AGE is a remarkable instance of the American press' hospitality to the public. This is "the National Newspaper of Marketing," and I am not even an American citizen; yet, on the strength of a 12-year-old onslaught on advertising, in which I condemned advertising as being contrary to the ideals of the American Revolution, ADVERTISING AGE has invited me to state my views today. I welcome this new opportunity that has been given to me so benevolently. The subject has become more topical than ever.

We are indeed living in an advertising age. It is also true that there are some kinds of advertisement that are uncontroversial. Examples are the announcements of births, deaths and marriages. This is a useful form of news-service, and here there is little incentive, and also little possibility, for masking the truth under an "image."

There are other forms of advertisement in which the presentation of a misleading image is the whole purpose of the exercise. When a peacock fans up his tail-feathers, he is trying to delude a peahen into imagining that he is a bigger and finer bird than he really is. In the history of human society, purposely deceptive advertising was first devised by apostles of the missionary religions. The word, propaganda, has been coined from the title of one of the organs of the Vatican. But advertising did not become a dominant feature of modern life in "developed" countries until the outbreak of the Industrial Revolution.

Drab Reality Camouflaged

The mechanization of industrial production has called the commercial advertising industry into existence because of the enormous cost of mechanized industrial plant. This initial outlay cannot be made to yield profit unless the conveyor-belt is kept moving, non-stop, at the maximum practicable speed. Production then threatens to exceed demand, and this threat is parried by trying to induce purchases in excess of the potential purchaser's inclination to buy.

Acquisitiveness has to be stimulated artificially by resorting to the peacock's device. Drab reality has to be camouflaged under an alluring image, and, if an image of drabness has to be alluring, it has also to be deceptive. When a majority of a country's population has come to be employed in urban factories and offices, the substitution of images for realities does not remain confined to commercial and industrial business; it pervades the whole of life.

This has happened in America. About half a century ago, President Calvin Coolidge remarked that "the business of America is business"; yet, by comparison with Britain and even Germany, America has industrialized herself relatively recently. Until within living memory, a majority of the nation was still rural and still self-employed. It was, in fact, still what the authors of the Constitution assumed the American citizen-body to be.

Insincerity a New Way of Life?

In the generation that waged the Revolutionary War, most Americans (with the glaring exception of slaves) were self-employed farmers who owned the land from which they made their living. Most other American citizens were self-employed storekeepers or members of the so-called liberal professions (lawyers, doctors, teachers, ministers of religion). In eighteenth-century America, private employers of other American citizens' labor were about as rare as private employers are in present-

116

British historian Arnold Toynbee is concerned about what he terms "the disastrous spiritual effects" of advertising and the Industrial Revolution. He and other academicians have expressed worry about such questions as these: Is advertising's stress on glamorizing goods making us overly acquisitive, materialistic? Is the sometimes dog-eat-dog competition of the marketplace making us predatory?

The conventional answer from admen is that the function of advertising is to sell, and therefore achieve distribution of goods, whereas solutions to such problems as the above are the function of the schools, the church. But, critics warn, can such institutions have much effect when we are bombarded almost incessantly through the day and evening with advertising, much of it very intrusive? That may be a social problem that advertising will find hard to ignore. Mr. Toynbee offers a solution that admen hardly will accept. Whether we accept it or not, if historian Toynbee's concern is in any way justified, the problem is worth thinking about.

Twelve years ago, Mr. Toynbee in a speech in Williamsburg, Va., urged Americans to turn away from creation of "artificial wants" through advertising and to switch efforts, instead, to meeting the "pressing needs of the majority of our fellow human beings." AA asked the historian if he has softened his views or maintained them in light of world events in the '60s and early '70s. In any case, Mr. Toynbee was invited to state his views for AA. In his reply, presented here, he urges curtailment not only of advertising, but of our entire industrial system.

day communist countries. Mechanized industry was still in its infancy. (Mercantilist governments in Britain had seen to that.) At that stage there was little demand in America for advertising, and there was therefore little temptation there to misrepresent realities by fabricating images.

Today, insincerity is a feature of American life that forces itself upon a foreigner's notice. The experience is disagreeable and disquieting. Photographing people on any and every occasion plays a prominent part in the present American advertising industry, and the professional photographer's victim is never allowed to be natural. If he is attending a funeral and is feeling grief, but happens to be well enough known to be worth photographing, he is made to assume a false smile. If he is a visiting professor, a bunch of students is rounded up, a book is thrust into his hands, and he is instructed: "Act as if you were talking to them; look as if you were teaching them."

The insincerity has infected the American vocabulary. All languages employ some euphemisms, of course—for instance, in describing "the calls of nature" and the "conveniences" provided for meeting them. But the American euphemistic vocabulary has been carried to unparalleled lengths: A latrine has become a "rest-room"; prostitutes have become "hostesses"; the places in which corpses are prepared for burial or cremation have become "funeral parlours" ("Come into my parlour," says Death, the spider, to Man, the fly); coffins have become caskets; death itself, the starkest of all realities, has become unmentionable and therefore impossible to prepare for spiritually. These pitiful euphemisms are symptoms of refusal to face facts.

God Is Greed in 'Advanced' Society

This is the effect of disingenuous commercial advertising on the rest of life. False images breed false souls, and "we are betrayed by what is false within." When we get into trouble, the mask is ripped off, and the reality remains—now laid bare. This is the terrible nemesis of trying to substitute images for realities. That, in turn, is the fate of societies whose god is greed. This is the present religion of all the so-called "advanced" societies. America is not the oldest of them, but she has traveled the farthest along their common road.

During the cold war, I was once shown an American anti-communist propaganda photograph. The photographees were a dejected-looking Russian peasant family. The caption ran: "Probably these poor people have never even seen an advertisement." My comment was "lucky dogs," and I remembered an indignant letter that the Emperor Theodore of Ethiopia is reported to have sent to the French Emperor Napoleon III. "Yesterday," so this letter is said to have run, "I gave an audience to a man because he said that he was your ambassador; but, as soon as he entered, he thrust a bundle of rags at me and asked me to buy them. Do you use ambassadors as pedlars?"

Well, this was in fact what Napoleon III was doing. The "bundle of rags" was a sheaf of samples of French silk fabrics. The French ambassador's job was to try to capture the Ethiopian market. The Emperor Theodore thought that this commercialism was beneath France's dignity, and he was right. Yet today every embassy has a "commercial counselor" on its staff.

'Undo Industrial Revolution, Reject Advertising'

Fortunately for the prospects of the human race, the industrialized peoples are still in a minority. The majority of mankind is not yet committed to our way of life. China, for instance, is still sufficiently uncommitted to be able to retain some freedom of maneuver, which gives her some freedom of choice. The committed countries—America, Western Europe, Japan—have, awaiting them, the formidable task of undoing the disastrous spiritual effects of the Industrial Revolution. To recover our sincerity, we must give up fabricating false images. This means that we must renounce advertising, and that probably means that we must abandon our present industrialized way of life and must look for an alternative way to replace it.

This may sound impracticable, but it may be inevitable; for we ourselves are now rejecting the industrial way of life. The more highly an industrial process is mechanized, the more lavishly the workers in it are paid; but pay-rises do not compensate for the increasing dreariness of their work. When the gods gave King Midas the golden touch, Midas found that his life was no longer worth living. Whatever the cost may be in material terms, I believe that we are going to pay it for the sake of liberating ourselves from a way of life that we are now finding intolerable. The generation that made the Industrial Revolution had a grim experience; the generation that breaks away from industrialism will pay a still higher price for the prize of self-emancipation.

The other day I was glancing through an illustrated history of the 20th-century western world, and I came across a picture of Henry Ford's first conveyor-belt, with the caption, "The Industrial breakthrough." The caption ought to have been "The spiritual breakdown." Conveyor-belts may be the necessary enabling condition for material affluence, but experience has already shown that they are incompatible with a human way of life. Achilles in Hades said that he would rather be the poorest serf in the land of the living than be king of all the ghosts of the dead. I guess that a hungry and destitute Indian peasant is less unhappy than a western conveyor-belt worker who eats steak for dinner and has a refrigerator, a tv set, an air-conditioning apparatus and a car.

Follow St. Francis to a Better Life?

In a town in western Christendom in the 12th century, the son of a successful wholesale cloth-merchant dropped out of the family business and espoused the Lady Poverty. This "drop-out" was St. Francis of Assisi. His example, not Henry Ford's, is the one that we westerners ought now to follow. St. Francis lived a life of voluntary physical hardship, but he was a happy man. He had set for himself a spiritual objective that was enormously ambitious. He set out to live the kind of life that Christ lived, as this is described in the Gospels. Before he died he had received the stigmata.

If we do follow St. Francis' example and espouse the Lady Poverty, will not this require the liquidation of the advertising industry? This industry has been called into existence in order to stimulate ever greater demands for material goods and services. What role can advertising men have in a society that has renounced material affluence? Well, advertising is the art of persuading, and persuasion can be used for preaching a new way of life. The members of the advertising profession throughout the western world might transform themselves into a new Franciscan Order. They might try, like St. Francis' followers, to give a new turn to the course of our western history. If even a fraction of the advertising fraternity were to devote themselves to this novel enterprise, they would win the gratitude of posterity.

Mankind is passing through a crisis. We need all the help that can be given to us by men of good will. The gap is widening between the rich minority and the poor majority, both in the world as a whole and inside each of the materially affluent countries. The growth of the minority's material wealth is being bought at the price of a spiritual impoverishment that leaves the "rich fool" dissatisfied and bewildered. The historic religions differ in their accounts of the nature of the Universe in which a human being awakes to consciousness, but, in their ethical precepts, they speak with one voice. They all preach abstinence, self-denial, self-sacrifice. Paradoxically, self-denial is the only possible way to survive in a habitat that is confined to the surface of this single planet, and which contains only a limited amount of irreplaceable material resources.

Can you imagine an advertising man devoting his ability and experience to the advertising of abstinence? I am not sure that I myself can imagine this. It would be a paradoxical *volte-face*. But I do not doubt that an advertising man who achieved this *tour de force* would be the happier for it. He might become almost as happy as St. Francis.

Reprinted from "Advertising Age," Nov. 21, 1973, pp. 194, 197

An interview with

Alvin Toffler

Author of "Future Shock" and "The Ecospasm Report"

JWT WORLD: How is future shock affecting our readers as they sit reading this interview?

Toffler: By future shock I mean the disorientation and decision overload produced by high-speed change—and that's something that people in communications are especially exposed to. The accelerated arrival of the future is forcing millions of us, not just people in advertising, to live at a faster tempo than our nervous systems can tolerate. It subjects us to dangerous over-stimulation. It predisposes us to disease. It creates psychological stress. And it sometimes leads to a breakdown of our capacity for rational decision making.

The pace of change in the high-technology societies is accelerating so fast that a lot of what I call our "durational expectancies" are beginning to be battered. Things are happening faster than we anticipate, and not just the big things, like technology and science; the little things in our daily lives come along at a faster and faster clip as well, so that we have to make more and more adjustments at an ever-accelerating pace. This conflicts with our need to process more information because of increasing novelty in the environment, and increasing choice. The result is an adaptational crisis that has powerful implications for the society.

For example, the extreme anxiety that we see among some of the hard-hats, the construction workers, has a lot to do with the rate at which they have been asked to adjust and readjust their habits and make sense of all kinds of strange inputs—beards and long hair on their kids, drugs, political oddities that they never had to face before, neighborhood integration, threats to their newly won middle-class status, and so on.

The same thing is true for some of the radical students. They react to what they see as the standardizing, brutalizing aspects of industrial society by either trying senselessly to destroy it or by just as senselessly dropping out of it and trying to build an alternate anti-technological life style based on a pastiche of 19th century Marxism and early 20th century Freudianism.

There is a concealed thread, a hidden unhappiness that unites both the hard-hats and the most dramatic and violent critics of the present society. Instead of beating each other on the skulls, it would be better if they found some opportunity to sit down and talk about what kind of future our society and our communities should be moving toward. If they did, I think they would be surprised to find wide areas of agreement. Both groups, it seems to me, are suffering from the stress of super-change. The hard-hats want change to stop. Many radicals want to bring about a simpler, more tranquil, less hassled way of life. Both groups, despite their rhetoric, are reacting against environmental over-stimulation. Both exhibit signs of future shock—confusional breakdown, violence, apathy.

JWT World: But haven't things always changed? What makes now different?

Toffler: Several things make the situation unique today. It is no longer a matter of cultures changing over the course of many lifetimes. The rate of change is now so fast that many significant changes become visible within the lifetime of the individual, and this radically alters the meaning of *time* in our lives. Time is telescoped.

What this means is that people are now asked to make and break their relationships with their environment more rapidly than ever before. The *duration* of their links with the environment is compressed, and this fact becomes the key to understanding the new world that is now exploding into being.

In the agricultural era, even in the early industrial period, people lived in communities where they had relatively fixed and stable personal ties, where the physical goods they lived with, the objects, the products they bought, the things they made, the buildings around them, endured through time. Individuals thus had long-lasting relationships with the objects around them.

In the last generation, and much more dramatically in the last decade, the duration of our ties with the physical environment has shrunk. We're now asked to cope with a never-ending flow of products that move into and out of our experience at an accelerating clip, rental products that we use for short-term purposes; architecture based on modular principles, so that it's constantly rearrangeable; buildings constructed for short-term use, temporary buildings, temporary classrooms; so that the individual is enveloped in a dynamic, fast-changing physical environment. His experience of "things" is cut into more discontinuous segments.

Whereas in the past he could go to sleep and wake up in the morning correctly assuming that he knew where the main features of the community were, this is less and less possible. I talked with a cab driver in Washington a few weeks ago, and he shook his head and said, "If I take a vacation for two weeks, I've got to relearn the streets because so many buildings have been torn down and changed." The same is true on a "micro" scale as well.

I would be willing to bet that X number of JWT's offices around the world are being remodeled right now, and that people who have an office or a cubicle today will have a different one tomorrow. That didn't used to be the case. People went to work, they were assigned a place, and they stayed put for the rest of their lives. The physical surrounding, instead of being permanent, is now increasingly transient.

JWT World: Does this change the way people feel about "things?"

Toffler: Yes. It produces new attitudes toward ownership. We are, for example, witnessing a decline in possessiveness. The consumer is no longer as concerned with *possession* as he is with *use*. Increasingly, he will be making less and less of a commitment to things, as such. I'm wearing a tie which is about twice as wide as some of the ties I've had recently. I know that this tie will not be in my life very long and, consequently, my attitude toward it is not the same as that of my father, who may have lingered lovingly over the ties on his rack, keeping them for years and years. It's much more casual.

So we have a powerful trend toward a faster "through-put" of things in the individual's experience. This is a major difference between the way we live and the way all previous generations lived. But it's not only a matter of material goods.

A second factor, which parallels this, is the faster through-put of places. Within the last 12 months, for example, I have been to Latin America, Bermuda, California, the desert in Arizona, Japan, Hong Kong, Manila, New Delhi, Paris and London. Just as *things* are streaming through my experience, *places* are also streaming through it at a faster and faster tempo. My family and I have moved some 15 times in the last 20 years, and, except for nomadic communities, that kind of movement was totally unknown in the previous experience of man. It is a new nomadism. Primitive nomads move, but they take their whole tribe with them. They take their culture, their goods, their horses and cattle with them. We take very little: A few books, clothing which is discarded shortly thereafter, furniture which is banged up by the movers and then often discarded after we get there; and we *don't* take our friends.

So just as we have things streaming through our experience, we have places streaming through. We might cope with even this more readily if we didn't, at the same time, have a third parallel process affecting us.

We are moving into a high transience environment, and people, too, move through our lives today at faster rates. We develop modular relationships with people —we "plug in" to small parts of many different peoples' personalities.

A lot of people don't yet see this situation as a function of future shock. They don't recognize the temporal dimension, and they flail out at society for its coldness and lack of involvement. We *need* new expectations in personal relationships. Everyone needs *some* holistic relationships in his life, but it is nonsense to say that man should have *only* such relationships. In fact, to prefer a society where you have holistic relationships with many, is to lock yourself into the past. People then may have been more closely bound together, but they paid the price in the form of tightly regimented sexual mores, and religious and political restrictions.

On the other hand, the time factor in all this, the extended duration of human ties, placed a lot less adaptive strain on the individual. It is the compression of these ties that explains the current passion for sensitivity training, encounter groups, group-grope, immediate sex, and a generalized search for instant intimacy —attempts to accelerate friendship.

JWT World: How does high transience manifest itself in business?

Toffler: The heightened transience is evident at many levels— products, images, even the terrifically rapid turnover of organizational relationships. We not only are geographical, but organizational nomads. How many JWT people have shifted from one department to another, or one account to another, in the past year? We not only produce throwaway products, and throwaway personal relationships, but throwaway jobs and organizations. In "Future Shock" I describe the rapid emergence of the new organizational system based on task forces, project teams, temporary forms—what I call "Ad-hocracy."

Transience challenges corporations today to reexamine their internal structure in terms of the novelty ratio in the environments they operate in, and to redesign their organizational arrangements to fit the adaptive capabilities of their own inhabitants. Companies will simultaneously need several different kinds of internal organization, different in kind and duration, rather than a single bureaucratic structure.

JWT World: Does advertising contribute to future shock?

Toffler: You cannot watch television for an evening without being literally bombarded by advertisements to a point at which it really represents a tax on your nervous system and viscera. Much of the resistance to advertising, and the positive hatred for it in some sectors of the public, derives from this fact.

It's not the message, it's not even the medium. It's the sensory and cognitive over-stimulation that the medium and the message produce. Moreover, the ephemerality of campaigns, symbols, images, and the products themselves, intensify the sense of impermanence in life.

A few years ago someone computed that the average American is exposed to 560 advertising messages a day, ranging from the covers of matchbooks to tv commercials. Of these 560, he notices only 76. The individual must block out the rest. But the fact that he doesn't "notice" the other 484 doesn't mean they have no effect. They add to the general environment shrill. They raise the level of background noise and the viewer-reader-consumer twitches in response to them even though he may never pay an instant's attention to their formal appeals.

This has physiological as well as psychological significance, and it has more to do with the negative response to advertising than to all the familiar rhetoric about the manipulation of needs, economic waste, and so on.

JWT World: Is this a consequence of what you call the "information-rich coded message?"

Toffler: In part. Advertising is to the information-rich coded message what the Apollo project is to technology—a fantastic laboratory for the creation of new technology, linguistic technology, new symbolism. Advertising people are well paid for doing very systematically what poets used to starve doing.

In some ways, as I have said, the advertising industry has succeeded only too well, and the onset of future shock has curbed its efficiency in this respect. It's because you compress maximum message into minimum time that many recipients of the message feel as though they were having arrows shot into them. As I show in "Future Shock," we've gone from the handcrafted message to the engineered message, and this carries a heavy load of frequently unwanted information.

121

Advertising has a much more positive function as an adaptive aid. Like art, it makes possible a lot of "no trial" learning; it broadens the behavioral repertoires of people; but much of this valuable result is cancelled out by the information-enriched, perhaps over-enriched messages, that bombard us, endlessly forcing us to switch our attention and recategorize our imagery.

The development of specialized advertising media may be a partial solution to this problem. Between 1959 and 1969, for example, the number of American magazines offering special editions jumped from 126 to 235. People don't resent a limited number of ads that are aimed directly at them, or are relevant to their own interests. It's the irrelevant advertising pounding away constantly that drives them up the wall. This shift toward more specialized media, which I document in "Future Shock," is a shift to a much more sophisticated information system in the society. But, as I suggest elsewhere, it heralds a lot more conflict in the social order.

JWT World: How will future shock affect the marketplace?

Toffler: People have a feeling that things are getting out of control, that things are moving too fast, that they're being asked to cope with events that are running away from them. There is panic in the air. This is going to have an effect on the kinds of products we buy, the kinds of advertising we respond to, and the attitudes with which we approach the marketplace . . . Now we're beginning to see—with respect to many kinds of products—a growing consumer rebellion against change.

This reaction may grow stronger as the present generation begins to move into the marketplace. This is not an attack on change, *per se,* however. It is an attack on our cultural-pacing system, on the accelerating turnover rates in daily life.

What is involved here is a totally new consumer response to time. This will have obvious effects on manufacturers. And advertising designers—the people who write copy, and the ones who prepare the visuals, the ones who plan the strategy of an ad campaign—are all going to have to refocus themselves with respect to time.

For example, they will have to think especially carefully about the *duration* of a campaign, the duration of the symbols, slogans and phrases used. They're going to have to be very conscious of the distinction between those elements in a campaign that represent novel inputs; and they are going to have to learn to understand the links between transience, novelty and diversity, and to play on these factors like a piano.

For example, as "Future Shock" suggests, if we were to survey consumers, we would find significant differences between various cultural and economic groups in the marketplace with respect to time, to their durational relationships. Some people hold on to things longer than other people. If we made a similar analysis of the *duration* of place relationships, the duration of friendships and acquaintances, the duration of the individual's affiliations with organizations, and the duration of key values, we would find fascinating and useful patterns. This "transience index" could be invaluable to the advertiser and marketer because durational patterns are likely to correlate with consumer patterns.

In short, if we want to understand consumer behavior better, we are going to have to introduce much more serious analysis of the temporal factor, and make a much clearer distinction between routine and un-routine elements, *i.e.,* novelty.

JWT World: Is what you call "psycholigization of production" a function of the high rate of transience?

Toffler: Partly, yes. But it is also linked to affluence. We're beginning to recognize that products have more than the obvious functions. A house houses many people—but it also does many other things. An automobile gets you from here to there—but it can pollute the sky at the same time, and also represent symbolic values for the individual, etc.

As a society gets richer, there are a number of different directions in which it can go. It can apply its new productivity to war, to space adventure, to foreign aid, to the creation of new products for ever more luxurious living, or to the psychologization of goods and services.

One of the things that we have done in America is to begin paying attention to the psychological overtones of our products and services, so that we engineer into them features which do not necessarily improve the basic performance, but which yield psychic payoffs to the consumer. There is nothing new or startling in this idea. But no one has examined the long-range significance of this trend very seriously. Yet this emphasis on psychology is beginning to take us beyond the traditional service economy toward what I call an "experiential economy."

In "Future Shock" I describe the move toward experiential industry. We've already seen the sudden rise of what might be called the sensitivity-training industry. The encounter group people are selling experiences. So is Club Mediterranee. The tv show "The Dating Game" is another example of people being paid off with psychic rewards instead of cold cash. The contestants compete for a date with a pretty girl, quite apart from whatever financial rewards there may be.

I see the possibility of our society pouring more and more of its resources into the provision of ever more refined psychological experiences which can be marketed or sold. This may be immoral in a world still struggling with belly-hunger. But it is a strong tendency that needs to be understood.

JWT World: You think, then, that advertisements can perform cultural functions as well as selling products?

Toffler: Not only can they, they already do, and can't avoid doing so. But we need a fresh definition of these functions. For example, certain ad campaigns are reassuring to the viewer or reader simply because they are repetitive over time. They are anchors in a sea of change. Of course, they may not sell the product, but they may serve as a kind of image prop, a bit of background continuity for the individual whose life is changing in so many other ways. This is—or may be—of crucial importance in a culture rocketing toward transience.

On the other hand, the constant shifting and changing of advertising themes, reflecting the repeated upheavals in the marketplace, generates a sense of discontinuity. These differences themselves affect different groups in society in different ways. Some groups are trapped in low-stimulation environments; others suffer from over-stimulation. Advertising forms a prominent part of everyone's environment, but it does not begin to do all it could to help people make the transition into super-industrial society. A carefully thought-out and future-conscious ad can help prepare the society for a more graceful entry into tomorrow, as well as sell more of the product than ever before.

JWT World: Then the responsibility and relevance of advertising to lead us into the future with minimum shock is very great?

Toffler: Right. The widespread interest in "Future Shock" by people in the advertising industry—the reason, I think, that it's been called a basic text for advertising and communications—has to do with the fact that ad people are among the groups in society who are most exposed to super-change. They are among the groups in society I call "people of the future."

People in advertising fight on the front lines of future shock because every day they confront the high rate of turnover, the rates of transience, and the necessity to make enormous and constantly changing kaleidoscopic adjustments on the job, with respect to consumer tastes, families, organizations, people, life styles. All the component elements of future shock, it seems to me, are raised to the nth degree in advertising and communications. I think this is why so many advertising and communications people have said, privately to me and even publicly on the air, that the book expressed what they have been feeling. A friend of mine got a letter from a well known advertising executive which said, "The book reads as though the author had been standing over my shoulder for the last six months."

In some sense, ad people are pre-tasting a possible and quite probable future, and they have some responsibility for either changing it or preparing us to cope with it better.

Advertising agencies can do a lot to help prepare society for the future—and also, of course, to keep their clients one step ahead of change. But they will need special resources to do so. They will have to draw on the new intellectual technologies being created by the people who are seriously studying the future. They will need direct ties with the futurist community worldwide. They will need to develop their own long-range planning operations. But not the old-style technocratic planning. They will need new, free-form post-technocratic planning—a style that takes into account all sorts of non-economic factors, that reaches beyond the 10- or 15-year horizon, and that taps into the feelings, wishes, hopes of people at all levels of the various social hierarchies.

Not only must advertising agencies move in this direction, if they are to survive the jolts that lie ahead, they ought to be educating their clients along these lines as well. Some of the best advertising agencies already are

doing this, encouraging their clients to reexamine not only strategies, but even their most fundamental goals, drawing on the help of specially equipped outsiders.

You know, we've been talking about the rate of change and keeping an eye on the future. In "Future Shock," I quote a very pertinent article written by JWT's Henry Schachte in which he points out that in almost no major consumer goods category is there a brand on top today that was No. 1 ten years ago. Well, ten years ago those top brands must have had some good advertising to make them "top." But advertising is being reconceptualized, and what we regard as "good" today is already more than half obsolete.

If advertising is to be effective, its creators must continually anticipate the future. And if it is to be moral, they must assume a social responsibility that they have never accepted: The task of educating people not simply about what or how to buy, but more important, how to cope with change. And this means probing behind the "content" of advertising to its temporal connotations.

For society itself, I think it's time to ask very serious questions about advertising. More serious than the usual ones. It's time we dug deeper than the cliches about manipulation, economic waste, lack of veracity, and so on. These criticisms of advertising are important, no doubt, and ought by no means to be shrugged aside. But advertising is doing far more fundamental things to our culture than these arguments even begin to suggest.

JWT World: In terms of "Future Shock's" analysis, what do you think of Marshall McLuhan's insight that the medium is the message?

Toffler: The best thing that I heard anybody say about McLuhan came from Kenneth Boulding [the economist], who said that McLuhan had hit a very large nail not quite on the head. That is, in my opinion, very high praise, indeed. Not many books even come close to that.

There is more mysticism in McLuhan's work than I am comfortable with. But there is also more imagination than the media has been subjected to in 50 years of academic analysis. McLuhan has explosively enlarged our concept of the "content" of communications.

As I read him, McLuhan says that the analysts, until now, have

been looking at what comes across the screen or the printed page, and examining it only on the most literal level. They have had a very limited notion of what actually happens between the receiver and the words, ideas, pictures or symbols, reaching him. McLuhan has forced us to broaden our conception of "content" to include many of the side-effects —the effect of communication on the individual or cultural sense ratios, for example. And McLuhan has forced us to understand that these side-effects, all the events happening below the literal level, may be more important than the actual words coming across the screen and telling us to "Buy Widgets!" or "Vote Republican!" To the degree that he's got that message across—and that is only a small fraction of what he has to say—he has enormously expanded our understanding of what is happening to us.

■ What I have tried to do in "Future Shock" is to show that the "content" of change is also much bigger than we suspect. When we talk about change, we ordinarily confuse the directions of change with the content of change, just as the media analysts mistook what came across the screen for the whole content of communications. Change, too, has to be understood in terms of its secondary and tertiary consequences, some of which may well be more important than the so-called primary consequence.

For example, "Future Shock" argues that the *rate* at which change occurs is sometimes more important than the kind of change involved. The duration of an ad campaign may turn out to be more important than the specific sales message it projects.

■ Admen and market researchers have analyzed the consumer in terms of everything from Freudian drives to class position and color preference, but they—like most of the rest of us—have missed one of the most crucial elements in human behavior, the temporal dimension. They pay no attention to durational expectancies, although they act on them all the time. They seldom ask how people react to any step-up or slowdown in the pace of daily life.

More broadly, it is no longer possible for us to evaluate political changes, technological changes, social changes without an expanded definition of change, one that takes into account its less immediately evident results. We have got to understand that acceleration, the continual speedup of the rate of change, has consequences apart from, and possibly more significant than, the nature of the specific changes involved.

For advertisers, this means you have to begin asking how any specific ad or campaign affects the individual's transience level; how it raises or lowers the novelty ratio in his environment; and what it does to the number of choices he has to make in his daily life. Unless you begin asking questions like these, you may completely misunderstand the real content of change—and of your own behavior.

Super-change, and the decision crisis it is provoking in our culture, will compel us to think about change in totally new ways. Those who cannot will fall by the wayside—casualties of the accelerative thrust, victims of future shock.

Reprinted from "Advertising Age," Nov. 21, 1973, pp. 198-203, from an interview in "JWT World," the J. Walter Thompson house organ.

Freedom must advertise

BY TOM DILLON
President, Batten, Barton, Durstine & Osborn, New York

What does advertising contribute to the world? Are we advertising men, as many people think, an expensive parasite on the social structure? You will not need to look far to find that point of view expressed.

And it would be odd, indeed, if everyone in advertising had not at some time or another wondered whether he was wasting his skills and his life in a meaningless exercise.

How, we may be asked, is mankind served by our efforts to show that this miracle suds gets your clothes whiter than that miracle suds? Why, the critics say, is $23.1 billion every year wasted in advertising—$23.1 billion that could better be used to rebuild the school system of America?

Furthermore, they say, wicked advertising people are so manipulating the public mind that spiritual values are being replaced by materialism and the shabby doodads of a chrome-plated economy.

Let's take a few of these garlands of roses and look at them. Let's look at the great big $23.1 billion hole in our economy that is made by advertising. In the first place, it frequently amazes people to learn that in the last 50 years the percentage of the gross national product of this country spent on advertising has remained practically the same. Whatever hole advertising makes in our economy, it is now no larger a hole, proportionately, than it was in 1925. It may make advertising people feel good and some other people feel bad to talk about the growing factor of advertising in our economy. The plain fact is that it is not a growing factor.

■ It also makes some of our agency people feel happy to talk about being in a $23.1 billion industry. Well, unfortunately for us, the advertising agency business is only a $9.5 billion industry. And

in this $9.5 billion industry, advertising agencies siphon off only 15%, or some $1.4 billion.

But it is all very well to say that advertising agencies handle only about a third of all advertising. The fact remains that $23.1 billion is a lot of money, and it's being spent on advertising.

Or is it being spent on advertising?

Here we come to one of those little tricks that are used intentionally or unintentionally by people to confuse an issue. It consists of counting the same figure twice. Of course, any of the $23.1 billion that goes into advertising agency income, outdoor advertising or into direct mail is spent on pure advertising. But agency income, outdoor and direct mail are about 23% of total advertising.

After that, what happens when you spend a dollar, for example, on tv advertising? Where does the dollar go? Probably not more than a nickel of it goes into producing the commercial and into the electrical energy that transmits it to your tv set. What becomes of the other 95¢? It goes, of course, into the cost of programing and operating television stations.

■ So you see that the $23.1 billion spent in advertising also includes, as part of that $23.1 billion, the entire cost of running all the radio and tv networks in the U.S. and all the 7,493 individual radio and tv stations.

Let's look at newspapers. Probably most people feel that they are paying for their newspaper when they lay out their 15¢. Of course, they are not. A city newspaper is lucky if its circulation revenue pays for those big rolls of white paper that the news is printed on. Everything else—the entire cost of worldwide and local news gathering, pictures, features, the actual engraving, typesetting and printing of the paper—has to be borne by local and national

advertising. And there, for the support of 1,809 daily and 8,682 weekly newspapers in the U.S., goes another part of that $23.1 billion.

Now, let's take the magazines—9,062 consumer, trade and technical. Those subscription prices which are offered so tantalizingly just about pay for the cost of rounding up subscriptions and putting the postage on the magazines. So when your doctor reads the *Journal of the American Medical Assn.*, that communication is brought to him through the courtesy of advertising. And that scientist working out in the Point Mugu missile center—his copy of *Rockets and Missiles* is brought to him paid by advertising.

If you'd like to try a little mental experiment, imagine that instead of the New York newspapers that were struck a few years ago, the advertising industry had been struck. Who now will pay for the Associated Press correspondent in Moscow? Who will now pay for Mr. Reston in Washington? Who pays for the coverage of the astronauts at Cape Kennedy? After about 60 days I assure you that no one will. Most publications would have to stop after the first issue, and very few could go for more than a few weeks. Radio, tv, magazines and newspapers in this country would have to go dead for lack of income.

■ For, you see, there really is no such thing as a $23.1 billion advertising industry. The cost of advertising overlaps the cost of a communications system that covers the whole U.S. The cost of preparing and producing the advertising is a relatively small fraction of it, but advertising pays the bulk of the cost of communications.

Now, what would happen if, in the long run, there were no advertising industry and people simply paid more for their publications? It would be a good guess that the *New York Sunday Times* would probably cost $6 or $7 an issue, and the daily edition $1, or $1.50, even after it had been cut down because of the elimination of advertising.

It's really not necessary to guess what would happen if there were no advertising, because there are other countries in the world in which advertising does not play the part in the economy that it does in the U.S. What happens in their internal communications systems?

Some countries, like Great Britain and West Germany, have advertising operations very much like our own, but there are other countries where advertising expenditures per capita are very low. There you will find that freedom of the press tends to be a fiction. To begin with, radio and tv must be supported by the state, and they become the official propaganda organs of the party in power. Indeed, the last thing that these parties want to see is commercial television. For commercial television is free-speech television.

■ And what happens to newspapers? They are, to begin with, small, miserable, badly written and badly edited sheets. In the majority of cases, because circulation revenue can't possibly support them, these newspapers are the official organs of various political parties and get their revenues from party funds. The fact of the matter is that, in the absence of advertising revenue, the concept of freedom of the press is a joke.

But, asks someone, isn't advertising, even if it doesn't cost us $23.1 billion a year, but only $9 or $10 billion, a terribly inefficient and expensive part of our economy? What possible good does it do America to have people sitting in front of a tv set looking at advertising for 15 or 20 kinds of beer? Aren't there more important things in the world than deciding which brand of beer to drink?

Isn't this an inefficient use of people's time and money?

Let's look for a moment at some other inefficient things in our society. We won't have very far to look. You could look at the Constitution of the U.S. You will very readily see that it is a blueprint for inefficiency. It has set up the most ridiculous and complicated method of electing two bodies, totaling more than 500 people, to argue within themselves and with each other. After they finish their interminable argumentation, they put it in the hands of a third party, the President of the U.S., to carry out their orders, whether he

agrees with them or not. Further than that, it arranged for nine old men to take anywhere from two to ten years to decide whether what these two wrangling bodies had told the President to do was or was not within their power.

■ As if this weren't confusing and inefficient enough, every four years the whole country spends about four months in a continual uproar while hundreds of men make speeches and promises they haven't the slightest intention of keeping to people who know perfectly well that it would be silly to believe them. Then everybody goes into a little booth and marks X's next to the names of men they never heard of.

Now, everyone can see that Plato had the right idea 2,100 years before the Constitution was framed. The most efficient way to run a country, of course, is Plato's suggestion that we breed philosopher kings. These people were going to be bred to be so smart and fair and honest and brilliant that you could put them in charge of a country and they would simply make the best possible decisions about what to do. Being very wise and very honest, philosopher kings could easily settle the amount of taxes, what brand of beer everyone should drink and who was innocent and who was guilty of a crime. They could pass laws quickly and enforce them instantly.

Now, I don't think the framers of the Constitution of the U.S. were so dull-witted that they couldn't see that this was the most efficient form of government. But they had noticed a very interesting thing. In 2,100 years, no one had ever found a satisfactory philosopher king and put him on a throne. They had found only Alexander and Caesar and Frederick the Great and George III.

They came to the conclusion that efforts to find philosopher kings for 2,100 years had proved that you would get nothing but tyranny for your trouble. So they set up the government of the U.S. with a mind to preventing tyranny. They created the giant debating society of Congress, the Supreme Court and the President of the U.S. so every point of view could be aired before a decision was formalized in law.

They tried to make sure that the advocate of any point of view would have an opportunity to express his advocacy.

■ It looks to me as if it will require at least 200 years of tampering with their system before we can completely restore tyranny.

The Amendments IV through VIII, which were immediately tacked on to the Constitution, are also frightful sources of inefficiency. Up to 100 years before the Constitution was written, many then-civilized countries had highly efficient ways of dealing with accused criminals. One of the best, of course, was the pot of boiling water. If the accused criminal put his hand in the pot for a minute and it came out unburned, he was innocent. This kind of system not only is inexpensive, but guarantees that no guilty man shall go unpunished. Some other countries did then and do now simply have a state-appointed judge make a decision as to the guilt or innocence of the accused with or without listening to what he has to say.

Now what did the framers of the Constitution do? They abandoned all of these simple, effective methods and set up a terribly complicated, long-drawn-out and expensive process. In the first place, they made it so you had to run around and get a judge to sign an order before you could even rummage through a man's basement. Then, when you nabbed a scoundrel, you had to get an indictment from a grand jury of some 24 people. Then you had to convince 12 other people that he was guilty and do this without even being able to force him to make a confession. You had to confront him with the witnesses against him, which is often very awkward. You had to shag out and get his own witnesses for him and even furnish him a free attorney if he was short of cash. You had to let him go out and run around on bail until the trial took place. Now, right away, you can see that this is not an efficient way of catching and imprisoning criminals.

■ Now why be so complicated? Only, of course, because the framers of the Constitution, having studied the 5,000 years of man's recorded history, decided that you can put up with quite a lot of inefficiency better than you can put up with a little tyranny. They had a choice between the freedom of mankind and efficiency. Thank God they took freedom.

Amendment I of the Constitution also provided a very grave source of inefficiency and confusion and did it in a very few words. The First Amendment to the Constitution states: "Congress shall make no law respecting an establishment of religion or prohibiting the free exercise thereof or abridging the freedom of speech or of the press or the right of the people peaceably to assemble and to petition the Government for redress of grievances."

Just in the field of religion alone, this created a very inefficient and uneconomical duplication of effort. According to the National Council of Churches, there are in the U.S. some 87 separate faiths having 50,000 or more members each. And of these, over 83 are variations of Christianity.

Now each one of these brands of religion exists because 50,000 or more people in each case feel that this particular brand of thought washes the soul whiter than the other 86. Yet for many thousands of years, people thought that this was a very illogical thing.

They thought it was so illogical and inefficient that the state establishment of a uniform religion was considered a necessity. The framers of the Constitution, some of whose forefathers had been prevented from advocating their deviations from the state-established Church of England by unpleasant remedies like jail and hanging, were again prepared to abandon logic and efficiency on behalf of freedom from tyranny.

■ And, finally, freedom of speech and of the press.

Now, anyone put in charge of running a country knows what a large pain in the neck freedom of speech and of the press is. Every President of the U.S. must, at least in some hour of his life, have been driven by the yammering of the press into wondering whether the First Amendment to the Constitution was not in contravention of another provision against cruel and unusual punishment. How inefficient and awkward it is to have every movement of the state under the piercing scrutiny of men who are anxious to seize upon every mistake and, perhaps, balloon it way out of proportion, to the embarrassment of our government both here and abroad.

Again, does anyone really think the founders of this country were so dull and so remote from the lessons of history and experience that they did not know the terrible risk they ran when they forged this freedom into the basic law of the land? If they didn't, they were soon to know. For the moment they were in office, the press began a barrage of invective against Washington, Adams, Madison, Jefferson and Hamilton unparalleled in modern political dogfights.

They knew, all right. But they were prepared to sacrifice themselves and their successors forever if they could hold back the tyranny of man over man. And,

perhaps incidentally, the framers of the Constitution could hardly have been unaware of advertising. For advertising supported the newspapers that carried the spirit of revolution to the people of the Colonies.

Do not think for a moment that the Declaration of Independence was carried around on parchment scrolls and read in town squares by men wearing funny hats and ringing bells. If you will examine the July 6, 1776, issue of the *Pennsylvania Evening Post,* you will find the Declaration of Independence requires two and one-half columns, and, at the end of those two and one-half columns, beneath the signatures of those who pledged their sacred honor and their fortunes, there are ten ads. It appears to me that if the framers of the Constitution had intended to exclude them from the protection of the First Amendment, they probably would have said so.

■ Freedom carries with it the opportunity for many evils. The freedom of those running for public office to promise what they cannot deliver has let evil men reach public power. The freedom given to our legislators on the floor of Congress has enabled them to blacken the names of honest men who have no recourse to law. The freedom of religion has permitted the teaching of tenets that have resulted in the needless deaths of helpless children.

Freedom of speech has caused senseless riots and suffering. Freedom of the press has ruined innocent people and possibly started needless wars. Freedom is an expensive thing. It is also extremely fragile.

For all tyranny does not come with tanks and jack boots. Tyranny also creeps in, like the fog, "on little cat feet." Softly, soothingly. Tyranny carries a nicely lettered sign on which it says, "This is being done for the public good." Tyranny is sly. It whispers to you and says, "You and I know what the best thing is to do. But those poor people over there are not as fortunate as you and I. They do not have the wisdom to know that what we want is really for their own good." Tyranny puts its arm around your shoulder and says, "Let's you and I save them from themselves. Let us force them to make the right choice, and later, when they are wiser, they will thank us." Tyranny says, "Let us draw up some rules to prevent the advocacy of ideas that we know are wrong. Come, let us go together and curb evil."

■ It is true that to live together

we must have some rules for some things. We cannot, after all, each decide for himself whether to drive on the right or the left-hand side of the street.

But watch out for tyranny's trick. Watch for the trick when tyranny shifts to rules that will prevent a man from advocating a point of view. For all those rules that the founders of the Republic tried so hard to rivet into the Constitution were to protect that right of advocacy.

There have been copies of our Constitution in other lands. And in these other lands they promise freedom of the press, speech and of religion. Yet there is no freedom. And how was that done? It's a very simple trick. It is easy to write into your Constitution that you have freedom of religious thought. All the state then has to do is to write a statute preventing you from building a church and holding a meeting in it. Oh, you have the right of your thought, all right. You can sit and think any religious thought you like.

■ But you can't talk to others about it, nor can you go and listen to anyone talk to you about it. If you have the freedom of religious thought without the right to advocate religious thought, then you have no freedom at all.

Or you can have a country in which there is freedom of the press. But what good is freedom of the press unless you have a press and the paper to put in it, and a way of distributing the paper? You may have freedom of speech even, but if you do not have access to a press or to a radio station, or to a television station, of what value is this freedom?

Many countries know this. Since they control the press and usually control radio and tv, they can cheerfully grant freedom of the press and freedom of speech with the full knowledge that there is no possibility of exercising those freedoms. All of the tools that make them possible are within the grasp of an all-powerful state.

What has advertising to do with all this? Well, in a country that gets above-subsistence living, man is presumed to be entitled to freedom of economic choice. He has the freedom of choosing whether he shall spend his money on a glass of beer or put it into the bank. He has the freedom to decide what he will pay his money for, in terms of what he thinks will best suit him. It is a freedom no less dear than the freedom of choosing the men who will govern him or the religious thought he will follow. The very essence of all of these freedoms is that he is free to do something that you and I might feel to be very foolish. He may elect Huey Long governor of his state, adopt a highly improbable religious belief or spend twice as much buying a car as he can afford.

■ You and I may deplore his decisions. But freedom from tyranny is freedom to make a mistake as well as freedom to be right.

To exercise true freedom of choice, we've got to know what we've got a choice of. This is the function of advertising. We do not have a free choice of religion unless there are people preaching various religions. We do not have a free choice of election unless there are speakers for a variety of candidates. We don't have a free economic choice unless there is some way in which our alternatives can be brought forcibly to our attention. What the orators and preachers are to politics and religion, advertising is to economics. Advertising presents in the best possible way the best possible case for an economic decision to buy certain products and services. Is this an economic and social waste?

Of course it isn't. It is only a waste if you don't believe in freedom. But can you point to cases where advertising has misled people? Yes, indeed, just as you can point to cases where attorneys have gotten guilty men free, where liars have had themselves elected to office and religious fanatics have caused a wholesale slaughter of children.

Presumably, every citizen in this country over the age of 18 is entitled to vote for the President of the U.S., not only the highest office in this land, but probably the most powerful office in the history of the world. In the 1960 Presidential election there was a difference of only 118,550 votes between the winner and the loser. Now, gentlemen, I ask you: If you are going to trust your fellow Americans to use their judgment on a matter in which the balance of the world hangs, are you going to deny them that judgment when it comes to the selection of their shaving cream? Are the people whose individual votes control the course of this planet too dim-witted to vote for the right soap powder?

I do not apologize for advertising. I think it is as vital to the preservation of freedom in my country as the free exercise of publishing a newspaper or the free exercise of building a church or the free exercise of the right of

trial by jury.

For not only is advertising the only practical source of advocating to the people of this country the economic choices they have before them, but it is also, as I have outlined before, practically the sole support of the only communications system that is not under the control of the state. Without the financial support of advertising, not only would there be no practical freedom of economic choice, but there is also a very serious question whether there would be any practical freedom in politics and religion.

■ If you think that is theoretical, I suggest you look at the record. Make up a list of the countries where you think that man is most free of tyranny. Where has he developed the highest social and economic values in the modern world? You will probably come up with, at the top of the list, countries like the U.S., Great Britain, Canada, West Germany, the Scandinavian countries, Australia, Japan, Switzerland, Holland, Belgium, France and perhaps Italy. Now you may not agree with me completely on this list of countries or the order in which I have put them. But now let me give you another list. This is a list of countries showing the amount of the gross national income spent on advertising. The countries are listed in order of percentage.

Per cent of national income spent for advertising

Ireland	2.23%
Switzerland	2.18
U.S.	2.11
New Zealand	1.65
Denmark	1.64
West Germany	1.56
Australia	1.44
Netherlands	1.38
Sweden	1.32
Austria	1.30
Argentina	1.28
Canada	1.25
Malaysia, Singapore & Brunei	1.23
Puerto Rico	1.18
Finland	1.17
Lebanon	1.15
Japan	1.14
United Kingdom	1.13
Norway	1.11
Aruba	1.10
Hong Kong	1.03
Costa Rica	1.02

So much for the top of the list. Now let's look at some of the countries on the bottom:

Bottom of list

USSR	0%
Red China	0%
East Germany	0%
Cuba	0%
Poland	0%
Hungary	0%
Czechoslovakia	0%

Now, do you think for a moment that this is a coincidence? Do you think that it is just a matter of luck that advertising and the freedom and dignity of man go hand in hand? Do you think that advertising is merely a frill that rich and successful nations can afford? If you do, I would like you to remember that in all countries where freedom of the press and freedom of speech and freedom of religion are suppressed, they are suppressed under the argument that the people are not yet rich enough for that luxury.

No Ads After Hitler

No, I would suggest a different thing to you. I would suggest that it was no coincidence that in the *Pennsylvania Evening Post* the Declaration of Independence was followed by ten ads. I don't think you'd expect to find the proclamations of Alexander, Frederick the Great, Napoleon, Mussolini, Hitler or Stalin followed by ten ads. Indeed, advertising is never welcome among the politically or intellectually arrogant who have appointed themselves the nursemaids of the people. Tyranny, gentlemen, hates advertising like the devil hates holy water.

■ If you believe, as I do, that advertising plays such a vital part in maintaining the freedom of our social structure, then we citizens charged with advertising bear some heavy responsibilities. I would like to list three of them briefly.

We bear, first, the obvious responsibility of so conducting advertising that it is as free as possible from legitimate criticism. This is not easy. Anyone can become an advertising agency by having a letterhead printed. Anyone can become an advertiser by the simple act of having money. But we can't get together and agree on details of our conduct lest we all go to the pokey for violation of the anti-trust laws.

Protect Our Freedom

Second, I am gravely concerned that we may not meet our responsibility to protect the principle of freedom of speech in advertising. For the first time in 238 years, we are finding a spate of cases where truth is no defense against suppression. I do not think that editors or advertisers should be complacent because it is happening to someone else. I think that history indicates that a man who mocks at others on their way to the guillotine may be premature in his laughter.

Finally, I believe that today it is more important that all of us in advertising continue in support of the long-standing American traditions of noninterference in the communications content of media. We have a grave responsibility to protect the independence of our communications media . . . for the day on which we do not do so we open up an additional opportunity for the management of news by the state. I happen to be very much in favor of having news managed by managing editors and advertising managed by advertising managers.

I hope you are, too.

Reprinted from "Advertising Age," Nov. 21, 1973, pp. 204-207, 210